The GOD of Covenant

The GOD *of* Covenant

Biblical, theological and contemporary perspectives

Edited by Jamie A. Grant
and Alistair I. Wilson

APOLLOS

APOLLOS (an imprint of Inter-Varsity Press)
38 De Montfort Street, Leicester LE1 7GP, England
Email: ivp@uccf.org.uk
Website: www.ivpbooks.com

First published 2005

British Library Cataloguing in Publication Data
A catalogue record for this book is available from the British Library.

ISBN 1–84474–065–X

Set in Monotype Garamond 11/13pt
Typeset in Great Britain by Servis Filmsetting Ltd, Manchester
Printed and bound in Great Britain by Creative Print and Design (Wales), Ebbw Vale

Inter-Varsity Press is the publishing division of the Universities and Colleges Christian Fellowship (formerly the Inter-Varsity Fellowship), a student movement linking Christian Unions in universities and colleges throughout Great Britain, and a member movement of the International Fellowship of Evangelical Students. For more information about local and national activities write to UCCF, 38 De Montfort Street, Leicester LE1 7GP, email us at email@uccf.org.uk, or visit the UCCF website at www.uccf.org.uk.

CONTENTS

CONTRIBUTORS

David L. Baker is Deputy Warden and Research Fellow at Tyndale House, Cambridge, England.

Harry Bunting is Lecturer in Philosophy at the University of Ulster, Northern Ireland.

Colin Chapman was Lecturer in Islamic Studies at the Near East School of Theology, Beirut, Lebanon, and is recently retired, living in Malvern.

David G. Firth is Tutor in Old Testament Studies and Third Year Course Leader at Cliff College, Derbyshire, England.

Jamie A. Grant is Lecturer in Biblical Studies at the Highland Theological College, Dingwall, Scotland.

James Hely Hutchinson is Associate Lecturer in Old Testament at the Faculté Libre de Théologie Évangélique, Vaux-sur-Seine, France.

A. T. B. McGowan is Principal of the Highland Theological College, Dingwall, Scotland, and lectures in Systematic Theology.

Kim Huat Tan is Chen Su Lan Professor of New Testament at Trinity Theological College, Singapore.

Alistair I. Wilson is Lecturer in New Testament at the Highland Theological College, Dingwall, Scotland.

Christopher J. H. Wright is International Ministries Director of the Langham Partnership International and was formerly Principal of All Nations Christian College.

ABBREVIATIONS

1Q28b (1QSb)	*Rule of the Blessings*
1Q34	*Festival Prayers*
1QpHab	*Habakkuk Pesher*
1QS	*Community Rule / Manual of Discipline*
1QSb	*Rule of the Blessings*
4Q504	*Words of the Luminaries*
4Q521	*Messiah of Heaven and Earth*
AB	Anchor Bible
ABD	*Anchor Bible Dictionary*, ed. David Noel Freedman (New York: Doubleday; electronic edition, 1996)
ABRL	Anchor Bible Reference Library
AcT	*Acta theologica*
AnBib	Analecta Biblica
BA	*Biblical Archaeologist*
b. Ber.	*bavli [Babylonian Talmud] Berakot*
BDAG	W. Bauer, F. W. Danker, W. F. Arndt and F. W. Gingrich, *Greek–English Lexicon of the New Testament and Other Early Christian Literature* (3rd. ed.; Chicago: University of Chicago Press, 1999)
BDB	F. Brown, S. R. Driver and C. A. Briggs, *A Hebrew and English Lexicon of the Old Testament* (Oxford: Clarendon, 1907)
BECNT	Baker Exegetical Commentary on the New Testament

BETS	Bulletin of the Evangelical Theological Society
Bib	*Biblica*
b. Sanh.	*bavli [Babylonian Talmud] Sanhedrin*
BST	Bible Speaks Today
BTB	*Biblical Theology Bulletin*
BZAW	Beihefte zur Zeitschrift für die alttestamentliche Wissenschaft
CBQ	*Catholic Biblical Quarterly*
CD	*Cairo Damascus Document*
CTJ	*Calvin Theological Journal*
CurBS	*Currents in Research: Biblical Studies*
DCH	*Dictionary of Classical Hebrew*, ed. D. J. A. Clines (Sheffield: Sheffield Academic Press, 1993–)
DPL	*Dictionary of Paul and His Letters*, ed. G. F. Hawthorne and R. P. Martin (Downers Grove: IVP, 1993)
EBC	Expositors' Bible Commentary
EBib	*Etudes bibliques*
EvQ	*Evangelical Quarterly*
ESV	English Standard Version
EvT	*Evangelische Theologie*
ExpTim	*Expository Times*
FB	Forschung zur Bibel
FCI	Foundations of Contemporary Interpretation
Gen. Rab.	*Genesis Rabbah*
IBD	*Illustrated Bible Dictionary*, IVP, 1980
ICC	International Critical Commentary
Int	*Interpretation*
JBL	*Journal of Biblical Literature*
JETS	*Journal of the Evangelical Theological Society*
JP	*Journal of Philosophy*
JRE	*Journal of Religious Ethics*
JPTSup	*Journal of Pentecostal Theology*, Supplement Series
JSHJ	*Journal for the Study of the Historical Jesus*
JSNT	*Journal for the Study of the New Testament*
JSNTSup	*Journal for the Study of the New Testament*, Supplement Series
JSOT	*Journal for the Study of the Old Testament*

JSOTSup	*Journal for the Study of the Old Testament,* Supplement Series
JSS	*Journal of Semitic Studies*
LD	Lectio divina
LXX	Septuagint
m. Ber.	*mishnah Berakot*
m. Naz.	*mishnah Nazir*
m. Šabb.	*mishnah Šabbat*
NASB	New American Standard Bible
NBD	*New Bible Dictionary*
NCBC	New Century Bible Commentary
NEB	New English Bible
NIBCOT	New International Biblical Commentary on the Old Testament
NICNT	New International Commentary on the New Testament
NICOT	New International Commentary on the Old Testament
NIDNTT	*New International Dictionary of New Testament Theology,* ed. Colin Brown (Grand Rapids: Zondervan; electronic edition 2001)
NIDOTTE	*New International Dictionary of Old Testament Theology and Exegesis,* ed. Willem A. Van-Gemeren, 5 vols. (Grand Rapids: Zondervan, 1997)
NIGTC	New International Greek Testament Commentary
NRSV	New Revised Standard Version
n.s.	new series
NT	New Testament
NTS	*New Testament Studies*
OBT	Overtures to Biblical Theology
OT	Old Testament
OTE	*Old Testament Essays*
OTL	Old Testament Library
OTS	Old Testament Studies
PPR	*Philosophy and Phenomenological Research*
REB	Revised English Bible

REV	Revised English Version
RevExp	*Review and Expositor*
SB	Stuttgarter Bibelstudien
SBLDS	Society of Biblical Literature Dissertation Series
SJOT	*Scandinavian Journal of the Old Testament*
SJT	*Scottish Journal of Theology*
s.v.	*sub verbo* (under the word given)
TDOT	*Theological Dictionary of the Old Testament*, ed. G. J. Botterweck and H. Ringgren, tr. J. T. Willis, G. W. Bromiley and D. E. Green, 8 vols. (Grand Rapids: Eerdmans, 1974–)
TB	Indonesian New Translation
TEV	Today's English Version
Them	*Themelios*
ThSt	Theologische Studien
TOTC	Tyndale Old Testament Commentaries
TynBul	*Tyndale Bulletin*
TZ	*Theologische Zeitschrift*
VT	*Vetus Testamentum*
VTSup	*Vetus Testamentum*, Supplement Series
WBC	Word Biblical Commentary
WMANT	Wissenschaftliche Monographien zum Alten und Neuen Testament
WTJ	*Westminster Theological Journal*
WUNT	Wissenschaftliche Untersuchungen zum Neuen Testament
ZAW	*Zeitschrift für die alttestamentliche Wissenschaft*
ZKT	*Zeitschrift für katholische Theologie*

INTRODUCTION

Alistair I. Wilson and Jamie A. Grant

Eclectic is perhaps the best word to describe this volume. There is a rich and wide diversity of material contained in this book, all based around a single theme – 'covenant'. Arguably, covenant is the single most significant theme in the whole of the Scriptures and it is the very breadth and magnitude of this biblical thread that makes possible the diversity of approach and discussion found in the pages that follow.

The idea of covenant is fundamental to the Bible's story. At its most basic covenant presents God's desire to enter into relationship with men and women created in his image. This is reflected in the repeated covenant refrain 'I will be your God and you will be my people' (Exodus 6:6–8; Leviticus 26:12 etc.). Covenant is all about relationship between the Creator and his creation. The idea may seem simple; however, the implications of covenant and covenant relationship between God and humankind are vast and it is from the expanse of these implications that the following articles are drawn.

Covenant begins (explicitly, at least) with the Noah account in the prehistory of the book of Genesis,[1] and its inclusion as part of this foundational pericope (Genesis 1 – 11) is significant. Covenant is essential to God's gracious dealings with his people after the fall.[2] This is further accentuated by the centrality of covenant to the Abraham narrative (the beginnings of 'salvation-history'). The Creator God has a plan to restore relationship with his people and this plan works by way of covenants.

The Abrahamic covenant is extended to his descendants Isaac and Jacob before being expanded to the nation of Israel via Moses, the mediator of the Sinai covenant. This 'law-based' covenant is reapplied to a new context prior to Israel's entry into the land (Deuteronomy), and the next sea-change comes in the form of the covenant with David (2 Samuel) – the promise of an eternal line of

---

1. Genesis 8:20 – 9:17.

2. There are those who would suggest that covenant is implicit to the creation account itself and, therefore, has an even more foundational role in the biblical narrative of God's dealings with humanity both before as well as after the fall. See, for example, O. Palmer Robertson, *The Christ of the Covenants* (Phillipsburg: Presbyterian & Reformed, 1980); or W. J. Dumbrell's *Covenant and Creation: A Theology of Old Testament Covenants* (Exeter: Paternoster, 1984). Of course, the word 'covenant' (*běrît* in Hebrew) is nowhere used in Genesis 1 – 3 nor is there any *explicit* indication of a covenant sign or ceremony or formula (classic indicators of a covenant relationship), which makes the argument complex. However, Genesis 1 – 3 does make it absolutely clear that Yahweh enters into special relationship with men and women, as those created in his image, and delegates special purpose and authority to them. Is this enough to indicate covenant relationship? Possibly. Equally the question may be asked, 'Should we expect all of the characteristics of post-lapsarian covenants to be present in a covenant made with humanity in its perfect state? Is it not reasonable to expect a pre-fall covenant to be somehow different from a divine–human covenant made after the fall?' Interesting though these questions are, this 'Introduction' is not the place for such lengthy discussion. The above works will provide a starting point for those who are interested.

kings, instruments of Yahweh's rule. Yet throughout the progressive development of the idea of covenant in the Old Testament the reader is confronted with a constant problem: covenant unfaithfulness. Covenants regulate the relationship between Creator and sinful creation, yet the problem of sin continues. So it is we come across discussion of a 'new covenant' in the prophets (Jeremiah, Isaiah) . . . a promise of relationship that will lead to a change of heart. By way of this enigmatic allusion to a radically different covenant, we as readers are prepared for the new covenant accounts of the Messiah and the guarantee of restored relationship with Yahweh.[3]

Covenant spreads its wings throughout the Bible. It is a theme we cannot ignore if we desire to know the God of the Scriptures, because he reveals himself as a 'covenant-making and covenant-keeping God' (Exodus 34:10; 1 Kings 8:23).

This volume is a collection of papers selected from those given at the Triennial Conference of the Tyndale Fellowship in Nantwich, UK, in July 2003. The Tyndale Fellowship is 'a fellowship of Christians engaged in biblical and theological research. Its aim is to promote the Christian faith through careful and honest study done in a spirit of loyalty to the historic Christian faith . . .'[4] The Tyndale Fellowship is made up of evangelical scholars from throughout the world who gather to discuss biblical and theological issues each year in subject-specific study groups (e.g. OT, NT, Christian Doctrine etc.), and every third year all of the study groups come together for a larger conference. The 2003 Triennial Conference was devoted to the topic of covenant and it resulted in the fascinating, multifaceted discussions contained within this book.

The first chapter of this book is David Baker's 'Covenant: an Old Testament study', which was delivered as the Biblical Theology Lecture. Baker provides us with an exhaustive study of the use of the term 'covenant' (*bĕrît*) in the Old Testament. He discusses the

---

3. The 'testaments' of the Old and New Testament are, of course, references to covenants.

4. See the Tyndale House website for more details:
   <www.tyndale.cam.ac.uk/Tyndale/Fellowship.htm>.

meaning of covenant and the significance of the covenant formula before taking the reader through a brief discussion of the main covenants of the OT. He points out the formative nature of the Abrahamic covenant (it is to some extent basic to the very idea of covenant), as a covenant of relationship between God and an elect group of people – this covenant becomes the basis for the prophets' presentation of the 'new covenant'. Baker then goes on to discuss the covenant ceremonies that confirm this covenant in the varying settings of the people of God (Sinai, Moab, Shechem etc.). Finally, he leads us through the covenant breaches and renewals that occurred throughout Israel's history – paving the way for the idea of a 'new covenant' in the OT prophetic books. This leads naturally to discussion of what these passages highlight as being 'new' about the new covenant. Baker's contribution provides us with a good, descriptive grounding with regard to the very essence of what covenant is all about.

Chris Wright develops many of these ideas, and goes on to show that the idea of covenant highlights the missionary heart of God. Wright's paper – entitled 'Covenant: God's mission through God's people' – argues that covenant essentially restores relationship and this is all part of the divine plan of salvation. There are, therefore, missional implications to be drawn from the biblical notion of covenant. Wright defines a 'missional' reading of the Bible in terms of being sensitive to God's *purpose* and, in a broad sweep through the key moments in God's covenantal relationship with humanity, he draws out various significant missional emphases. In God's covenant with Noah, Wright notes God's commitment to life on this earth and draws out the ecological dimension to this commitment. The covenant with Abraham, Wright claims, is 'the most significant of all the biblical covenants' from a missiological perspective. God promises blessing to the nations through the particular means of Abraham and his descendents, who will form a community that embodies righteousness. Turning to the Sinai covenant, Wright notes that Exodus 19:3–6 emphasizes the priority of God's initiative, a universal perspective and the character of Israel as priestly (i.e. making God known to the nations) and holy (i.e. representing God's character to the nations). He also argues that Deuteronomy has several emphases suggestive for reflection

on mission: that Israel is a people 'on the boundary' and is called to
loyalty in the face of cultures that would impose themselves on
Israel; that Yahweh is God and there is no other, not only for Israel
but for all the nations; that Israel is an ethical model to the nations,
as they embody the character of the God they worship; and that
Israel's lack of covenant faithfulness is portrayed frankly, yet hope
of restoration remains. Wright also highlights further hints of universality in God's purposes from the Davidic Covenant and briefly
notes several passages in Jeremiah, Ezekiel and Isaiah that point
towards the universal significance of a *new* covenant. Wright leaves
us with a powerful plea that the covenants be integrated into a
Christian reading of the Old Testament that is 'both messianic and
missiological'.

We move from the general to the specific in chapter 3, where
David Firth examines the Davidic Covenant ('Speech acts and
covenant in 2 Samuel 7:1–17'). One of the interesting things about
the passage, which describes the 'covenant' with King David and
his line, is that the word 'covenant' is nowhere used in this passage.
This has led some commentators to question whether 2 Samuel 7
actually contains a covenant at all. Firth examines this text from
the perspective of the speech acts of Yahweh, David and the narrator and concludes that (while the word does not appear) clearly
the language used indicates that a covenant relationship is formed
between Yahweh and the house of David. He goes on to examine
the overlap between 2 Samuel 7 and the 'Last Words of David',
where the reference to a covenant with David adopts similar language to that used in 2 Samuel 7. Firth also adds some helpful
discussion of the whole question of faithful response and conditionality in 'unconditional' covenants formed at the sovereign
behest of Yahweh. This is also a useful introduction to speech act
theory, if this is something new to you.

In chapter 4 ('A new-covenant slogan in the Old Testament')
James Hely Hutchinson suggests that the phrase 'Give thanks to
Yahweh, for his steadfast love (*ḥesed*) endures for ever' should
actually be understood as a covenant formula. He examines the
contextual usage of each occurrence of this phase in the light of
the 'base text' found in Jeremiah 33:11, which connects the phrase
with the 'new covenant' idea. Hutchinson's canonical analysis of the

occurrences in the psalter, Ezra and Chronicles points to a similar conclusion – this formulation points to an understanding of this repeated phrase in terms of the eschatological framework of the new covenant. Obviously, any distinctively Christian discussion of covenant will find a focal point in the 'new covenant' (the fulfilment of the covenant ideal in Jesus the Messiah) and Hutchinson points out that there is a strong line of continuity between the OT covenants with Abraham and David and the new covenant. One substantive difference, according to Hutchinson, between the new covenant and other covenants is that Jeremiah seems to suggest that the former will provide a permanent solution to the problem of 'exile' – a covenant that somehow deals with the problem of covenant unfaithfulness.

Hutchinson's consideration of this (new) covenant formula leaves us knocking at the door of the New Testament, and in chapter 5 ('Community, kingdom and cross') Kim Huat Tan takes us over the threshold with his discussion of the covenant in Jesus' conception. Moving from predominantly OT-centred discussion of covenant in the previous chapters, Tan leads us into the Gospels and argues that, despite the infrequent use of explicit covenant terminology, the teaching of Jesus must be understood in covenantal terms. Tan lays out the foundations of his argument by highlighting the relational character of the covenant, with its intimate relationship to community and by arguing that the anticipated goal of the covenant is the final establishment of Yahweh's kingdom. Tan believes that these covenantal themes of 'kingdom' and 'community' in Jesus' ministry are exemplified in the parable of the good Samaritan. In a careful study of the text, he argues firmly for the historical plausibility both of the parable itself and its original relationship with its narrative setting or 'frame'. Tan argues that the conversation between the lawyer and Jesus should be understood in covenantal terms as the lawyer's question is thoroughly Jewish ('How can I share in the life of the age to come?') and Jesus' reply is thoroughly covenantal in that he draws the lawyer's attention to OT texts that define the covenant relationship. Finally, Tan presents a reading of the Last Supper narratives that integrates the cross into this covenantal reading of Jesus' mission as the means by which God will inaugurate the eschatological/new covenant.

In chapter 6 Alistair Wilson picks up again on the 'new covenant theme' but this time drawing conclusions from Luke's take on the idea. It is interesting that Luke alone among the Gospel writers describes the Last Supper covenant meal in terms of the *new* covenant, so Wilson asks whether the new covenant theme is apparent elsewhere in Luke. Luke does not cite Jeremiah in his Gospel, but his work is steeped in new covenant thought. Zechariah's *Benedictus* highlights the fact that God is beginning a radically new work in the coming of the Messiah, and Luke's framing of Jesus' ministry in the Isaianic terms of 'release' and forgiveness of sins draws further allusion to the prophetic presentation of the new covenant. Wilson asks (from a NT perspective this time), 'What's new about the new covenant?' and his conclusions provide an interesting supplement to the discussions of this question found in earlier chapters of this book. Wilson also takes on some ideas found in recent scholarship: he stresses a Lukan emphasis on the continuity of the covenants where some have called this into question, and he also suggests that Luke frames his understanding of the new covenant more in terms of 'release from sin' than return from exile.

The remaining three chapters of this book move beyond analysis of the biblical material to discuss the theological and practical implications of this magisterial theme. Chapter 7 sees Andrew McGowan write 'In defence of "headship theology"'. Having defined 'Federal Theology' (FT) as theology that describes the relationship between God and humanity in covenantal terms, McGowan sketches the shape of classical FT, noting the foundational biblical texts in Romans and 1 Corinthians and then tracing the historical development of the system from Ursinus to its expression in the Westminster Confession of Faith. McGowan then takes us into the eighteenth century, highlighting two strands of thought among adherents to the Westminster Confession, as exemplified by James Hadow and Thomas Boston. He argues that, despite claims to the contrary, Boston represents an expression of FT that emphasizes grace rather than law. Moving into the twentieth century, McGowan highlights the significance of John Murray as a theologian standing in the tradition of Boston, and notes that his views on the original relationship between God and humanity have been challenged by Meredith Kline and some of his students, who have argued for a 'covenant of works'. McGowan defends Murray's view that all of God's dealings with humanity have been based on grace and the initial pre-fall relationship with Adam might best be described as the 'Adamic Administration'. Building on Murray's work and drawing on insights from Dietrich Bonhoeffer, McGowan argues that, in the interests of linguistic precision, we should speak of a 'Messianic Administration' and replace 'FT' with 'Headship Theology' so as to draw attention to the distinctive characteristic of FT.

In chapter 8 ('Covenants, special relationships and a perfectly loving God'), Harry Bunting discusses the implications of covenant from the perspective of contemporary philosophy and ethical theory. Bunting 'takes on' the popular notion that the 'partiality' of (particularly OT) covenant relationship is incompatible with the concept of an 'all-good, all-loving moral being' – is not such partisanship inherently wrong? First, he challenges utilitarian notions of moral impartiality by examining 'agent-centred' theories of morality and 'hybrid concepts' of ethics. Essentially, Bunting argues that 'partial' relationships can ultimately be beneficial to broader cross-sections of society if they fulfil certain criteria ('seriousness' and being 'other-regarding'), which the OT covenants clearly do. Bunting then goes on to examine the 'internal critique' of covenant (namely, that the particularity of the OT covenants stands in irreconcilable conflict with the universality of the new covenant) and he challenges this notion by examining the three types of love highlighted in contemporary moral philosophy. Bunting suggests that a right understanding of the concepts of 'instrumental, non-instrumental and pure love' resolves the prima facie tensions often highlighted between the covenants of Old and New Testaments.

This type of discussion may be very new to many, but is worth devoting attention to, as the discussion adds a helpful 'external and contemporary' perspective to the biblical material we have been examining.

In the final chapter of this book ('God's covenant – God's land?'), Colin Chapman demonstrates with a degree of passion that the idea of covenant is not purely academic, but has far-reaching implications for the world in which we live. There is much talk about 'the war on terror', 'the Palestinian problem' and 'radical Islamism' in the media presently and one aspect that plays into this ferment of debate is the idea (popular in certain Christian circles, especially in North America) that the OT covenant promises with regard to the land apply today with regard to the secular state of Israel. Covenant is not just an abstract theory – its implications can be huge. Chapman discusses the biblical issues regarding covenant and land, and the theological implications, and this leads him on to consider the Christian's involvement in politics. The biblical idea of covenant may well have deeply profound implications for the individual believer and the Christian community in spiritual terms, but do the implications go beyond the spiritual to the literal? Chapman helpfully discusses the spiritualization of the covenant idea, the implications of this for world politics and challenges the reader as to the Christian's proper response to social injustice.

Eclectic? Certainly. There is a broad range of material contained within this book, but our hope is that you will find it as fascinating as it is varied. Few things in life are as profound as the promise 'I will be your God, and you will be my people'. We hope you will enjoy these deliberations upon such a rich theme.

Alistair I. Wilson
Jamie A. Grant
June 2004

1. COVENANT: AN OLD TESTAMENT STUDY

David L. Baker

Introduction

The word 'covenant' is rarely used in modern English but its meaning is essentially an 'agreement', 'contract', 'treaty' or 'commitment' between two or more parties. Such an agreement may create a new relationship between the parties, or formalize a relationship that already exists. Generally there will be written documentation, and often witnesses, though where the respective parties trust each other a verbal agreement may be sufficient, as in the London Stock Exchange where deals are traditionally made verbally and the dealers hold to their motto 'My word is my bond'. Individuals, groups and nations usually enter into contracts voluntarily, for mutual advantage, though in some cases one party may impose a contract or treaty on another (e.g. a creditor on a defaulting debtor, or a victorious country on another defeated in war). There are also acts of commitment, such as marriage or confirmation, intended to express mutual love in a way that defines obligations and promises faithfulness, without necessarily conferring specific benefits on either party.

Hebrew terms for 'covenant'

The most important term in Hebrew for covenant is *běrît*, found 287 times in the Old Testament and generally translated 'covenant', though occasionally 'treaty', 'agreement' or 'alliance'. It refers to the establishment of a specific relationship between two parties, human and/or divine (Eichrodt 1961: 36–45; Kalluveettil 1982; Mendenhall and Herion 1992; McConville 1997).[1] The word is commonly used with the verb *kārat*, 'cut', perhaps because the making of a covenant was often accompanied by sacrifice, but various other verbs also occur, including *hēqîm*, 'establish' (e.g. Genesis 9:11; 17:7), *nātan*, 'give' (e.g. Genesis 17:2) and *ṣiwwâ*, 'command' (e.g. Psalm 105:8; Jeremiah 11:4).

The term *'ēdût* (46 times in the Old Testament) is translated by some versions as 'covenant', especially in relation to the ark, tablets and tabernacle, though others prefer 'testimony' or 'treaty'. Several other terms are also related in meaning to covenant and occasionally interchangeable (Weinfeld 1977: 256–259), for example:

'ālâ, 'oath' (Genesis 26:28; Deuteronomy 29:12, 14; Nehemiah 10:29; Ezekiel 16:59; 17:18);

dābār, 'word' (Deuteronomy 9:5; cf. 8:18; Haggai 2:5);

ḥesed, 'steadfast love' (Deuteronomy 7:9, 12; Isaiah 54:10; 55:3);

šālôm, 'peace' (Numbers 25:12; Joshua 9:15);

tôrâ, 'law, instruction' (2 Kings 23:3; cf. verse 24; Hosea 8:1).

The 'covenant formula'

The so-called 'covenant formula' has been studied in detail by several scholars (Smend 1963; Lohfink 1969; Rendtorff 1998; van den Eynde 1999). Its full form is found first of all (canonically) in Exodus 6:7:

---

1. Some scholars have argued that the original meaning was 'obligation', imposed by one party on themselves and/or others, and that the idea of a mutual agreement that created and defined a relationship was a later development (Kutsch 1973; Weinfeld 1977: 255). For a summary and critique of Kutsch's view, see Nicholson (1986: 89–99, 104–109); cf. Barr (1977).

I will take you as my people, and I will be your God.[2]

Leviticus 26:12 is identical in content, but the order is reversed:

I . . . will be your God, and you shall be my people.

With very similar wording the formula is found in Deuteronomy (26:17–19; 29:12–13), 2 Samuel (7:24), and frequently in the prophets (Jeremiah 7:23; 11:4; 24:7; 30:22; 31:1, 33; 32:38; Ezekiel 11:20; 14:11; 36:28; 37:23, 27; Zechariah 8:8).
Two brief forms of the covenant formula are common.[3] 'I will be your God', or something similar, is used in the first four books of the Pentateuch (Genesis 17:7, 8; Exodus 29:45; Leviticus 11:45; 22:33; 25:38; 26:45; Numbers 15:41) and once in Ezekiel 34:24. The other half of the formula 'You shall be my people' or its equivalent, is characteristic of Deuteronomy (4:20; 7:6; 14:2; 27:9; 28:9) and occurs in 1 Samuel 12:22; 2 Kings 11:17; and Jeremiah 13:11.
There are also allusions to the formula, or at least expressions very similar in content, in Exodus 19:4–6; Deuteronomy 4:7; 27:9; 2 Kings 11:17 ‖ 2 Chronicles 23:16; Psalm 33:12; 95:7; 100:3; Ezekiel 34:30–31; Hosea 1:9; 2:23; and Zechariah 2:11.[4]

Covenants in the Old Testament
Many covenants and treaties in the Old Testament are between human beings, both individuals and groups, for example:

• Abraham and Abimelech, Genesis 21:22–32

---

2. All quotations are taken from the NRSV, unless otherwise stated.
3. It is commonly assumed that the bilateral form is original, and the others are 'halves', though Rendtorff (1998: 12) questions this assumption.
4. The similarity between covenant forms in the Old Testament and treaty forms in the ancient Near East is well known and has been studied by many scholars but will not be discussed here (see Mendenhall 1954a; 1954b; Muilenburg 1959; Calderone 1966; Hillers 1969: 25–71; Baltzer 1971; Weinfeld 1972; McCarthy 1978; Lucas 1982; Nicholson 1986: 56–82; Mendenhall and Herion 1992).

- Isaac and Abimelech, Genesis 26:26–31
- Jacob and Laban, Genesis 31:43–54
- Jonathan and David, 1 Samuel 18:1–4; 20:8, 16–17; 23:18
- David and Abner, 2 Samuel 3:12–13; cf. verses 17–21
- David and Israel, 2 Samuel 5:3 || 1 Chronicles 11:3
- Nebuchadnezzar and Zedekiah, Ezekiel 17:12–19

The people of Israel are warned not to make covenants or treaties with pagan nations and their gods (Exodus 23:32; Deuteronomy 7:2), though in fact they often do so (e.g. treaties with Gibeon, Joshua 9; Tyre, 1 Kings 5:1–12; cf. 2 Samuel 5:11; 1 Kings 16:30–31; Amos 1:9; Aram, 1 Kings 15:19; 20:34; 2 Chronicles 16:3; Assyria, Hosea 12:1). Marriage is occasionally referred to as a covenant (Proverbs 2:17; Malachi 2:14; cf. Job 31:1), as is friendship (Psalm 55:20).[5]

There are several covenants between God and human beings. The first mentioned is God's covenant with *Noah* and the whole earth (Genesis 6:18; 9:1–17).[6] God also makes covenants with *Levi* and the priesthood (Numbers 18:19; 25:10–13; Deuteronomy 33:8–9; Nehemiah 13:29; Jeremiah 33:20–22; Malachi 2:4–8), and with *David* and his dynasty (2 Samuel 7;[7] 23:5; 1 Kings 8:23–25; 2 Chronicles 6:14–16; 7:17–18; 13:5; 21:7; Psalms 89; 132:11–12; Jeremiah 33:17–26). All three covenants are described as 'everlasting' or 'perpetual' (*běrît 'ôlām*, Genesis 9:12, 16; Numbers 18:19; 25:13; 2 Samuel 23:5; 2 Chronicles 13:5; Psalm 89:29). They are unilateral in nature, in the sense that God initiates them and commits himself to keeping them, whereas little is said about

---

5. On secular covenants in the Old Testament and the ancient Near East, see Kalluveettil (1982).

6. Some scholars have suggested an even earlier covenant with creation (e.g. Robertson 1980: 17–25; Dumbrell 1984: 11–43), and this is the starting point for seventeenth-century federal theology (Visser 1996), but the exegetical basis for this is disputed (Williamson 2003: 141–143) and the word *běrît* is certainly not used before the flood story.

7. Even though the word *běrît* is not used, this is clearly the fundamental text (together with its parallel in 1 Chronicles 17:1–15) which establishes God's special relationship (i.e. covenant) with David and his descendants.

human response and obligations (though a positive response is implied).

However, by far the most important covenant in the Old Testament is the one made by God with Abraham and his descendants, and confirmed to the people of Israel at Sinai, Moab and Shechem. It does not invalidate the prior covenant with Noah, which included all human beings, but is more specific and focuses on the election of the people of God. It is also divinely initiated, but is bilateral in the sense that human response is specifically invited and documented (e.g. Exodus 24:3, 7). This too is an everlasting covenant (Genesis 17:7, 13, 19; 1 Chronicles 16:15–17 ‖ Psalm 105:8–10), and God is always faithful to that intention (Judges 2:1; Psalms 105:8; 111:5, 9) though it is repeatedly broken by Israel (as we shall see later). It is primarily this covenant that becomes the basis of the prophecies of a new covenant in the future, also to be everlasting (Isaiah 59:21; 61:8; Jeremiah 31:31–34;[8] 32:40; 50:5; Ezekiel 16:60; 37:26; cf. Isaiah 55:3).

Many interpreters distinguish the Abrahamic and Mosaic covenants, considering them to be quite separate, but the position taken here is that – at least from a canonical perspective – the Mosaic covenant is a confirmation and elaboration of that made with Abraham, not something new or different. There are of course widely varying views among scholars concerning the origins of the covenant traditions, and whether they can in fact be traced back as far as Abraham and Moses, but issues of dating and historicity will not be discussed in this chapter.[9] The focus here is on understanding the Old Testament as we now have it, and from that perspective it is

---

8. The term *bĕrît 'ôlām* is not actually found in this text, the only one that specifically uses the term 'new covenant'; nevertheless it is clear from the description that it is intended to be everlasting.

9. Wellhausen believed that the covenant was a late development in Israelite religion, resulting from the preaching of the prophets. This view was largely abandoned in the twentieth century through the research of Gunkel, Weber, Mowinckel, Alt, Noth, Eichrodt, Mendenhall and others; then revived by Perlitt (1969) and Kutsch (1973). Two recent studies have argued that the idea of covenant originated in the kinship bonds of

one covenant that God initiates with Abraham, then confirms and elaborates to his promised descendants after they are liberated from Egypt, and before and after they enter the Promised Land (Exodus 6:2–8; Leviticus 26:42, 45; Deuteronomy 4:31; 9:27; Judges 2:1; 1 Chronicles 16:15–17; Nehemiah 9:7–15).[10] As Fretheim (1991: 208–214) demonstrates, Israel does not become the people of God at Sinai, but their election is already assumed as an established fact in the early chapters of Exodus (e.g. 3:7–10; 4:22; 5:1 etc.). They are inheritors of the promises to the ancestors (Exodus 3:15–17; 32:13) and the covenant that God made with Abraham *and his offspring* (Genesis 17:7). They believe the word of God spoken by Moses, witness God's saving power and worship him (Exodus 4:31; 12:27; 14:31–15:21). Thus 'the covenant at Sinai is a specific covenant within the context of the Abrahamic covenant', made with an already existing covenant community (Fretheim 1991: 209).[11]

God's covenant with Abraham and his descendants

Abraham
When God first calls Abraham, he establishes a special relationship with him as he promises him a new land, many descendants and great blessing (Genesis 12:1–3, 7). This may be seen as the basic biblical promise, which is elaborated and [partially] fulfilled throughout the Pentateuch, and indeed the whole Bible (Baker 1991: 215–231). The word 'covenant' is first used to express this relationship in Genesis 15:18:

> On that day the LORD made a *covenant* with Abram, saying, 'To your descendants I give this land, from the river of Egypt to the great river, the river Euphrates …' (my emphasis)

---

ancient Israelite tribal society (Cross 1998; McKenzie 2000: 11–39). For a historical survey, see Nicholson (1986: 3–117).

10. It may be significant here that the noun *bĕrît* (covenant) is never found in the plural in the Old Testament (cf. Barr 1977: 29–31).

11. See also Robertson (1980: 27–52) on the unity of the divine covenants.

It is in the context of a covenant ceremony involving sacrifices and a theophany (verses 7–17).

In Genesis 17 the covenant becomes the main topic. God takes the initiative by appearing to Abraham, now 99 years old, and informing him that he is intending to make a covenant with him; namely that Abraham will be the 'ancestor of a multitude of nations' (verses 2–6). He explains that this will be an everlasting covenant (verse 7) and that the land where they reside as immigrants will become theirs forever (verse 8). As a sign of Abraham's acceptance of the covenant, he is instructed to perform the rite of circumcision (verses 9–14; cf. 23–27). God adds that although Ishmael (already 13 years old) will also be blessed with many descendants (verses 18, 20), the covenant will be established with Isaac, the child to be conceived by Sarah and born the following year (verses 15–16, 19, 21).

The essence of this covenant is a special relationship with God, stated with a double use of the covenant formula (in short form):

> I will establish my *covenant* between me and you, and your offspring after you throughout their generations, for an everlasting *covenant, to be God to you* and to your offspring after you. And I will give to you, and to your offspring after you, the land where you are now an alien, all the land of Canaan, for a perpetual holding; *and I will be their God.* (Genesis 17:7–8, my emphasis)

It is sometimes thought that the covenant with Abraham was unconditional, but the fact that circumcision is the only obligation specified in this text does not mean there were no other conditions. To accept the LORD as God surely implies obligations of worship, obedience and faithfulness, even if the details are not elaborated here. Genesis 17 begins with an ethical imperative ('walk before me, and be blameless', verse 1) and ethical implications are referred to later in the Abraham story (18:19; 22:18; 26:5).

In later days the covenant with Abraham is celebrated in a psalm of David (1 Chronicles 16:15–17 || Psalm 105:8–10) and a prayer of Ezra (Nehemiah 9:7–8), and the Deuteronomic historian considers it to be the reason why Israel continued to exist and

occupy the land for so long in spite of their repeated disobedience
(2 Kings 13:23; cf. Joshua 24:3–13).

God's covenant with Abraham and his descendants is confirmed in special ceremonies at three crucial points in the history
of the people of God, namely:

- after the exodus from Egypt (at Mount Sinai)
- at the end of Moses' life, before the people enter the Promised
  Land (on the plains of Moab)
- after the settlement in the land (at Shechem)

We will consider these one by one.

Sinai

Several hundred years later God has fulfilled his promise to
Abraham of many descendants, but those descendants are slaves in
Egypt and feeling far from blessed. Now the narrator tells us that
'God heard their groaning, and God remembered his covenant with
Abraham, Isaac, and Jacob' (Exodus 2:24). He declares to Moses:

> I am the LORD. I appeared to Abraham, Isaac, and Jacob as God
> Almighty, but by my name 'The LORD' I did not make myself known to
> them. I also established my *covenant* with them, to give them the land of
> Canaan, the land in which they resided as aliens. I have also heard the
> groaning of the Israelites whom the Egyptians are holding as slaves, and
> I have remembered my *covenant*. Say therefore to the Israelites, 'I am the
> LORD, and I will free you from the burdens of the Egyptians and deliver
> you from slavery to them. I will redeem you with an outstretched arm
> and with mighty acts of judgement. *I will take you as my people, and I will be
> your God.*' (Exodus 6:2–7, my emphasis)

It is on the basis of his covenant with the ancestors that God
intends to set his people free from Egypt, and once again the
essence of the covenant is affirmed; namely their special relationship with God. This time the covenant formula appears in its full
form.

After the exodus the people travel to Sinai, and there the
essence of the covenant is restated:

You have seen what I did to the Egyptians, and how I bore you on
eagles' wings and brought you to myself. Now therefore, if you obey my
voice and keep my *covenant, you shall be my treasured possession out of all the
peoples.* Indeed, the whole earth is mine, but you shall be for me a priestly
kingdom and a holy nation. (Exodus 19:4–6, my emphasis)

The expression 'you shall be my treasured possession out of all
the peoples' in verse 5b is very close to the covenant formula
(Rendtorff 1998: 26–28), and specifically related to the word
'covenant' in the first part of the verse. It indicates God's love for
his chosen people, and this is the motivation for the covenant
rather than mutual advantage (cf. Exodus 34:6–7; Deuteronomy
7:6–9).

This is followed by an awesome theophany (Exodus 19), the
giving of the Ten Commandments (Exodus 20), the so-called
Book of the Covenant (Exodus 21–23; cf. 24:7), and finally a ceremony to confirm the covenant (Exodus 24), which includes

- a statement of intent between the LORD and the people
  (verse 3)
- writing the covenant document (verse 4a)
- building an altar and twelve pillars (verse 4b)
- sacrifices (verses 5–6)
- reading the covenant document and acceptance by the people
  (verse 7)
- sprinkling the people with blood, to seal the covenant (verse 8)

Then Moses and the leaders climb the mountain and meet with
God (verses 9–11), and Moses himself stays a further forty days to
receive the tablets of stone (verses 12–18).

In Leviticus the covenant formula appears five times (11:45;
22:33; 25:38; 26:12, 45). Two of the occurrences are in chapter 26,
together with a sevenfold use of the word 'covenant'. Thus the
conclusion to the Holiness Code reaffirms the covenant with an
assurance that God will maintain the covenant (verse 9), promising
rewards if the people are obedient (verses 3–13) and warning of
the consequences if they break the covenant (verses 14–39).
However, even if Israel does break the covenant, God will always

remember it and be prepared to renew it if they repent (verses
40–45).

Moab

Forty years later, on the plains of Moab, Moses and the people of
Israel have reached the border of the Promised Land. The two
addresses in the first eleven chapters of Deuteronomy review the
history of the preceding years and reflect on the covenant and its
implications for the people of God. The next fifteen chapters
present the distinctive Deuteronomic Laws, and are followed by
confirmation of the covenant in chapters 26:16 – 30:20.[12]

The word *běrît* is used twenty-seven times in Deuteronomy, more
than in any other Old Testament book apart from Genesis; the
covenant formula is used directly in seven texts (4:20; 7:6; 14:2; 27:9;
26:17–19; 28:9; 29:13) and alluded to elsewhere (e.g. 4:7; 27:9).
Clearly the covenant relationship between God and his people is a
major theme and focus of the book. The covenant, expressed in the
Ten Commandments and inscribed on the two tablets, had been
declared to the people at Sinai/Horeb (4:13; 5:2), as a confirmation of God's covenant with their ancestors (4:31; 7:12; cf. 1:8;
26:3–10). They must therefore observe the covenant (4:23, 40; 5:33;
6:3, 17; 7:11; and passim), just as God will surely keep his part of the
deal (7:9).

As the covenant with the ancestors had been confirmed to the
people at Sinai, so it is confirmed once again to the next generation in Moab:

---

12. Olson (1994: 126–158) argues that the next two chapters present parallel
    versions of the Moab covenant, characterized by word (Deuteronomy 31,
    on the leadership succession) and song (Deuteronomy 32, the Song of
    Moses). Against those who consider Deuteronomy 29 – 32 to be appen-
    dices largely unrelated to the preceding laws, he argues that they are 'a
    climactic extension and reinterpretation of the Horeb commandments'
    (152).

    Cholewinski (1985) considers the covenant with Israel in Moab to be
    even more significant than that at Sinai, and to prefigure the 'new
    covenant' spoken of by the later prophets.

The LORD our God made a *covenant* with us at Horeb. Not with our ancestors did the LORD make this *covenant*, but with us, who are all of us here alive today. (Deuteronomy 5:2–3, my emphasis)[13]

Remember the LORD your God, for it is he who gives you power to get wealth, so that he may confirm his *covenant* that he swore to your ancestors, as he is doing today. (Deuteronomy 8:18, my emphasis)

These are the words of the *covenant* that the LORD commanded Moses to make with the Israelites in the land of Moab, in addition to the *covenant* that he had made with them at Horeb. (Deuteronomy 29:1, my emphasis)

These texts make it clear that the covenant at Sinai is understood to be still operative for the new generation of Israelites, and Deuteronomy intends to confirm and supplement its provisions. The term 'confirmation of the covenant' is preferable to 'covenant renewal' (because the old one has not been broken) or 'new covenant' (because the new one does not replace the old).

Exodus has no description of a covenant ceremony like that, though many key elements of a ceremony are stated or implied:

- a statement that the LORD and the people have agreed to the covenant (26:16–19; cf. 27:9–10)
- provision for further confirmation of the covenant after entering the Promised Land (27:1–8, 11–26)
- blessings for obedience and curses for disobedience (28:1–68)
- assembly of the whole people to 'enter into the covenant of the LORD your God' (29:1–15)
- warnings and assurances (29:16 – 30:10)
- concluding call to commitment (30:11–20)

Shechem
When they have occupied the Promised Land, the people of Israel

---

13. This is of course not a literal historical statement, but hyperbole intended to actualize the covenant for the hearers of Moses' sermon, and no doubt also for later readers and hearers of these words (cf. Olson 1994: 41).

are instructed to set up stones inscribed with the words of the law and to build an altar on Mount Ebal (Deuteronomy 27:1–8), and then to hold a ceremony declaring the blessings and curses of the covenant on Mount Gerizim and Mount Ebal respectively (27:11–26; cf. 11:29–30). These two mountains overlook Shechem, an ancient city in the heartland of northern Canaan that was significant in the lives of Abraham (Genesis 12:6) and Jacob (33:18–20; 35:4).

The book of Joshua twice records Israel assembling at Shechem to reconfirm their covenant with God, though some commentators consider both texts to refer to the same event (e.g. Soggin 1972: 220–244). According to Joshua 8:30–35, after the conquest of Ai (which was the earliest point in the settlement that it was feasible to access Shechem), Joshua builds an altar and offers sacrifices on Mount Ebal, in conscious fulfilment of Moses' instructions. He then inscribes a copy of the law of Moses on stones and holds a ceremonial reading in the presence of all Israel, including the blessings and curses. In Joshua 24, at the end of Joshua's life and after the completion of the settlement, the tribes of Israel are gathered once again in Shechem. In his farewell speech, Joshua has previously warned the people of the danger of breaking the covenant (23:16), and now he negotiates their renewed commitment. There is a clear structure to the account of the assembly:

- opening ceremony (24:1)
- historical introduction (verses 2–13)
- call to decision (verses 14–15)
- the people's response (verses 16–21)
- confirmation of the covenant, including
  oath of allegiance (verses 22–24),
  writing of the covenant document (verses 25–26a),
  setting up a stone as witness to the agreement (verses 26b–27)
- closing ceremony (verse 28)

The covenant and Israel's worship
The covenant is a key theme in the worship of Israel, as it sums up the relationship between God and his people, and several artefacts and symbols have a role in this connection.

The most important artefact is the *ark* of the covenant,[14] the making of which is prescribed and recorded in Exodus (25:10–22; 26:33–34; 30:26; 31:7; 37:1–9; 39:35; 40:3, 20–21; cf. Deuteronomy 10:1–5). It functions as a focal point for the people during their wandering in the wilderness (Numbers 4:5–6; 7:89; 10:33–36; 14:44; Deuteronomy 10:8), on the plains of Moab (Deuteronomy 31:9, 25–26) and during the settlement of the Promised Land (Joshua 3 – 4; 6:3–13; 7:6; 8:33). In the historical books the ark is mentioned intermittently, particularly in the stories of Eli (1 Samuel 3:3; 4:1–7:2), David (2 Samuel 6; 7:2; 11:11; 15:24–29; 1 Chronicles 13; 15–16; 22:19) and Solomon (1 Kings 3:15; 6:19; 8:1–21; 2 Chronicles 5 – 6), and presumably it was captured or destroyed in the fall of Jerusalem.[15]

The primary stipulations of the covenant are written on the *tablets* of the covenant (Exodus 31:18; 32:15–19; 34:29; Deuteronomy 9:9–17; 1 Kings 8:9 || 2 Chronicles 5:10), sometimes referred to simply as 'the covenant' (Exodus 25:16, 21; 40:20; 1 Kings 8:21 || 2 Chronicles 6:11), which are kept in the ark. And the ark is kept in the *tabernacle*, which is occasionally called the tabernacle of the covenant (Exodus 38:21; Numbers 1:50–53; 10:11) or tent of the covenant (Numbers 9:15; 17:7–8; 18:2; 2 Chronicles 24:6) and is once associated with the covenant formula (Exodus 29:42–46).[16]

The covenant is often mentioned in the psalms, reminding worshippers of God's faithfulness to his covenant (Psalms 106:45; 111:5, 9) and encouraging them to keep his covenant (25:10, 14; 103:17–18), unlike those ancestors who broke it (78:10, 37). One

---

14. Both *běrît* and *'ēdût* are used interchangeably in this term, and it is also often called 'the ark of the LORD' or 'the ark of God' or simply 'the ark'.

15. It is also referred to briefly in Judges 20:27, in the time of Saul (1 Samuel 14:18) and Josiah (2 Chronicles 35:3; cf. 33:7?) and by Psalm 132:8 and Jeremiah 3:16.

16. Other artefacts and symbols related to the covenant include the book and blood of the covenant (Exodus 24:7–8), the sabbath (31:16), the salt that accompanies grain offerings (Leviticus 2:13), the curtain (24:3), the holy bread (Leviticus 24:5–9) and fringes on garments (Numbers 15:37–41).

psalmist protests that he and his people have been faithful to the
covenant, whereas God appears not to be keeping his part of the
agreement (44:17). The covenant formula is alluded to in Psalms
33:12 (Lohfink 2000); 95:7; and 100:3.[17]

Covenant-breaking and renewal

Tragically the covenant between God and Abraham, thrice confirmed to his descendants with great ceremony, is repeatedly
broken in the succeeding years (Judges 2:2, 11–21). Eventually this
leads to expulsion from the Promised Land, first for the ten tribes
of northern Israel (2 Kings 17:7–23; 18:11–12) and later for
the remaining people of Judah in the south (2 Kings 24:20;
2 Chronicles 36:15–21; Jeremiah 22:4–9; 25:8–11).[18] However, this
does not mean that God has given up on the covenant, and
prophets assure the exiles in Babylon of his continued concern for
his people and plans for their restoration (Isaiah 40:1–11; 41:8–10;
Jeremiah 29:10–14).

God is not taken by surprise when Israel breaks the covenant. It
is specifically predicted in Deuteronomy (e.g. 29:18–21; 31:16, 20),
and their 'stiff-necked' nature is noticed immediately after the confirmation of the covenant at Sinai in the incident of the golden
calf (Exodus 32:9; 33:3, 5; 34:9). A major part of the prophetic
role is to remind the people of their covenant obligations and call
them to repentance.

We will now look briefly at ten examples of covenant-breaking
and renewal in the Old Testament, in order to gain a clearer
picture of what is happening and why.

---

17. Other references to covenant are found in Psalms 50:5, 16; 74:20.
18. Are there echoes of the expulsion from Eden (Genesis 3:22–24) here?
    Of course neither the term nor the concept of covenant is found in the
    early chapters of Genesis, but there is a parallel in the idea of God giving
    the land and its produce to human beings and later retracting that gift
    when they fail to follow the conditions laid out beforehand.

Moses

It is never said that Abraham himself broke the covenant, but 'the ink is scarcely dry' on the Mosaic tablets before Israel has broken the covenant by making a golden calf. There is a certain ambivalence in the narrative as to whether or not it is a conscious rejection of YHWH as God, and it appears that Aaron is attempting a compromise between the demands of the people for visible gods (Exodus 32:1–4) and his own loyalty to Moses and belief in the unseen God (verses 5, 21–24). However, the narrator clearly understands it as a breaking of the covenant by the people (verses 7–10), so serious that it would have been cancelled there and then, were it not for Moses' appeal to the promise to the ancestors (verses 11–14).

An extraordinary succession of events is then set in motion. The impetuous breaking of the tablets of the covenant is followed by destruction of the calf, execution of three thousand rebels, a further appeal by Moses to God, a plague, God's statement that he will no longer accompany his people to the Promised Land, mourning by the people, a third appeal by Moses to God, the cutting and inscribing of two new tablets, a theophany on Mount Sinai, Moses' confession of sin on behalf of the people and finally the renewal of the covenant (34:10, 27–28).[19] Various laws are included here, including a prohibition of making treaties (= covenants) with the inhabitants of Canaan (verses 12, 15).

Joshua

The next time the covenant is broken is not long after its second confirmation on the plains of Moab. Shortly after entry to the Promised Land and the dazzling victory at Jericho, Achan son of Carmi son of Zabdi son of Zerah of the tribe of Judah helps himself to some of the 'devoted things', plunder that according to the principles of holy war should have been destroyed or placed in

---

19. Fretheim describes it as a new covenant, rather than simply a renewal of the Sinai covenant, which is 'grounded in a new act of God on behalf of Israel' (1991: 308). But most interpreters understand it as a renewal of the original covenant of Sinai (e.g. Segal 1967).

the sanctuary (Joshua 7:1). This is a serious transgression of the covenant, involving stealing from God and deception (verse 11), and results in God's withdrawal from the people so that they are no longer able to stand against their enemies (verse 12).

As Moses had done before him, Joshua acts decisively. In accordance with divine instructions, a ceremony of sanctification is held to determine who is responsible for the crime, so that:

> The one who is taken as having the devoted things shall be burned with fire, together with all that he has, for having transgressed the *covenant* of the LORD, and for having done an outrageous thing in Israel. (Joshua 7:15, my emphasis)

The guilty party is found and stoned by 'all Israel', and the matter is considered closed (verses 24–26). No specific covenant renewal ceremony is recorded at this point, but it is hardly coincidental that no sooner is the battle of Ai over than the Israelites travel north to Shechem for the confirmation of the covenant (8:30–35; see above).

Samuel

During the time of the judges the covenant is repeatedly broken, and a pattern appears of apostasy, punishment, God's provision of a deliverer ('judge'), temporary improvement, then further relapse (Judges 2:11–21). However, no specific covenant renewal ceremonies are described until the time of Samuel.

After the proclamation of Saul as first king of Israel, and the defeat of Ammon, Samuel assembles the people at Gilgal to 'renew the kingship' (1 Samuel 11:14 – 12:25). The assembly may be understood as a covenant renewal ceremony (Vannoy 1978), with several features of the covenant form visible:

- appeal to antecedent history (12:6–12)
- blessing and curse sanctions (12:14–15, 25)
- a theophanic sign (12:16–18)
- challenge to allegiance to the Lord (12:20–21, 24)

The word *běrît* is not used in the passage, and it is not actually said that the covenant has been broken. Nevertheless, the demand for a king 'like the nations' is understood as rejection of God as King (12:19; cf. 8:4–8), and the use of the covenant formula in verse 22 is a reminder of God's faithfulness to the covenant, implicitly in contrast to Israel's unfaithfulness.

Asa

Solomon breaks the covenant by following other gods (1 Kings 11:1–11), and his son Rehoboam (14:21–24) and grandson Abijam (15:1–3) do likewise. It is not until the time of King Asa (15:11–14) that there is a change in attitude. The Chronicler records Asa's reform in some detail (2 Chronicles 15), after his account of an extraordinary victory over an invading Ethiopian army (14:9–15). He tells us that the reform takes place at the instigation of the prophet Azariah, who encourages the king to take action and assures him of God's favourable response. Throughout Judah and Benjamin, and also in parts of Ephraim that he controls, Asa does away with idols (15:8); and in Judah he also destroys sacred pillars and poles, and abolishes pagan places of worship and incense altars (cf. 14:3–5). Then he repairs the altar of the Lord (15:8) and holds a covenant renewal ceremony, consisting of

- assembly of the people in Jerusalem (verses 9–10)
- sacrifice (verse 11)
- renewal of the covenant with the God of the ancestors (verse 12)
- penalty for any who refuse to cooperate (verse 13)
- oath of allegiance to the LORD (verses 14–15)

Elijah

Ahab's marriage to a foreign princess is probably politically motivated and the religious implications from his perspective are secondary. However, Jezebel turns out to be a fanatic proponent of her religion, persuading her husband to worship Baal and eliminating prophets of the LORD (1 Kings 16:31–33; 18:4). Elijah's subsequent confrontation with the prophets of Baal on Mount Carmel is well known (18:20–40), but even after that triumph Elijah's assessment of the situation is that Israel has broken their covenant with God, having torn down his altars and killed his prophets (19:10, 14).

The situation is the reverse of what we might expect. Most often the divine assessment is more negative than the human one, but this time God reassures his prophet that things are not so bad as they seem (19:18) and that he has plans to remove Ahab and Jezebel (verse 16; cf. 21:18–24). There is no covenant renewal ceremony, though certain features in the narrative imply a change of direction in the national religion:

- the people's confession on Carmel (1 Kings 18:39)
- execution of the prophets of Baal (verse 40)
- Jehu's subsequent massacre of Baal worshippers and destruction of their temple (2 Kings 10:18–28)[20]

Jehoiada

The next recorded renewal of the covenant is in Judah, during the reign of the usurper Queen Athaliah (who takes advantage of Jehu's murder of her son to take the kingdom for herself). The rightful heir to the throne, Joash, is just a baby and is hidden away by his aunt so that he escapes Athaliah's massacre of the royal family. After six years the priest Jehoiada makes a covenant (*běrît*) with key military leaders to protect the king's son (2 Kings 11:4–8 || 2 Chronicles 23:1), and according to the Chronicler also obtains the support of religious and tribal leaders (2 Chronicles 23:2–3). He then arranges a coronation, at which the seven-year old king is presented with 'the covenant' (*'ēdût*, verse 12 || 2 Chronicles 23:11).[21] Athaliah's protest and summary execution is followed by renewal of the covenant with God, including an allusion to the covenant formula:

---

20. Apart from this, no other renewal of the covenant is recorded among the ten tribes of northern Israel.

21. NRSV and NIV translate *'ēdût* as 'covenant', though REV translates it as 'testimony' and TEV expands it to 'a copy of the laws governing kingship'. Whichever is preferred, the reference is presumably to the Davidic rather than the Abrahamic/Mosaic covenant (though the Indonesian New Translation translates *'ēdût* as *hukum Allah*, 'the law of God', perhaps thinking of Deuteronomy 17:18).

Jehoiada made a *covenant* between the LORD and the king and people,
that they should be the LORD's people; also between the king and the people.
(2 Kings 11:17 || 2 Chronicles 23:16, my emphasis)

Details of the ceremony are not recorded, except that it is followed
by destruction of the temple of Baal and repair of the temple of
the LORD.

Hezekiah

One hundred and twenty years later Hezekiah begins his reign
with a major religious reform, abolishing pagan practices introduced during the sixteen years' reign of his father Ahaz (2 Kings
18:1–4; 2 Chronicles 29–31). The problem, as he sees it, is that the
people have forsaken God by introducing 'unclean things' to the
holy place, and failing to maintain the regular temple-worship
(2 Chronicles 29:5–7, 16). Thus Hezekiah states his intention 'to
make a covenant with the LORD, the God of Israel, so that his fierce
anger may turn away from us' (verse 10). The destruction of
Samaria and end of the northern kingdom just seven years earlier,
interpreted as divine punishment for covenant-breaking, will no
doubt have been a major stimulus in this.

After the offending objects have been removed from the temple,
and the original altar, table and utensils have been resanctified,
Hezekiah assembles the political and religious leaders of the
city for a ceremony to reinstate authentic worship in the temple
(2 Chronicles 29:20–36), involving vast numbers of sacrifices inter-
spersed with choral and instrumental music. Then he summons the
entire people, including those remaining in northern Israel, to come
to Jerusalem for an extraordinary Passover (ch. 30). He appeals to
them to remember the covenant with their ancestors and return to
the Lord (verses 6–9; the word 'covenant' is not actually used in this
text but the concept is implied) and there is a massive though not
unanimous response. This success in Jerusalem is followed by
extension of the reform throughout Judah and parts of northern
Israel, reorganization of the priesthood, and reinstatement of
tithes and offerings (ch. 31).

Josiah

King Hezekiah dies and is succeeded by his son Manasseh, who promptly reverses his father's policies. His long reign (fifty-five years) is characterized by idolatry, spiritism and violence. As a result he is considered by both the Deuteronomic historian and the Chronicler to be even more evil than the Canaanites, though the latter also records his repentance. Amon, his son and brief successor, is also categorized as a bad king, and it is not until the reign of Josiah that things change for the better.

The 'discovery' of the book of the law in the eighteenth year of his reign is well timed, for Josiah has been seeking the Lord since his youth and has already taken some steps to purify the worship of Israel (2 Kings 22 || 2 Chronicles 34). (If the book's existence had been known to Manasseh or Amon, it would very likely have suffered the same fate as Jeremiah's scroll in the time of Jehoiakim [Jeremiah 36].) This book becomes the basis for Josiah's reformation, the essence of which is renewal of the covenant:

> The king went up to the house of the LORD, and with him went all the people of Judah, all the inhabitants of Jerusalem, the priests, the prophets, and all the people, both small and great; he read in their hearing all the words of the book of the *covenant* that had been found in the house of the LORD. The king stood by the pillar and made a *covenant* before the LORD, to follow the LORD, keeping his commandments, his decrees, and his statutes, with all his heart and all his soul, to perform the words of this *covenant* that were written in this book. All the people joined in the *covenant*. (2 Kings 23:2–3 || 2 Chronicles 34:30–32, my emphasis)

The assembly of the people is followed by a celebration of Passover, 'as prescribed in this book of the covenant' (2 Kings 23:21).

Zedekiah

Covenant is not mentioned again until the reign of Zedekiah, Judah's last king. Apparently Zedekiah had made a covenant with the people, before the LORD in the temple, to free their Hebrew slaves in accordance with the law of the seventh year (Jeremiah

34:8–10, 14–15; cf. Deuteronomy 15:12–15). However, the people then change their mind and take back their former slaves (verses 11, 16). They are reprimanded by the LORD, through Jeremiah, who reminds them of his covenant with their ancestors at the time of the exodus (verse 13) and declares them to be covenant-breakers (verse 18). There is no indication of repentance as a result of this message, simply an announcement of doom (verses 17–22).

Ezra and Nehemiah

After the return from exile, worship of the Lord in his temple in Jerusalem is reinstated, implicitly a renewal of the covenant (Ezra 3 – 6). However, even now God's people are ambivalent in their devotion and the issue of mixed marriages is highlighted as a serious breach of the covenant (9:1–4). After prayer, Ezra succeeds in persuading the people to make a covenant with God, whereby they separate themselves from the inhabitants of the land and send away their foreign wives and children (ch. 10).

Nehemiah 8 – 10 records the renewal of the covenant, spread over most of the seventh month (Duggan 2001). There is reason to think that the event actually took place earlier than its place in the canon suggests, perhaps very soon after Ezra's return to Jerusalem (Ezra 7 – 8), before the problem of the mixed marriages mentioned above (Clines 1984; Williamson 1985). The covenant with Abraham (Nehemiah 9:7–8), confirmed to Israel at Sinai (verses 9–15), has been kept by God (verses 17b, 19–25, 31–32; cf. 1:5) but broken by his people (verses 16–18, 26–30, 33–37). The key elements of the covenant renewal are as follows:

Day 1
reading of the law by Ezra to the people (8:1–8)
response of the people (8:9–12)

Days 2–14
study of the law by the leaders (8:13–15)
preparation for the feast of Tabernacles (8:16)

Days 15–22
celebration of Tabernacles, with daily reading of the law
(8:17–18a)
solemn assembly (8:18b)

Day 24
reading of the law and national confession (9:1–37)
signing the covenant document by political and religious leaders
(9:38 – 10:27)
oath of allegiance by the people (10:28–29)
declaration of the obligations of the covenant (10:30–39)

Note the emphasis on the reading and study of the book of the
law throughout the whole process.

The new covenant

One thing is clear from this survey of the making, breaking and
remaking of the covenant over fifteen centuries: the people of
Israel have an inherent inability to stick with their God for much
more than a few decades. The prophets are acutely aware of this
and begin to point towards a 'new covenant'. The precise term is
actually used only once in the Old Testament, in Jeremiah 31:31,
but the idea is also present in Isaiah, Ezekiel and several other
prophets. The idea is taken up at Qumran and in the New
Testament, but we will concentrate on its meaning in the Old
Testament here.

A major question of interpretation is whether this new covenant
is to be yet another renewal of the old covenant or a completely
new covenant that replaces the old. Some scholars have argued for
the former (Welch 1951: 229–231; Wallis 1969; Lohfink 1991: 45–51;
Holmgren 1999: 75–95), others for the latter (von Rad 1965: 212;
Zimmerli 1965: 79–80; Gross 1996; Robinson 2001), while others
have looked for a middle way between these two alternatives
(Kaiser 1972). Let us see what conclusions we can draw from the
texts. We will look at them in canonical order, which is not the same
as their chronological order.

Isaiah

Isaiah 1 – 39 mentions the covenant only once,[22] when the prophet complains:

> The earth lies polluted under its inhabitants;
> for they have transgressed laws,
> violated the statutes,
> broken the everlasting *covenant*. (Isaiah 24:5, my emphasis)

Other prophecies of judgment also imply the breaking of the covenant, even if that is not stated in so many words (e.g. 1:2–4; 5:1–7).[23]

However, in the last few chapters of the book the covenant becomes a major topic. In Isaiah 54 the prophet promises an eternal 'covenant of peace' to the exiles who return from Babylon, comparable to that made with Noah (verses 9–10); and in the following chapter the covenant with David is remembered and becomes the prototype for an 'everlasting covenant' (55:3; cf. 61:8). This new covenant will include many who were excluded by the Abrahamic-Mosaic covenant, such as foreigners and eunuchs (56:3–8; cf. Deuteronomy 23:1, 3). It will be spiritual in nature, but that does not mean that the words of the law will be forgotten:

> This is my *covenant* with them, says the LORD: my spirit that is upon you, and my words that I have put in your mouth, shall not depart out of your mouth . . . from now on and forever. (Isaiah 59:21, my emphasis)

Jeremiah

The word 'covenant' and the 'covenant formula' are found more often in Jeremiah than in any other Old Testament prophetic book. Jeremiah reminds the people of Judah about God's covenant with their ancestors when he brought them out of Egypt

---

22. The word *běrît* is also used in 28:15, 18 and 33:8, but not in reference to God's relationship with his people.

23. Twice it is said that the servant has been given by God 'as a covenant to the people' (42:6; 49:8), though the meaning of this phrase is not entirely clear.

(11:2–5) and how their ancestors had broken the covenant (verses 6–8), then he accuses the present generation of doing the same thing (verses 9–10), which will result in disaster (verses 11–17; cf. 16:10–13).[24]

A prayer for mercy is recorded once, pleading with God to remember his covenant and spare his people punishment (14:21), but it is too late (15:1–9). The reason for the subsequent destruction of Jerusalem is clearly stated to be that its inhabitants have 'abandoned the *covenant* of the LORD their God, and worshipped other gods and served them' (Jeremiah 22:9, my emphasis). Yet even the devastation of their homeland and desolation of exile do not mean that the people have been abandoned by God. The exiles are reassured in the words of the covenant formula that they will return to God and he will restore them as his people (24:5–7; 30:22; 31:1).

How will this happen? Jeremiah explains:

> The days are surely coming, says the LORD, when I will make a *new covenant* with the house of Israel and the house of Judah. It will not be like the *covenant* that I made with their ancestors when I took them by the hand to bring them out of the land of Egypt – a *covenant* that they broke, though I was their husband, says the LORD. But this is the *covenant* that I will make with the house of Israel after those days, says the LORD: I will put my law within them, and I will write it on their hearts; and *I will be their God, and they shall be my people*. No longer shall they teach one another, or say to each other, 'Know the LORD,' for they shall all know me, from the least of them to the greatest, says the LORD; for I will forgive their iniquity, and remember their sin no more. (Jeremiah 31:31–34, my emphasis)

The prophet gives four characteristics of the 'new covenant':

- internalization of the law (verse 33b)
- personal relationship between God and his people (verse 33c)

---

24. The covenant formula is used here (verse 4), and also in a similar prophecy of judgment in Jeremiah 7:23 (cf. 13:11).

- knowledge of the Lord (verse 34a)
- forgiveness of sins (verse 34b)

As Fretheim (2002) points out, all of this is expected to happen in the context of a renewed people of Israel. There will be a new historical basis for their faith: the archetypical saving event had been the exodus from Egypt, but now it will become the return from exile (Jeremiah 16:14–15 || 23:7–8). Jeremiah does not promise that they will immediately become perfect, for there will still be sin and death (31:30), but they will no longer follow their 'evil will' (3:15–18;[25] cf. 7:24; 11:8; 18:12) and forgiveness of sins will be assured (31:34).

In the following chapters it is clarified that this new covenant – like the old – is to be everlasting (32:40; 50:5; cf. 33:25–26), and the use of the covenant formula makes it clear that the focus is precisely as before; namely the relationship between God and his people (32:38).

Ezekiel

By the time of Ezekiel, judgment is past history and present experience, so his prophecies are very much focused on the future. He promises the exiles that God will give them a new heart and spirit, to obey his laws and to remake them as his people (11:19–20; 36:26–28; 37:12–14; cf. Jeremiah 32:39–40). He will establish an everlasting covenant with them (16:59–63; cf. 37:26), on the basis of the earlier covenant (16:60; cf. 20:36–37), whereby they will know that he is the LORD (16:62) and receive forgiveness of their sins (verse 63). It will be a 'covenant of peace' (34:25; 37:26; cf. Isaiah 54:10), which includes both material and spiritual security. Throughout the book the covenant formula reverberates like a refrain, so that the reader is continually reminded of the goal: 'They shall be my people, and I will be their God' (Ezekiel 11:20; cf. 14:11; 34:24, 30–31; 36:28; 37:23, 27).

---

25. On this passage and its relationship to Jeremiah 31:31–34, see Gosse (1989).

Other prophets

Three of the minor prophets refer to the covenant, and look forward to its future renewal.[26]

Hosea graphically describes the breaking of the covenant (6:7; 8:1), elaborating the painfully lived-out allegory of his own wayward wife, and her children with their strange names: 'God sows', 'Not Pitied' and 'Not my People' (1:2–9). However, his message also portrays God's amazing grace shown to sinners, and promises future restoration for the people of God through the remaking of the covenant (1:10–11; 2:14–23). An ancient Near-Eastern suzerain whose vassal broke their treaty would be likely to act swiftly and ruthlessly to punish the offender, without offering any opportunity for repentance. But God is more like a husband or wife whose spouse is unfaithful, feeling jealous and angry but longing for the relationship to be restored.[27]

After the exile and restoration, it might have seemed that the covenant had been renewed and the people of God reinstated to their former position. Yet *Zechariah* still looks to the future for the realization of such hopes (8:7–8; cf. 2:11; 9:11); while *Malachi* reports continuing covenant-breaking in Judah (2:10–11) and envisages no further renewal before the coming of the Messiah (3:1). Until that time, the people should revere the LORD (3:16) and remember the teaching of his servant Moses (4:4), trusting that in this way they will be prepared for the new covenant (3:17) and be able to stand on the day of judgment (4:1–2).[28]

---

26. There are also several references to covenant in Daniel (9:4, 27; 11:22, 28, 30, 32), which will not be discussed here.

27. On new covenant in Hosea, see Light (1993).

28. McConville (1997) adds that the idea of new covenant may 'loosely be extended to all those OT expectations that, in spite of and beyond the falling of the covenantal curses, picture a future, living relationship between God and his people' (e.g. Hosea 14; Amos 9:11–15; Micah 4:1–8; cf. Deuteronomy 30:1–10). Dumbrell (1984: 188–189) also includes Ezekiel 40 – 48 in his discussion of new covenant.

What is 'new' about the new covenant?

Nothing, and yet everything! A great deal that is said about the new covenant is not in fact 'new'. Its essence is still a personal relationship between God and his people, expressed by the covenant formula 'I will be their God, and they shall be my people' (Jeremiah 31:33c; cf. 32:38; Ezekiel 11:20; 14:11; 34:24, 30–31; 36:28; 37:23, 27), just as before.

It is to be an *everlasting covenant* (Isaiah 61:8; Jeremiah 32:40; 50:5; Ezekiel 37:26), based on the earlier covenant with Abraham and Israel (Ezekiel 16:59–63; 20:36–37), and comparable to the covenants made with Noah (Isaiah 54:9–10) and David (Isaiah 55:3), all of which were to be everlasting. It is described as a *covenant of peace* (Ezekiel 34:25–31; 37:26; cf. Isaiah 54:10), implying both material and spiritual security and recalling the covenant blessings of Deuteronomy 28:1–14. The new covenant will make possible *forgiveness of sins* (Jeremiah 31:34b; Ezekiel 16:63; cf. Isaiah 43:25), and the forgiveness of sins is certainly part of the old covenant, at least from Sinai onwards (Exodus 34:6–10; Numbers 14:17–20).

So where does its newness lie? The *scope* of the new covenant is wider, including foreigners and eunuchs who were excluded under Mosaic legislation (Isaiah 55:3–5; 56:3–8; cf. Deuteronomy 23:1, 3). Egypt and Assyria will become peoples of God, sharing in the Abrahamic blessing alongside Israel (Isaiah 19:18–25; cf. 42:6; 49:6; Jeremiah 12:14–17)! But even this is not an unprecedented idea, since the covenant with Abraham was potentially universal in scope (Genesis 12:3), we are told that 'a mixed crowd' went up with the Israelites from Egypt (Exodus 12:38), and there are hints of a universal perspective in Exodus 19:5 ('the whole earth is mine') and Deuteronomy 4:6 (Israel's ethical behaviour will amaze other nations).

It will be *spiritual* in nature, as God gives his people a new heart and spirit (Ezekiel 11:19–20; 36:26–27; 37:12–14). The law will be written on their hearts instead of on tablets of stone (Jeremiah 31:33b) and God's words will be continually in their mouths (Isaiah 59:21). This internalization of the law is not entirely new, since Moses in Deuteronomy exhorts the people to 'put these words of mine in your heart and soul' (Deuteronomy 11:18; cf. 30:14) and twice refers to circumcision of the heart (10:16; 30:6), but it may be true to say that it is emphasized more strongly in the new covenant than in the old (cf. Swetnam 1974; van den Busch 1980).

One important characteristic of the new covenant, according to Jeremiah 31:34a, is *personal knowledge of God*.[29] This is not stated explicitly in the earlier covenant. Throughout the Old Testament certain individuals are singled out because they have a close relationship with God and know him personally, such as Enoch (Genesis 5:24), Abraham (2 Chronicles 20:7; Isaiah 41:8) and Moses (Deuteronomy 34:10), perhaps implying that this is an exceptional experience. Although Israel knows intellectually that the LORD is their God (Exodus 6:7; 29:45–46; Deuteronomy 7:9) – unlike Pharaoh who does not know the LORD (Exodus 5:2) – they do not all know him in a personal way but rely on priests and prophets to teach them and approach God on their behalf.[30] Indeed, earlier prophecies of Jeremiah refer specifically to the lack of knowledge of God among the people, including the king (5:4–5; 8:7; 22:15–17). The great commandment of Deuteronomy 6:4–9 makes love of God the prime responsibility of his people, and a relationship of love surely presupposes personal knowledge, but this is implicit rather than explicit. So the explicitness and universality in Jeremiah's prophecy is new. Just as God knows his people intimately (Exodus 33:17; Jeremiah 1:5) and loves them passionately (Exodus 34:6–7; Deuteronomy 7:6–9; Psalm 103:13; Isaiah 43:1–4), the prophets make clear that he longs for them to know and love him (Jeremiah 9:24; Hosea 6:4, 6; 11:1–11). In the

---

29. Not just *savoir* but *connaissance* (French), not just *pengetahuan* but *pengenalan* (Indonesian). Cf. Jeremiah 24:7; Ezekiel 16:62; Daniel 11:32. The phrase 'are loyal to their God' (NRSV) in the latter text is literally 'know their God' (SO NIV, TB).

30. There may well have been many individuals who had a meaningful relationship with God, as the example of Hannah suggests (1 Samuel 1), though even here the role of the sanctuary and the priest are significant. Some of the psalms may have been written by lay people (David himself was neither priest nor prophet). However, we know little of the personal piety of the ordinary 'Israelite in the street'.

new covenant such unmediated knowledge of God will be a daily reality for every member of the community.[31]

So is the new covenant a further renewal of the old one or something completely different? Undoubtedly, the aim and content of the new covenant are substantially the same as the covenant with Abraham, confirmed to Israel at the time of the exodus and settlement of the Promised Land, and repeatedly broken and renewed in the succeeding years. The new covenant is therefore a renewal of the *one* covenant, albeit with certain distinctive emphases. However, there is a crucial difference, not in the covenant itself but in the people. It has become clear that they are incapable of loving God, and never will do so unless they are renewed from within (cf. Miskotte 1967: 409–415; Robinson 2001: 197–198). And this is precisely what the prophets promise: their hearts of stone will be turned to hearts of flesh, as the Spirit is poured out on all (Ezekiel 36:26; Joel 2:28–29). Knowledge of God will no longer be restricted to a few privileged individuals but will become a reality for all (Jeremiah 31:34). And at last God's passionate love for his people will be reciprocated (Hosea 2:14–23).

Two questions remain: 'How can this be, since all previous attempts to renew the covenant have failed?' And, 'When will this be?'[32] The prophets do not give the answers,[33] and to find them we have to turn to that collection of books known as the

---

31. Does Jeremiah 31:34a mean that teachers of the law will be redundant? Perhaps this is hyperbole. Jeremiah 3:15 suggests that the renewed people will still need to be fed with 'knowledge and understanding', though verses 16–17 indicate that the ark of the covenant, containing the tablets of the law, will be obsolete. Fretheim (2002: 443–444) interprets Jeremiah 31:34 in terms of the democratization of the people of God, who will no longer need teaching since there will be no spiritual elite with special access to the knowledge of God or the forgiveness of sins (cf. Swetnam 1974; Potter 1983).

32. No doubt many Israelites hoped that the return from exile would bring the fulfilment of these prophecies, but the reality of post-exilic Judah fell far short of these expectations.

33. But see chapters 4, 5 and 6 in this volume.

'New Covenant'. However, that is beyond the scope of the present chapter.[34]

Bibliography

Baker, David L. (1991), *Two Testaments, One Bible: A Study of the Theological Relationship between the Old and New Testaments* (2nd ed.; Leicester: Apollos).

Baltzer, Klaus (1971), *The Covenant Formulary: In Old Testament, Jewish, and Early Christian Writings* (Oxford: Blackwell; tr. from German, 1964, 2nd ed.).

Barr, James (1977), 'Some Semantic Notes on the Covenant', in *Beiträge zur Alttestamentlichen Theologie: Festschrift für Walther Zimmerli zum 70. Geburtstag* (Göttingen: Vandenhoeck & Ruprecht), 23–38.

Bright, John (1977), *Covenant and Promise* (London: SCM).

Buis, Pierre (1976), *La Notion d'Alliance dans l'Ancien Testament* (LD 88; Paris: Éditions du Cerf).

Busch, Roger J. van den (1980), 'Jeremiah: A Spiritual Metamorphosis', *BTB* 10: 17–24.

Calderone, Philip J. (1966), *Dynastic Oracle and Suzerainty Treaty: 2 Samuel 7, 8–16* (Manila: Loyola House of Studies).

Cholewinski, A. (1985), 'Zur Theologischen Deutung des Moabbundes', *Bib* 66: 96–111.

Clines, David J. A. (1984), *Ezra, Nehemiah, Esther* (NCBC; Grand Rapids: Eerdmans/London: Marshall, Morgan & Scott).

Cross, Frank Moore (1998), 'Kinship and Covenant in Ancient Israel', in *From Epic to Canon: History and Literature in Ancient Israel* (Baltimore: Johns Hopkins University Press), 3–21.

Davidson, Robert (1989), 'Covenant Ideology in Ancient Israel', in Ronald E. Clements (ed.), *The World of Ancient Israel: Sociological, Anthropological and Political Perspectives* (Cambridge: Cambridge University Press), 323–347.

Duggan, Michael W. (2001), *The Covenant Renewal in Ezra–Nehemiah (Neh 7:72b–10:40): An Exegetical, Literary, and Theological Study* (SBLDS 164; Atlanta, GA: Society of Biblical Literature).

---

34. I am grateful to Terence Fretheim and Elizabeth Baker, who read drafts of this chapter and made many helpful suggestions.

Dumbrell, William J. (1984), *Covenant and Creation: An Old Testament Covenantal Theology* (Exeter: Paternoster).

Eichrodt, Walther (1961), *Theology of the Old Testament* (OTL; Philadelphia: Westminster; tr. from German, 1959, 6th ed.).

Eynde, Sabine van den (1999), 'Covenant Formula and *Bryt*: The Links between a Hebrew Lexeme and a Biblical Concept', *OTE* 12: 122–148.

Fretheim, Terence E. (1991), *Exodus* (Interpretation; Louisville: John Knox).

— (2002), *Jeremiah* (Smyth & Helwys Bible Commentary; Macon, GA: Smyth & Helwys).

Gosse, Bernard (1989), 'L'Ouverture de la Nouvelle Alliance aux Nations en Jérémie iii 14–18', *VT* 39: 385–392.

Gross, Walter (1996), 'Erneuerter oder Neuer Bund? Wortlaut und Aussageintention in Jer 31,31–34', in Friedrich Avemarie and Hermann Lichtenberger (eds.), *Bund und Tora: Zur Theologischen Begriffsgeschicte in Alttestamentlicher, Frühjüdischer und Urchristlicher Tradition* (WUNT 92; Tübingen: Mohr), 41–66.

— (1998), *Zukunft für Israel: Alttestamentliche Bundeskonzepte und die Aktuelle Debatte Um den Neuen Bund* (SB 176; Stuttgart: Katholisches Bibelwerk).

Hillers, Delbert R. (1969), *Covenant: The History of a Biblical Idea* (Baltimore: Johns Hopkins University Press).

Holmgren, Fredrick C. (1999), *The Old Testament and the Significance of Jesus: Embracing Change – Maintaining Christian Identity* (Grand Rapids: Eerdmans).

Kaiser, Walter C. (1972), 'The Old Promise and the New Covenant: Jeremiah 31:31–34', *JETS* 15: 11–23.

Kalluveettil, Paul (1982), *Declaration and Covenant: A Comprehensive Review of Covenant Formulae from the Old Testament and the Ancient Near East* (AnBib 88; Rome: Biblical Institute).

Kutsch, Ernst (1973), *Verheißung und Gesetz: Untersuchungen zum Sogenannten »Bund« im Alten Testament* (BZAW 131; Berlin: de Gruyter).

Light, Gary W. (1993), 'The New Covenant in the Book of Hosea', *RevExp* 90: 219–238.

Lohfink, Norbert L. (1969), 'Dt 26,17–19 und die "Bundesformel"', *ZKT* 91: 517–553; reprinted in *Studien zum Deuteronomium und zur deuteronomistischen Literatur* (Stuttgart: Katholisches Bibelwerk, 1990), 1: 211–261.

— (1991), *The Covenant Never Revoked: Biblical Reflections on Christian–Jewish Dialogue* (New York: Paulist; tr. from German, 1989).

— (2000), 'The Covenant Formula in Psalm 33', in Norbert L. Lohfink and Erich Zenger (eds.), *The God of Israel and the Nations: Studies in Isaiah and the*

Psalms (Collegeville, MN: Liturgical; tr. from German, 1994), 85–122.

Lucas, Ernest C. (1982), 'Covenant, Treaty, and Prophecy', *Them* 8.1: 19–23.

Lundbom, Jack R. (1992), 'New Covenant', *ABD* (electronic edition).

McCarthy, Dennis J. (1978), *Treaty and Covenant: A Study in Form in the Ancient Oriental Documents and in the Old Testament* (AnBib 21a; 2nd ed; Rome: Biblical Institute).

McConville, J. Gordon (1997), '*běrît*, Treaty, Agreement, Alliance, Covenant', *NIDOTTE* (electronic edition).

McKenzie, Steven L. (2000), *Covenant* (Understanding Biblical Themes; St Louis, MO: Chalice).

Mendenhall, George E. (1954a), 'Ancient Oriental and Biblical Law', *BA* 17: 26–46.

— (1954b), 'Covenant Forms in Israelite Tradition', *BA* 17: 50–76.

Mendenhall, George E., and Gary A. Herion (1992), 'Covenant', *ABD* (electronic edition).

Miskotte, Kornelis H. (1967), *When the Gods Are Silent* (tr. John W. Doberstein; London: Collins; tr. from Dutch, 1956 / German, 1963).

Morrice, William G. (1975), 'New Wine in Old Wine-Skins: XI. Covenant', *ExpTim* 86: 132–136.

Muilenburg, James (1959), 'The Form and Structure of the Covenantal Formulations', *VT* 9: 347–365.

Neef, Heinz-Dieter (1996), 'Aspekte Alttestamentlicher Bundestheologie', in Friedrich Avemarie and Hermann Lichtenberger (eds.), *Bund und Tora: Zur Theologischen Begriffsgeschichte in Alttestamentlicher, Frühjüdischer und Urchristlicher Tradition* (WUNT 92; Tübingen: Mohr), 1–23.

Nicholson, Ernest W. (1986), *God and His People: Covenant and Theology in the Old Testament* (Oxford: Clarendon).

Oden, Robert A. (1987), 'The Place of Covenant in the Religion of Israel', in Patrick D. Miller et al. (eds.), *Ancient Israelite Religion: Essays in Honor of Frank Moore Cross* (Philadelphia: Fortress), 429–447.

Olson, Dennis T. (1994), *Deuteronomy and the Death of Moses: A Theological Reading* (OBT; Minneapolis: Fortress).

Perlitt, Lothar (1969), *Bundestheologie im Alten Testament* (WMANT 36; Neukirchen-Vluyn: Neukirchener Verlag).

Potter, Harry D. (1983), 'The New Covenant in Jeremiah xxxi 31–34', *VT* 33: 347–357.

Rad, Gerhard von (1965), *Old Testament Theology* (Edinburgh: Oliver & Boyd; tr. from German, 1960).

Rendtorff, Rolf (1998), *The Covenant Formula: An Exegetical and Theological Investigation* (OTS; Edinburgh: T. & T. Clark; tr. from German, 1995).

Robertson, O. Palmer (1980), *The Christ of the Covenants* (Grand Rapids: Baker).

Robinson, Bernard P. (2001), 'Jeremiah's New Covenant: Jer 31,31–34', *SJOT* 15: 181–204.

Segal, Moses H. (1967), 'Renewal of the Covenant at Sinai: An Essay in Exegesis', *Seventy-Fifth Anniversary Volume of The Jewish Quarterly Review:* 490–497.

Smend, Rudolf (1963), *Die Bundesformel* (ThSt 68; Zurich: EVZ).

Soggin, J. Alberto (1972), *Joshua: A Commentary* (OTL; London: SCM; tr. from French, 1970).

Swetnam, James (1974), 'Why Was Jeremiah's New Covenant New?', in George W. Anderson et al. (eds.), *Studies on Prophecy* (VTSup 26; Leiden: Brill), 111–115.

Vannoy, J. Robert (1978), *Covenant Renewal at Gilgal: A Study of 1 Samuel 11:14–12:25* (Cherry Hill, NJ: Mack).

Visser, Derk (1996), 'Covenant', in Hans J. Hillerbrand (ed.), *The Oxford Encyclopedia of the Reformation* (New York: Oxford University Press), 1: 442–445.

Wallis, Wilber B. (1969), 'Irony in Jeremiah's Prophecy of a New Covenant', *BETS* 12: 107–110.

Weinfeld, Moshe (1972), *Deuteronomy and the Deuteronomic School* (Oxford: Clarendon).

— (1976), 'Jeremiah and the Spiritual Metamorphosis of Israel', *ZAW* 88: 17–56.

— (1977), '*běrît*', *TDOT*, 2: 253–279.

Welch, Adam C. (1951), *Jeremiah: His Time and His Work* (Oxford: Blackwell).

Williamson, Hugh G. M. (1985), *Ezra, Nehemiah* (WBC 16; Waco: Word).

Williamson, Paul R. (2003), 'Covenant', in T. Desmond Alexander and David W. Baker (eds.), *Dictionary of the Old Testament: Pentateuch* (Downers Grove: IVP), 139–155.

Zimmerli, Walther (1965), *The Law and the Prophets: A Study of the Meaning of the Old Testament* (James Sprunt Lectures; Oxford: Blackwell; tr. from German, 1963).

2. COVENANT: GOD'S MISSION THROUGH GOD'S PEOPLE

Christopher J. H. Wright

Introduction: definitions and approach

'The mission of God'

I use the phrase here, not in the sense of its earlier use, *missio Dei*, in terms of the inner sending of the Trinity (the Father's sending of the Son, and their joint sending of the Spirit).[1] That limits the word 'mission' to its etymological roots in the Latin verb *mittere*, to send, and places too much emphasis on the idea of sending or being sent. I use it in its more general sense of a purpose or objective, something to be achieved. Thus I use the phrase 'mission of God' as a shorthand for the goal and purpose of God throughout history. The God revealed in the Bible is personal,

---

1. For a survey of the early use of this term in ecumenical theology, see L. A. Hoedemaker, 'The People of God and the Ends of the Earth', in A. Camps, L. A. Hoedemaker and M. R. Spindler (eds.), *Missiology: An Ecumenical Introduction* (Grand Rapids: Eerdmans, 1995), pp. 157–171.

purposeful and committed to explicit goals that he intends to accomplish for the whole of his creation.

'The people of God'

By this expression I refer to that community within history through whom God has committed himself to the goal of blessing the nations – which in the canonical Scriptures includes, of course, Israel in the Old Testament and the church as the messianic heirs of Israel in the New Testament. This people also has a mission, derived from the mission of God. Again the word is used to mean that this people exists for a purpose, or more precisely, have been brought into existence for the sake of the purpose of God. But in their case, especially in the New Testament (though not absent from the Old Testament), the concept of mission as 'sending and being sent' is an essential component in that overall orientation towards the goal of God's mission.

A missiological hermeneutic of Scripture

For a number of years now I have been exploring what it means to practise a missiological hermeneutic in reading the Bible. By this I mean much more than simply finding biblical texts that appear to support the missionary enterprise of the Christian church. I mean the habit of reading all biblical texts in the theological light of the mission of God, conceived as an overarching biblical theme. From that perspective a number of other key theological themes take on particular importance, since they are foundational to that mission of the biblical God and the derivative mission of the people whom he has called to be witnesses to his identity, character and actions. These would include, for example, the uniqueness and universality of YHWH as God (i.e. the missiological significance of Israelite monotheism), and the universal significance of the particular election of Israel (i.e. that Israel was uniquely chosen but for the sake of the blessing of all nations).[2]

---

2. At All Nations Christian College (where I was Academic Dean and then Principal from 1988 to 2001) I encouraged several candidates for the MA in Missiology to devote their dissertations to missiological readings of

The sequence of covenants

If we have learnt anything from a century of Old Testament theology it is that it is futile to isolate any one theme or category as the
sole organizing centre for the whole. Nevertheless, it will be
granted that the sequence of covenants in the canonical narrative
does offer us *one* fruitful way of presenting the grand narrative that
embodied Israel's coherent worldview – a worldview that included
their own sense of election, identity and role in the midst of the
nations. There are many ways in which one can present, organize or

---

specific Old Testament books or themes. These included Paul Davies,
'"A Wise and Understanding People": The Deuteronomic Portrait of
Community and Discipleship as a Pattern for Christian Mission' (1994);
Jonathan Y. Rowe, 'Holy to the LORD: Universality in the
Deuteronomistic History and its Relationship to the Author's Theology
of Idolatry' (1997); David A. Williams, '"Then they will know that I am
the LORD": The Missiological Significance of Ezekiel's Concern for the
Nations as Evident in the Use of the Recognition Formula' (1998); John
S. Harverson, 'Exploring the Missiological Coherence of the Book of the
Twelve Minor Prophets: A Thematic Approach' (2001). Though unpub-
lished, these dissertations may be obtained on temporary loan from the
Librarian, ANCC, Easneye, Ware, Herts., SG12 8LX. In my own work
I sought to develop missiological perspectives in my commentaries on
Deuteronomy (NIBCOT; Peabody: Hendrikson/Carlisle: Paternoster,
1996); and *The Message of Ezekiel* (BST; Leicester: IVP, 2001). Pending a
more substantial monograph on the subject, several articles express my
perspectives, including 'Truth with a Mission: Reading Scripture
Missiologically', in Paul Gardner, Chris Wright and Chris Green (eds.),
Fanning the Flame: Bible, Cross and Mission (Grand Rapids: Zondervan,
2003), pp. 221–239; also published in *Princeton Theological Review* 9.1 (March
2003), pp. 16–24; 'The Old Testament and Christian Mission', *Evangel* 14.2
(1996), pp. 37–43; 'Old Testament Theology of Mission', in A. Scott
Moreau (ed.), *Evangelical Dictionary of World Missions* (Grand Rapids:
Baker/Carlisle: Paternoster, 2000), pp. 706–709; 'Mission as a Matrix for
Hermeneutics and Biblical Theology', in Craig Bartholomew et al. (eds.),
Out of Egypt: Biblical Theology and Biblical Interpretation (Grand Rapids:
Zondervan/Carlisle: Paternoster, forthcoming).

summarize that story (as Jesus demonstrated with his parable of the tenants in the vineyard). But the key point is that it *is* a narrative – a narrative in which we can look backwards (to its beginnings, redemptively, with Abraham), and forwards (to its climax in the new creation). The sequence of covenants is one way through the narrative. Accordingly, the intention of this chapter is to observe some of the missiological dimensions of that most central of all biblical themes, the covenants between God and his people as they develop through the canonical story.

Noah

The narrative of the covenant that God made with Noah in Genesis 8:15 – 9:17 is the first explicit reference to covenant-making in the text. Although some theological systems speak of an Adamic covenant, the relationship between God and Adam is not described in that way in the text itself. The Noachic covenant establishes at least two foundational points that are relevant to the rest of the biblical concept of mission.

God's commitment to creation and life on earth
In the context of God's radical judgment upon the comprehensive nature of human sin (repeatedly portrayed as 'violence and corruption'), God still commits himself to the created order itself and to the preservation of life on the planet. While it is true that we live on a cursed earth, it is also true that we live on a covenanted earth. There is an unambiguous universality about God's covenantal self-commitment here: his promise is not only with humanity, but also with 'every living creature on earth' (9:10). This Noachic covenant provides the platform for the ongoing mission of God throughout the rest of human and natural history, and thereby also, of course, the platform for our own mission in participation with his. Whatever God does, or whatever God calls us to do, there is a basic stability to the context of all our history. This does not of course preclude God's use of his natural creation in judgment as well as in blessing (as the rest of the Old Testament amply testifies). But it does define the limits of such actions within

history. This is God's earth and God is covenantally committed to
its survival, just as later revelation will show us that God is also
covenantally committed to its ultimate redemption.

The ecological dimension to mission

The language with which God addresses Noah at the end of the
flood clearly echoes Genesis 1. In a sense this is a fresh start for
creation. So Noah and his family are blessed and instructed to fill
the earth and (though not with the same phrase) to have dominion
over it. The creation mandate is renewed. The human task remains
the same – to exercise authority over the rest of the creation, but
to do so with care and respect for life, symbolized in the prohibition on eating animal blood (9:4). So there is a human mission,
built into our origins in God's creation and God's purpose for creation. To care for creation is in fact the first purposive statement
that is made about the human species; it is our primary mission on
the planet. The covenant with Noah effectively renews it, within
the context of God's own commitment to creation.

Abraham

From a missiological perspective the covenant with Abraham is
the most significant of all the biblical covenants. It was the origin
of Israel's election as the means God would use to bless the
nations, and it undergirds Paul's theology and practice of mission
to the Gentiles in the New Testament. Within the Old Testament
context it is theologically proper to see the covenants at Sinai and
with David not as wholly distinct covenantal arrangements, but as
developments of the Abrahamic in new circumstances (as David
L. Baker points out in his chapter). Richard Bauckham, reflecting
on the missiological aspects of these three covenants, sees them
all as characteristically moving from the one to the many – the
dynamic of the key biblical category of election:

> God singles out first Abraham, then Israel, then David. The three
> movements that begin with these three choices by God each has its own
> distinctive theme, one aspect of God's purpose for the world. We could

call these the thematic trajectories of the narrative. The trajectory that moves from Abraham to all the families of the earth is the trajectory of blessing. The trajectory that moves from Israel to all the nations is the trajectory of God's revelation of himself to the world. The trajectory that moves from God's enthronement of David in Zion to the ends of the earth is the trajectory of rule, of God's kingdom coming in all creation. Of course, these three movements and themes are closely interrelated. [3]

The canonical context: Genesis 1 – 11

The Old Testament begins on the stage of universal history. After the accounts of creation we read the story of God's dealings with fallen humanity and the problem and challenge of the world of the nations (Genesis 1 – 11). After the stories of the fall, Cain and Abel, the flood and the tower of Babel, could there be any future for the nations in relation to God? Or would judgment have to be God's final word? It is against this background of universal sinfulness and divine judgment that we are introduced to God's determination to 'bless'. Blessing, of course, had been a key work in the early chapters of Genesis. Now it becomes God's answer to a broken world.

The universality of the ultimate goal: 'all families / nations of the earth will find blessing'

The covenant with Abraham is God's answer to the problems posed by Genesis 1 – 11. God's declared commitment is that he intends to bring blessing to the nations: 'all the families of the earth will be blessed through you' (Genesis 12:3; my tr.). Repeated six times in Genesis alone, this key affirmation is the foundation of biblical mission, inasmuch as it presents the mission of God. The creator God has a purpose, a goal, which is nothing less than blessing the nations of humanity. So fundamental is this divine agenda that Paul defines the Genesis text as the Scripture declaring 'the gospel in advance' (Galatians 3:8). And the concluding vision of the

---

3. Richard Bauckham, *Bible and Mission: Christian Witness in a Postmodern World* (Carlisle: Paternoster/Grand Rapids: Baker Academic, 2003), p. 27.

whole Bible signifies the fulfilment of the Abrahamic promise, as
people from every nation, tribe, language and people are gathered
among the redeemed in the new creation (Revelation 7:9). The
gospel and mission both begin in Genesis, then, and both are
located in the redemptive intention of the Creator to bless the
nations, as the bottom line of God's covenant with Abraham.
Mission is God's address to the problem of fractured humanity.
And God's mission is universal in its ultimate goal and scope.

The particularity of the means: 'through you': the missiological significance of election

The same Genesis texts that affirm the universality of God's
mission to bless the nations also, and with equal strength, affirm the
particularity of God's election of Abraham and his descendants to
be the vehicle of that mission.[4] The election of Israel is assuredly
one of the most fundamental pillars of the biblical worldview, and
of Israel's historical sense of identity.[5] It is vital to insist that
although the belief in their election could be (and was) distorted
into a narrow doctrine of national superiority, that move was
resisted in Israel's own literature (e.g. Deuteronomy 7:7ff.). The
affirmation is that YHWH, the God who had chosen Israel, was
also the creator, owner and Lord of the whole world (Deuteronomy

---

4. There is, of course, considerable exegetical debate over the precise
   meaning of *běkā*, 'through you', in Genesis 12:3. Is it instrumental ('by
   means of you'), or associative ('in connection with you')? Furthermore
   there is the question regarding the niphal form of *bārak*. Is it to be understood reflexively ('the nations will bless themselves' – i.e. pronounce or
   seek for blessing upon themselves), or passively ('the nations will be
   blessed')? The matter is thoroughly discussed in the commentaries. What
   is unmistakeable is that God's goal is the blessing of the nations and that
   Abraham/Israel are key to the fulfilment of that goal.
5. This has been shown clearly, and in a way that underlines its importance
   for the whole mission of the biblical God through the people of God for
   the world, in the works of N. T. Wright, especially his *New Testament and the
   People of God* (London: SPCK, 1992), pp. 244–279; and *Jesus and the Victory
   of God* (London: SPCK, 1996).

10:14–15; cf. Exodus 19:4–6). That is, he was not just 'their God' –
he was God of all (as Paul hammers home in Romans 4). YHWH
had chosen Israel in relation to his purpose for the world, not just
for Israel. The election of Israel was not tantamount to a rejection
of the nations, but explicitly for their ultimate benefit. If we might
paraphrase John, in a way he would probably have accepted, 'God
so loved the world that he chose Israel'.[6]

The ethical connection: election, ethics and mission (Genesis 18:18–19)

The debate over whether the Abrahamic covenant was unconditional or not seems somewhat beside the point. It was unconditional
in the sense that it was initiated by God without regard for any conditions Abraham had hitherto fulfilled. But it certainly comes with
commands and expectations that Abraham is urged to fulfil, and he
is commended for it when he does. There is not, as Walter Moberly
has pointed out,[7] an explicit demand for holiness such as dominates
the Sinai covenant. But there are some texts in which a clear ethical
agenda is explicitly connected to the universal goal of blessing the
nations.

The clearest of these is Genesis 18:18–19. This little divine
soliloquoy comes in the middle of a narrative that spans Genesis
18 – 19, the story of God's judgment on Sodom and Gomorrah.
So this reminder of God's universal promise of blessing comes in
the midst of a story of God's historical judgment. Somewhat like
the story of the flood, Sodom and Gomorrah represent the way
of the fallen world of human wickedness. Their evil is pro-
totypical and proverbial. We hear of the 'outcry' ($s\check{e}\,{}^{c}\bar{a}q\hat{a}$) that
betrays oppression and cruelty (Genesis 18:20–21); of the per-
verted and violent immorality of the inhabitants (Genesis 19).
Later accounts of Sodom and Gomorrah draw comparisons with
the bloodshed, corruption and injustice of Jerusalem (Isaiah

---

6. Stimulating missiological reflection on the particularity and universality
   dimensions of the Abrahamic covenant and of the nature of God himself
   is found throughout Bauckham, *Bible and Mission*.
7. In *The Old Testament of the Old Testament* (Philadelphia: Fortress, 1992).

1:9ff.), and itemize their arrogance, affluence and callousness to the needy (Ezekiel 16:49).

In that very context, God recalls his universal covenant purpose in Genesis 18:19. God's promise of a son in the first part of the chapter, on which the fulfilment of the covenant depended, is now seen in the light of this expression of God's universal mission in the second part. The central phrases of verse 19, however, indicate God's more immediate thinking:

> For I have chosen him, so that he will direct his children and his household after him to keep the way of the LORD by doing what is right and just, so that the LORD will bring about for Abraham what he has promised him.

In the context of a world going the way of Sodom, God wanted a community characterized by the 'way of the LORD'. This rich OT expression describes not only God's own characteristic behaviour, but also our imitation of him (cf. Deuteronomy 10:12ff.). It is further defined by that pair of words that virtually summarizes OT ethics, 'doing righteousness and justice'. This, God reminds himself, was the purpose of having chosen Abraham in the first place, and the means to fulfilling his promise to him of blessing the nations in the future. Thus the syntax and logic of Genesis 18:19 (three clauses connected by two purposive conjunctions, 'so that'), binds together election, ethics and mission in a single sentence. The ethical quality of life of the people of God is the vital link between their calling and their mission. There is no mission without ethics.

Genesis 26:3–5 is one of the passages in Genesis where the original covenant with Abraham is repeated, this time with Isaac. It is remarkable in that it connects the universality of the final goal of that covenant (that all nations should be blessed) with Abraham's ethical obedience:

> and through your offspring all nations on earth will be blessed, because Abraham obeyed me and kept my requirements, my commandments, my decrees and my laws.

The use of terms so reminiscent of Sinai lead many critics to see here an intrusion of Deuteronomic redaction. Theologically it suggests that Abraham's faith and obedience, even in its pre-Sinai form, was counted as faithfulness to the requirements of God's law as given later.[8] Missiologically it is further evidence of the close link between God's intention to bless the nations and the ethical demand on God's people.

Sinai

As David L. Baker argues elsewhere in this volume, the covenant with Abraham is the basic biblical covenant declaring God's missional intention to bless the world through the people he calls into existence and into covenant relationship with himself. That covenant, however, is reconfirmed and given broader substance in subsequent covenant arrangements, of which the first is the national covenant with Israel at Mount Sinai. The volume of relevant textual material would be overwhelming at this point, so for our more limited purpose I will look at two major articulations: the preamble to the covenant in God's address to Israel in Exodus 19:3–6, and the renewal of the covenant in Moab as presented in the book of Deuteronomy. In each case we shall be thinking of the missiological dimensions of the material before us.

Exodus 19:3–6: the preamble to the Sinai covenant

Exodus 19:3–6 is a key programmatic statement by God, coming, like a hinge in the book of Exodus, in between the exodus narrative (Exodus 1 – 18) and the giving of the law and covenant (Exodus 20 – 24). It defines the identity and agenda God has for Israel and sets both in the context of God's own action and intention. It functions as a narrative and theological preamble to the covenant to follow, so that we must view all the specific

---

8. One might say that Genesis 26:3–5 is to James what Genesis 15:6 is to Paul. Faith and obedience are inseparable – the latter being the evidence of the former.

details of the covenant itself from the perspective of this word of orientation.

YHWH's redemptive initiative (verse 4)

'You have seen what I have done . . .' God points to his own initiative of grace and redemption, which was a matter of historical fact and recent memory. The priority of grace is a fundamental theological premise in approaching Old Testament law and ethics.[9] Obedience to the law was based on, and was a response to, God's salvation. Exodus has eighteen chapters of redemption before a single chapter of law. The same is true in relation to Israel's mission among the nations. In whatever way Israel would be or become a blessing to the nations would be on the grounds of what God had done for them, not on the basis of their own superiority in any sense.

The universal perspective (verse 5b)

'Out of all nations . . .' 'The whole earth is mine . . .' God's very special place for Israel ('treasured possession'), along with their identity and task, is here set in the context of YHWH's universality as God in relation to the nations of the earth.[10] Therefore, the ethical and missional agenda for Israel has to be motivated by the same universal concern that characterizes YHWH as God. Israel is to be the holy priesthood of the God to whom all nations and the whole earth belong.

The identity and role of Israel (verse 6)

'You will be for me a kingdom of priests and a holy nation.'

1. Priestly. To understand what this meant for Israel as a whole in relation to the nations, we have to understand what Israel's

---

9. I have discussed this much more fully in *Old Testament Ethics for the People of God* (Leicester: IVP, 2004). This is a revised, updated and expanded edition of *Living as the People of God* (1983).

10. Interestingly, Peter's use of this text in relation to the identity and role of Christians likewise emphasizes our living 'among the nations' (*en tois ethnesin* – unfortunately often translated 'pagans', 1 Peter 2:12).

priests were in relation to the rest of the people. They had a twofold task: (a) *Teaching the law* (Leviticus 10:11; Deuteronomy 33:10; Jeremiah 18:18; Malachi 2:6–7; Hosea 4:1–9). Through the priests, God would be known to the people. (b) *Handling the sacrifices* (Leviticus 1 – 7 etc.). Through the priests and their work of atonement, the people could come to God. The priesthood was thus a two-directional representational task between God and the rest of the Israelites. In addition to this, it was of course a prime privilege and responsibility of the priests to bless the people in the name of YHWH (Numbers 6:22–27)

It is thus richly significant that God confers on Israel as a whole people the role of being his priesthood in the midst of the nations. As the people of YHWH they would have the historical task of bringing the knowledge of God to the nations, and bringing the nations to the means of atonement with God. The task of blessing the nations also put them in the role of priests in the midst of the nations. This dual movement is reflected in prophetic visions of the law/light/justice and so on of YHWH going out to the nations from Israel/Zion, and of the nations coming to YHWH/Israel/Zion. The metaphor easily connects with the centrifugal and centripetal dimensions of OT eschatology. The priesthood of the people of God is thus a missional function.

In the NT Peter sees the priestly nature of the church as 'declaring the praises' of our exodus God, and living in such a way among the nations that they come to glorify God (1 Peter 2:9–12). Significantly also, in the only New Testament text to speak of any individual Christian's ministry in priestly terms, Paul describes his *evangelistic* mission of bringing the gospel to the nations and bringing the nations to God as his 'priestly duty' (Romans 15:16).

2. Holy. For Israel to fulfil their mission of being YHWH's priesthood in the midst of the nations, they must be 'holy'. Israel was to be a nation among the nations, but to be recognizably, visibly and substantively *different*, as the people belonging uniquely to YHWH and therefore representing his character and ways to the nations who did not yet know him as God. Holiness is both a fact (it is something God does; cf. Leviticus 20:8, 26; 21:8, 15, 23; 22:32), and a command (it is something to be worked out in life; cf. Leviticus 18:3; 19:1; 20:7, 23, 26). Leviticus 19, prefaced by the command to be holy as YHWH is holy (verse 2), is a key text, giving practical down-to-earth content to holiness. The list of ethical distinctives for God's people include family and community respect (verses 3, 32); religious loyalty (verses 3b, 4–8, 12, 26–31); economic relationships (verses 9–10); workers' rights (verse 13); social compassion (verse 14); judicial integrity (verse 15); neighbourly attitudes and conduct (verses 11, 16–18); symbolic distinctiveness (verse 19); sexual integrity (verses 20–22, 29); exclusion of idolatrous and occult practices (verses 4, 26–31); racial equality (verses 33–34); commercial honesty (verses 35–36). The holiness by which Israel would be faithful to their priestly mission among the nations is remarkably comprehensive and predominantly ethical.

This densely packed text, Exodus 19:3–6, then, prefaces the Sinai covenant with several affirmations central to a biblical theology of mission. If Israel were to be God's priesthood in the midst of the nations, then they had to be holy, which (among other things) meant being different from the nations. This reinforces again the integral relationship between mission and ethics in biblical thinking. The chief agent of God's mission to the nations is the people of God. The chief requirement on the people of God is that they should be what they are; live out their identity.

Missiological dimensions of Deuteronomy's portrayal of the covenant[11]

Deuteronomy is a book for a people on the move,[12] literally at first, spiritually and morally thereafter. It sets Israel on the boundary of the land and looks beyond that boundary to what lay in store for Israel as it moved into the future with God. Furthermore, it is a

---

11. The section below on Deuteronomy is an abbreviated extract from the introduction to my commentary on the book, *Deuteronomy*, pp. 8–17 (see n. 2 above).

12. J. Gary Millar, who emphasizes the theme of 'journey' as a key to the theology of Deuteronomy as a whole, has interesting perspectives on the ethics of the book, including in its relation to the nations, in *Now Choose Life: Theology and Ethics in Deuteronomy* (Leicester: Apollos, 1998).

book addressed in the name of a God on the move – YHWH, the God who has been dramatically involved in Israel's own past movements, and indeed also in the movements of other nations on the great chessboard of history. It presents, therefore, a God of sovereign worldwide purpose and a people with a sharp spiritual mandate and moral agenda. And between this God and this people Deuteronomy records the renewal of the covenant to which each was committed and through which God's purposes for the world would be carried forward.

From a missiological perspective, we may take note of four features of Deuteronomy's message.

The challenge to loyalty in the midst of culture change (e.g. 6:4–5; 12:29–31)
Mission is sometimes defined (from the human angle) as the crossing of boundaries (cultural, geographical, linguistic, religious etc.). On this definition, since Israelites were not 'sent' anywhere, the Old Testament (with the exception of Jonah) is often regarded as decidedly non-missionary, in comparison with the centrifugal missionary expansion of the New Testament church.[13] Yet Deuteronomy is a book on the boundary.[14] The people of Israel faced the challenge of an idolatrous and polytheistic culture that, in spite of initial hostility, would prove enormously enticing and seductive. Would they remain loyal to the knowledge and love of the living God that had been entrusted to them through exodus and Sinai, or would they succumb to the pressures of syncretism by treating YHWH as one among the gods of Canaan? Would they live as a distinctive ('holy') community by the standards of justice and compassion that characterized YHWH, or would they sink to the inequalities, corruptions and perversions Baalism sanctioned? Inasmuch as the relationship

---

13. This understanding of the non-missionary nature of the Old Testament accounts for the mere four pages devoted to it in David Bosch's magisterial theology of mission, *Transforming Mission* (Maryknoll: Orbis, 1991).

14. This aspect of the book is emphasized especially by P. D. Miller, *Deuteronomy: Interpretation: A Bible Commentary for Teaching and Preaching* (Louisville: John Knox, 1990), and shapes the interpretive framework for his exposition.

between the gospel and human cultures is a central missiological
issue, the story of Israel's engagement with Canaanite culture is a
rich vein for cross-cultural missiological reflection, though not as
yet greatly exploited for that purpose. It is significant, though not
surprising, that when Jesus crossed his personal Jordan from the
obscurity of village craftsman to the temptations and hostilities of
public ministry, he turned to Deuteronomy for the resources to
confirm his own loyalty and obedience as he wrestled with the
implications of the mission he had embarked upon (Matthew
4:1–11).[15]

The uniqueness and universality of YHWH (4:32–40)

Deuteronomy is uncompromisingly, ruthlessly monotheistic. It
affirms that YHWH alone is God and there is no other (4:35, 39).[16]
Monotheism here is no mere philosophical abstraction. The
purpose of Deuteronomy is not to posit the singularity of deity,
but to define the character of deity. God is God as revealed in
YHWH. It is crucial to insist on the specificity of biblical covenantal monotheism. The first commandment was not 'You shall
believe that there is only one God', but 'I am YHWH, the God of
redemptive power and action demonstrated in the exodus liberation; you shall have no other gods to rival me.' But alongside this

---

15. Cf. Christopher J. H. Wright, *Knowing Jesus through the Old Testament*
    (London: Marshall Pickering/Downers Grove: IVP, 1992), pp. 181–191.
16. There is an unsatisfactorily a priori character about the tendency among
    commentators to diminish the force of such statements by saying that
    they 'cannot' have implied full monotheism, but only mono-Yahwism for
    Israel. The latter is obviously intended. But if an Israelite had wanted to
    make an explicitly monotheistic declaration in absolute terms, what more
    could he (or she; cf. 1 Samuel 2:2) have said than Deuteronomy 4:39 or
    32:39? For a fine exploration of the question of Old Testament covenan-
    tal monotheism, and critique of some current historical reconstructions,
    see Richard Bauckham, 'Biblical Theology and the Problems of
    Monotheism', in Craig Bartholomew et al. (eds.), *Out of Egypt: Biblical
    Theology and Biblical Interpretation* (Grand Rapids: Zondervan/Carlisle:
    Paternoster, forthcoming).

exclusiveness of YHWH in covenant relation with Israel there was also a definite universality regarding YHWH's dealings with the nations. Their movements are under YHWH's control (2:9–12, 19–23). By identifying YHWH with El Elyon, the Most High God, the Israelites accept his disposition of the boundaries and destinies of the nation also (32:8–9). Two missiological implications of Deuteronomy's covenantal monotheism may be mentioned.

First, there is a clear contrast between such historico-redemptively defined monotheism and all forms of polytheism and idolatry, whether fertility cults (7:5), astral deities (4:19) or gods of national pride (32:31). A primary feature of Israel's mission (i.e. a major reason for their election) was to be the stewards of the knowledge of this unique God. '*You* were shown these things *so that you might know* . . .' (4:35). The reason, therefore, for the totally uncompromising attitude to all forms of idolatry was not a racist hatred of foreign religions, but a total commitment to the saving truth. The tragedy of polytheism and idolatry is not the arithmetic (many gods instead of one), but that they exchange the only true source of salvation for lifeless and powerless substitutes, and in doing so, introduce injustice, bondage and cruelty into human life (cf. Romans 1:21–32). Baalism is an example, but it has many modern counterparts in Western and other cultures. The category of the idolatrous in every culture (including especially one's own, where it is most invisible) is one that needs far more careful attention and exposure than most biblical and theological scholarship currently affords it. For it is surely still as much the responsibility of the people of God to confront human idolatries with the reality of the living and saving God as it was for those addressed by Deuteronomy. Methods may change radically, but the mission is the same in principle.

Secondly, there is the relevance of Old Testament monotheism to the uniqueness of Christ – the key missiological issue today as it has always been. In the dialogue between Christians and those of other faiths there is a temptation to regard Jesus as simply the founder of Christianity in a way that cuts him loose from his deep roots in the Hebrew scriptures. Both in his own understanding of his mission, and in the interpretation of his identity and significance by his immediate followers in the New Testament church, Jesus shared in the uniqueness of Israel and in the uniqueness of YHWH the God of Israel. The historical particularity and redemptive character of Old Testament covenantal monotheism come together in the person of Jesus. It is not enough to acclaim merely the unique power of Jesus' life, or insights, or teaching, or example. The New Testament witness is that in Jesus the mission of *Israel* was accomplished (as the gospel went to the nations in fulfilment of the covenant with Abraham) and that in Jesus *YHWH himself* had been encountered in human life. God is God as revealed in Jesus of Nazareth. Reflection, therefore, on such heartbeat texts as Deuteronomy 4:32–40 and 6:4–5 must go on to detect their monotheistic but now Christocentric pulse in texts like 1 Corinthians 8:5–6.[17]

Israel as an ethical model to the nations

Deuteronomy is sometimes accused of being narrowly focused on Israel alone with no regard for the wider vision of Israel's role in God's purpose for the nations. Certainly its primary focus is on Israel as a society, but it would be unfair to take this as signifying either unawareness, or a deliberate exclusion, of the tradition of the blessing of the nations through Israel. The emphasis on the Abrahamic covenant alone would make such an oversight unlikely. Furthermore, the broader issue of YHWH and the nations is to be found quite explicitly in the theology of the Deuteronomic History (cf. Joshua 4:23–24; 1 Samuel 17:46; 2 Samuel 7:22–26; 1 Kings 8:41–43, 60–61; 2 Kings 5:15; 19:15–19). In Deuteronomy itself the nations are treated in a broadly dual role: on the one hand, as a problem and snare to be resisted, and on the other hand, as the observers of Israel. In the latter role the nations appear as witnesses to the quality of Israel's life or the blessing of God on them (4:6–8, 28:10), as well as to the judgment that

---

17. Cf. Christopher J. H. Wright, *Thinking Clearly about the Uniqueness of Jesus* (Crowborough: Monarch, 1997), pp. 65–82. N. T. Wright argues strongly for the Deuteronomic basis (Deuteronomy 6:4–5, the *šĕma*ʿ) of Paul's Christological monotheism in 1 Corinthians 8, in *The Climax of the Covenant: Christ and the Law in Pauline Thought* (Edinburgh: T. & T. Clark, 1991), pp. 120–136.

YHWH would pour out on Israel for their sin (28:37; 29:22–25). In either case, positively or negatively, it is the ethical quality of Israel's social life (for good or ill) that will draw the nations' attention and comment. This is consistent with the points made above about the strong connection between the missional and the ethical dimensions of the Abrahamic vision for Israel.

The most significant of these texts for the case being made here is Deuteronomy 4:6–8:

> Observe them [these laws] carefully, for this will show your wisdom and understanding to the nations, who will hear about all these decrees and say, 'Surely this great nation is a wise and understanding people.' What other nation is so great as to have their gods near them the way the LORD our God is near us whenever we pray to him? And what other nation is so great as to have such righteous decrees and laws as this body of laws I am setting before you today?

Its point is that if Israel would be shaped and characterized by the laws and institutions of the Sinai covenant, then they would be a highly visible exemplar to the nations both as to the nature of the God they worshipped and as to the quality of social justice embodied in their community. This seems to be a deliberate linking of Israel's role among the nations to the socio-ethical structure of their corporate life: mission and ethics combined.[18] The mission of Israel was to be a model to the nations. Mission for Israel was not a matter of *going* but of *being*; to be what they were, to live as the covenant people of the God YHWH in the sight of the nations.

Deuteronomy's theology of history

At its simplest, Deuteronomy's anticipation of history was that, although Israel was called and given every possible incentive to live in loyalty to its covenant Lord, it would in fact fail to do so. The Israelites' endemically stiff-necked nature would lead to rebellion and disobedience. As a result, the curses of the covenant would

---

18. I have commented further on the ethical and missiological significance of this text in *Deuteronomy* (see n. 2 above).

fall, including the terrible threat of scattering among the nations. However, beyond that judgment there lay the expectation of restoration and new life, if the people would return and seek God once more. This is the scenario that flows through the great concluding section of the book, chapters 27–32 especially. While the dominant issue is undoubtedly the fate of Israel, the nations are woven into the picture in several ways. They witness Israel's failure and judgment and are shocked by it (28:37; 29:22–28). They are also the human agents through which that judgment (the execution of the covenant curses) is carried out (28:49–52; 32:21–26). And yet finally, in the amazing inversion and paradox of chapter 32, God vindicates his people in the midst of the nations (as enemies) in such a way that the nations are called upon to praise YHWH and to rejoice *with* his people (32:27–43). Thus, the history that will see the judgment and restoration of Israel will also see the judgment and blessing of the nations, each pair interwoven with the other.

The influence of this Deuteronomic and covenantal theology of anticipated history upon the New Testament understanding of the mission of the church is profound. It is clear that Jesus linked his own mission to the hope of the restoration of Israel and that the Gospel writers had the same interpretation of the significance of his ministry. N. T. Wright, for example, suggests that Matthew has shaped his Gospel not merely in terms of the five books of the Torah (a common scholarly view), but specifically in terms of the sequence of thought in the great final section of Deuteronomy 27 – 34. In doing so, Matthew brings out the significance of the story of Jesus 'as the continuation and climax of the story of Israel, with the implicit understanding that this story is the clue to the story of the whole world'.[19] Although Jesus limited his own ministry to the primary objective of the restoration of Israel, he left in his actions and words many hints of an expected ingathering of the nations, and he made that ingathering the explicit mission of his disciples after his resurrection.

It was, however, the apostle Paul who made the most use of Deuteronomy in his theological and missiological reflection. Not

19. Wright, *New Testament and the People of God*, pp. 387–390.

only did he see in the continued suffering of Israel a kind of pro-
longation of the curse of exile (a view shared by many
first-century Jews), but he also saw in the death and resurrection
of Jesus as the Messiah the climax of the judgment and the
restoration of Israel respectively. Linking this with his central
understanding of the significance of Israel for the nations (as the
purpose of the Abrahamic covenant), Paul recognized that the
fulfilment of God's purpose for Israel could never be complete
without the ingathering of the nations as well. At the heart of
Paul's whole theological system was his redefinition of the
meaning of Israel's election in relation to the nations. It was for
their sake that Israel was elect and for their sake also that the
Messiah had come in fulfilment of Israel's election and mission.[20]
Hence the apparent paradox of Paul's sense of personal calling as
the 'apostle to the *nations*', and his actual missionary strategy of
'to the *Jew* first'. The failure of many Jews to respond to the
message of Messiah Jesus led to the extension of the Good News
to the Gentiles (e.g. Acts 13:44–48; Romans 11). But never in
Paul's thinking did this mean a final rejection or replacement of
the Jews. Rather, Paul picks up a rhetorical pun in Deuteronomy
32:21, on God making Israel 'jealous', and develops it into a theology of history and mission: the ingathering of the Gentiles will
arouse jealousy among the Jews, so that ultimately 'all Israel',
extended and inclusive of believing Jews and Gentiles, will share
in salvation (Romans 10:19 – 11:26). Clearly Paul reflected deeply
on the song of Moses in Deuteronomy 32 especially (it has been
called 'Romans in a nutshell'), and quotes its final doxology
(32:43) in his exposition of the multinational nature of the gospel
and its implications for the need for cross-cultural acceptance
and sensitivity between Jewish and Gentile Christians (Romans
15:7–10).[21]

---

20. This crucial theme is thoroughly expounded in Wright, *Climax of the
    Covenant*.

21. On the full extent of Deuteronomy's influence on Paul's missiology, cf. J. M.
    Scott, 'Restoration of Israel', in G. F. Hawthorne and R. B. Martin (eds.),
    Dictionary of Paul and his Letters (Downers Grove: IVP, 1993), pp. 796–805.

It can be seen, therefore, that although it is true to say that
Deuteronomy is primarily absorbed with God's covenantal dealings with Israel, it contains perspectives on Israel and the nations
that ultimately led 'over the horizon' of its own context and that
influenced and shaped the mission of Jesus and Paul in theory and
in practice.

David

Growing hints of universality

Obviously the primary focus of the covenant with the house of
David, as recorded in 2 Samuel 7 is on the role of David and his
successors in earthing the rule of YHWH in Israel. There is
however an awareness that, just as Israel itself had a more-than-
local significance in the purposes of God, so did their king. The
David/Zion/Temple nexus of theological traditions is at one
level highly centralized and particular (*this* is the place and the
sanctuary where YHWH is to be sought). Yet in other respects it
has a remarkable openness and incipient universality that surfaces
at times.

The prayer of Solomon at the dedication of the temple in the
Deuteronomistic History invites YHWH to pay attention to the
prayers not only of Israelites, but also to those of foreigners, in
the remarkable passage 1 Kings 8:41–43. It is first of all significant
in its simple expectation that foreigners will be attracted to come
and worship and invoke the God of Israel for blessing. No explanation is given other than that they will have heard of his 'great
name' – or reputation. Secondly, it is amazing that Solomon prays
that God should do for the foreigner what God had never
promised, in quite so many words, to do for Israelites; namely
'whatever the foreigner asks'. And thirdly the motivation offered to
God for answering such prayers of non-covenant people is
expressly 'missional' – namely that 'all the peoples of the earth may
know your name and fear you, as do your own people Israel'. The
same chapter includes the hope, very reminiscent of Deuteronomy
4:35, 39, 'that all the peoples of the earth may know that the
LORD is God and that there is no other' – a hope immediately

conditioned on God's own covenant people living in faithful commitment to obedience (1 Kings 8:60–61 – mission connected to ethics yet again).

Some of the Davidic/Zion Psalms also have this note of universality. Psalm 2:7–9, for example, celebrates the universal rule of the son of David, addressed as the son of God. The language may originally have been coronation hyperbole, but the theological and messianic implications certainly envisage the extension of the tiny kingdom of the historical David into the ultimately universal kingdom of 'great David's Greater Son'. The same kind of hope is found in Psalm 72:8–11, and is phrased in terms that very clearly echo the Abrahamic covenant in verse 17 of that psalm:

> All nations will be blessed through him,
> And they will call him blessed.

Eschatological ingathering of the nations

Since Zion had become the place of YHWH's dwelling at the heart of Israel, and since Israel was to be God's means of blessing the nations, it is not surprising that one of the themes within the broad range of traditions associated with the Davidic covenant and its Zion centralism was the eschatological hope of the nations coming up to Zion, in a universalized version of their own pilgrim feasts when Israelites would stream up to Jerusalem. The most notable of these are the twin texts Isaiah 2:1–5 and Micah 4:1–5. What is noticeable in both cases is the strong ethical content. The nations will come to Zion for the purpose of learning of the law of YHWH, and the effect of YHWH's accepted rule will be justice and peace. In the meantime, the challenge to Israel as the present people of YHWH is to walk in his ways. Again the strong connection between the ethical demand on Israel and the universality of God's mission to the nations through Israel is plain.

Isaiah 60 – 62 adds to this motif the concept of the tribute of the nations, which they will bring to Zion in honour of YHWH, with Israel functioning as priests (Isaiah 61:6). It is likely that Paul viewed his financial collection from among the Gentile churches for the impoverished Jerusalem church theologically as a token of the eschatological fulfilment of such prophetic visions.[22]

Psalm 87 is a celebration of the 'glorious things' spoken about Zion, among which is the remarkable claim that many surrounding nations are listed as having been 'born' there. The expectation seems clearly to be that 'Zion' will ultimately come to include not just native-born Israelites, but people of other nations who will be adopted and enfranchised as citizens of the city, with as much right as the native-born to be registered there by YHWH (also named Elyon, the original name of the God of Jerusalem, verse 5; cf. Genesis 14:18–20).

The specific promise to Zion in Zechariah 2:10–13 is that 'many nations will be joined with the LORD in that day and will become my people. I will live among you . . .' This combines the Davidic covenant (since the choice of Jerusalem is renewed in verse 12) with the language of the Sinai covenant, and extends both to the nations. Even the Philistines, most remarkably of all, will be cleansed and a 'remnant' of them will 'become leaders in Judah' (Zechariah 9:6–7).

A new covenant and wider expectation

The new covenant is discussed elsewhere in this volume.

1. In the one text that explicitly uses those words, Jeremiah 31:31–37, there is no clear indication of its universality. However, elsewhere the book of Jeremiah indicates the wider offer of God, not only to Israel, but to the nations. They are offered the same hope of restoration and establishment on the same conditions (repentance and true worship) that were held out to Israel (Jeremiah 12:14–17). And repentance on the part of Israel is seen as key to God fulfilling the Abrahamic promise of blessing the rest of the nations (Jeremiah 4:1–2).

---

22. This is argued by C. H. H. Scobie, 'Israel and the Nations: An Essay in Biblical Theology', *TynBul* 43.2 (1992), pp. 283–305.

2. Ezekiel envisages the future restoration and re-establishment of Israel in language that has echoes of the covenants with Noah, David and Sinai in Ezekiel 34 – 37 (e.g. 34:23–31). But did Ezekiel hold out hope for the salvation of the nations? Not explicitly, but his silence on the matter should not be used to prove too much. Ezekiel's passion was that the whole earth should come to know the true identity of God as YHWH. For Israel, that would be known both through judgment and future restoration. For the nations, it would be known through witnessing God's acts in and for Israel, and through their own judgment. Ezekiel never quite says that the nations will come to know YHWH through future salvation. However, it has been pointed out that, standing as he did at the beginning of the exile, Ezekiel's overriding concern was for the future of Israel. Unless Israel could be brought to repentance and saving knowledge of God, there was no hope for Israel themselves, let alone the rest of the world. Any hope for the nations depended entirely on Israel being put right. Later prophecy, discerning that God was about to restore Israel, could draw further conclusions for the nations and all the earth; for Ezekiel, Israel itself had to be the dominant horizon.[23]

3. Isaiah uses the language of covenant in explicitly universalizing ways. In Isaiah 42:6 and 49:6 the mission of the servant of YHWH is, among other things, to be a 'covenant for the people' – a mysterious phrase and something of an exegetical *crux*, but is surely to be understood in its parallelism with 'light for the nations' (cf. 49:6, which further explicates it in terms of YHWH's salvation going 'to the ends of the earth'). The language of justice and *tôrâ* in the Isaiah 42 context is reminiscent of the Sinai covenant, but it is the Davidic covenant that is referred to in Isaiah 55:3–5, and its universalizing tendency is actualized. Here we have an 'everlasting covenant' in which 'David' (probably to be identified with the servant figure of neighbouring texts), becomes the leader of peoples and of nations as yet unknown. Even the covenant with Noah is harnessed to the certainty of God's promise of future blessing for his people, in Isaiah 54:7–10).

---

23. I have discussed these dimensions of Ezekiel's message in relation to the nations further in *Message of Ezekiel*, pp. 35–38.

So we find that the new covenant picks up themes from all of the preceding covenants – Noah, Abraham, Sinai and David and in several places expands them to include the nations within the ultimate scope of God's saving covenantal mission.

Conclusion

We may never know for sure what scriptures Jesus expounded to the two disciples on the road to Emmaus, or which passages he may have had in mind when he told the rest of the disciples on the same evening that 'this is what is written . . .' (Luke 24:45–48). We can be fairly confident, however, that, having explicitly identified his own death with the new covenant (Luke 22:20), the covenants we have surveyed above would have been at least part of the path he trod through the scriptures. Certainly, in relation to our theme, it is significant that Jesus urged his disciples to 'understand the scriptures' not only in relation to himself as the messiah ('the Christ will suffer and rise from the dead on the third day'), but also in relation to themselves and their mission ('and repentance and forgiveness of sins will be preached in his name to all nations, beginning in Jerusalem'). The covenants thus form a part of a Christian reading of the Old Testament that must be both messianic and missiological.

3. SPEECH ACTS AND COVENANT IN 2 SAMUEL 7:1–17

David G. Firth

Introduction

It has for some time been a standard expression of Old Testament theology to speak of a Davidic covenant in which the key text is found in the promise to David in 2 Samuel 7:1–17[1] (a text that is

---

1. For a recent example, cf. Bernhard W. Anderson, *Contours of Old Testament Theology* (Minneapolis: Fortress, 1999), pp. 206, 209. Horst Dietrich Preuss, *Old Testament Theology* (Edinburgh: T. & T. Clark, 1996), vol. 2, pp. 25–26, recognizes some of the literary critical problems associated with the text but still sees it as having a central role. Gerald Eddie Gerbrandt, *Kingship According to the Deuteronomistic History* (Atlanta: Scholar's Press, 1986), pp. 16off., is also somewhat circumspect about the use of the term 'Davidic covenant', seeing it as much as a scholarly convention of naming as an actual covenant. Similarly, Gary N. Knoppers, 'David's Relation to Moses: The Contexts, Content and Conditions of the Davidic Promises', in John Day (ed.), *King and Messiah in Israel and the Ancient Near East: Proceedings of the Oxford Old Testament Seminar* (Sheffield: Sheffield

largely repeated in 1 Chronicles 17:1–15). This promise is spoken
of in covenantal terms and developed in a number of poetic texts
outside the books of Samuel such as Psalms 2, 78, 89[2] and 132,
whilst the Zion theme that was integrated to this promise was also
developed through the book of Isaiah.[3] Within the books of
Samuel, though, there is also the significant reference back to this
tradition in 2 Samuel 23:1–7, the 'Last Words of David,' which lie
at the heart of the so-called Samuel Appendix. Taken at face value,
it might seem that the concept of a Davidic covenant was a secure
element within Old Testament theology. But appearances can be
deceiving, and one of the points that has frequently been noted is
that the keyword in covenant texts, *běrît*, is absent from 2 Samuel
7:1–17, though it is found in 2 Samuel 23:5.[4] Scholars committed
to the idea of a Davidic covenant have not normally been overly
troubled by this situation. Gordon, for example, finds the absence

---

Academic Press, 1998), pp. 91–118 (p. 115), suggests that if a formal
document ever existed for the Davidic covenant, then it is no longer
extant, and we must deal only with the echoes of it found in various texts.
However, it can be argued that the elements of covenant are contained in
this passage.

2. The exact relationship between 2 Samuel 7:1–17 and Psalm 89 is somewhat complicated and beyond the bounds of this chapter to explore, with
some holding the priority of the psalm or arguing that both passages
are based on a common source. The priority of 1 Chronicles 17:1–15
has also been defended. For a handy summary of these debates,
cf. A. A. Anderson, *2 Samuel* (Dallas: Word, 1989), pp. 113–114. More comprehensive surveys are offered by William M. Schniedewind, *Society and the
Promise to David: The Reception History of 2 Samuel 7:1–17* (New York: Oxford
University Press, 1999), pp. 30–33; and Gwilym H. Jones, *The Nathan
Narratives* (Sheffield: Sheffield Academic Press, 1990), pp. 60–70.

3. This observation holds true irrespective of literary critical decisions about
the origins of the book, as the whole of the Isaianic corpus displays considerable interest in the ultimate outcome of Zion.

4. *běrît* could also be used in reference to David in 1 Kings 8:23, but this is by
no means clear, and it is more likely to refer back to either the Abrahamic
or Sinai covenants.

of the word *běrît* within the passage to be surprising, but insists that the tradition's interpretation of the promise as a covenant is entirely correct.[5] Wider concerns are judged to demonstrate that the tradition was correct in the way in which it interpreted the material, and Birch suggests that it can accordingly be considered to be the theological high point of the whole of the books of Samuel, and possibly even the whole of the Deuteronomistic History.[6]

However, a number of recent analyses have found the evidence as a whole much less compelling. On tradition critical grounds Mettinger has argued that there was no attempt to describe the promise to David as a *běrît* before the exile,[7] with the result that the idea of a Davidic covenant is something that is well removed from the period of David. But a far more trenchant criticism is offered by Eslinger who argues that in its present form 2 Samuel 7:1–17 does not represent a radically new promise from Yahweh to David,[8] and, indeed that 'the Davidic covenant never existed except in the minds of those taken in by Yahweh's seductive rhetoric in 2 Samuel 7'.[9] Eslinger's view is not dependent upon the absence of the word *běrît* from the text, but is based upon his reading of the rhetoric that is worked out by Yahweh and David as each seeks to persuade the other of their position. Nevertheless, it is a supporting point for his view, for which we can additionally note that the most obvious of the synonyms for *běrît* mentioned

---

5. Robert P. Gordon, *I & II Samuel* (Grand Rapids: Zondervan, 1986), p. 236.

6. Bruce C. Birch, 'The First and Second Books of Samuel', in L. E. Keck (ed.), *The New Interpreter's Bible* (Nashville: Abingdon, 1998), p. 1254; Dennis J. McCarthy, 'II Samuel 7 and the Structure of the Deuteronomistic History', *JBL* 84 (1965), pp. 131–138.

7. Tryggve N. D. Mettinger, *King and Messiah: The Civil and Sacral Legitimation of the Israelite Kings* (Lund: GWK Gleerup, 1976), p. 282; though he is forced to admit that 2 Samuel 23:5 poses a problem for his view before assigning it to the exile as well.

8. Lyle Eslinger, *House of God or House of David: The Rhetoric of 2 Samuel 7* (Sheffield: Sheffield Academic Press, 1994), p. 90.

9. Ibid., xi.

by DCH, *'ālâ* (oath), does not occur in the passage either.[10] Eslinger's view is thus a significant challenge to a traditional reading of 2 Samuel 7:1–17, and any attempt to address his challenges must take the rhetorical concerns of the text seriously.

Since rhetoric is ultimately an attempt to persuade, and thus 'do (some)things with words',[11] it is appropriate to consider the light that a speech act reading of 2 Samuel 7:1–17 can shed on the debate. As a method, speech act theory recognizes that a speaker can use the same words (illocutions) to create different effects (perlocutions), or seek to generate the same effect through the use of different words. That is to say, its focus is on what a speaker is attempting to achieve through the words rather than on the words themselves, acknowledging that a speaker may have subsidiary intentions with any given utterance.[12]

This is important in considering rhetoric, since we need to examine the point toward which the rhetoric seeks to move the hearer. It is, therefore, useful to note the distinction that the study of rhetoric is concerned with how a speaker or text seeks to

---

10. *DCH* also points to *ḥesed* which does occur, and *'ôr*, which does not. The significance of *ḥesed* will be considered below, but its role in covenantal texts should be noted. Cf. Brian Britt, 'Unexpected Attachments: A Literary Approach to the Term *Ḥesed* in the Hebrew Bible', *JSOT* 27.3 (2003), pp. 295–296, 301–302.

11. The best way to commence study of speech act theory is to begin with the pioneering work of J. L. Austin, *How to Do things with Words* (Oxford: Oxford University Press, 1962). On speech act theory generally, see also John R. Searle, *Speech Acts* (Cambridge: Cambridge University Press, 1969). For a helpful and accessible introduction to speech act theory, see Keith Allan, 'Speech Act Theory – an Overview', <http:|| www.arts.monash .edu/ling/speech_acts_allan.html> (accessed 21 July 2003).

12. According to the model developed by Searle, this would mean distinguishing between direct and indirect speech acts. However, Allen, 'Speech Act Theory', p. 9, points to theorists who prefer simply to recognize the possibility of multiple speech acts within a given illocution. What is clear, though, is that secondary speech acts need in some way to be dependent on the primary speech act.

persuade, whereas speech act theory is concerned with the goal of the locutions employed. Complicating this, though, is the fact that speech act theory is normally concerned with the spoken word rather than the written one, principally because the social setting in which something is said has an effect on its intended outcome. But it is still possible to apply the method to a written text, even an ancient one, though some care is needed.[13] Nevertheless, to do so will also mean recognizing two levels at which the text operates.

First, there is the level of the conversation recorded between David and Yahweh, though the bulk of our focus will be on the oracle that Yahweh directs Nathan to give in verses 8–16, which is the core of the dynastic promise. Secondly, there is the level of the narrator of the books of Samuel. Although the speech acts of the narrator might be considered to be identical with those of the characters presented in the text, the possibility exists that in taking over an existing source the narrator has included speech acts that, though consistent with the narrator's overall view, might within themselves be ambiguous. Consideration of the narrator's own speech acts, though, indicates the ways in which we are intended to read these texts. What will be argued is that while Eslinger is correct to note the presence of possible ambiguities in Yahweh's speech, the speech acts of the narrator determine the way in which Yahweh's announcement is to be applied, and this application is that the promise to David in 2 Samuel 7:1–17 is indeed to be

---

13. For the general possibility of applying speech act theory to literature, Allan, 'Speech Act Theory', p. 17, points to D. Harrah, 'On the Vectoring of Speech Acts', in Savas L. Tsohatzidis (ed.), *Foundations of Speech Act Theory: Philosophical and Linguistic Perspectives* (London: Routledge, 1994), pp. 374–392. On the applicability of speech act theory to the Old Testament, cf. H. Irsigler, 'Psalm-Rede als Handlungs-, Wirk-, und Aussageprozeß: Sprechtanalyse und Psalmen-interpretation am Beispiel von Psalm 13', in E. Zenger (ed.), *Neue Weg der Psalmforschung: Festschrift W. Beyerlin* (Freiburg: Herders, 1994), pp. 63–104; 'Speech Acts and Intention in the "Song of the Vineyard" Isaiah 5:1–7', *OTE* 10.1 (1997), pp. 39–68; and David G. Firth, 'Psalms of Testimony', *OTE* 12.3 (1999), pp. 440–454.

understood as a covenant.[14] Eslinger's insistence on focusing only on the rhetoric of the characters within the narrative and not on the level of control provided by the authorial voice is thus fundamentally flawed.[15] As such, a point-by-point rebuttal will not be offered. Rather, the point is to be established by a close reading that attends to the textual pragmatics.

Yahweh's speech acts in 2 Samuel 7:4–17

Verses 1–3 of this chapter set the scene for all that follows – David approaches Nathan with his plan to build a temple, a plan that Nathan initially accepts on the grounds that Yahweh was with David. Such a conclusion is, in fact, presumed by the opening of the chapter, which is said to be the time when David was securely on his throne, with Yahweh having given him rest from his enemies all around. Nathan's acceptance of David's proposal is at that level entirely understandable, even though David's own motivation in seeking to build a 'house' for Yahweh is less than clear.

What is apparent, though, is the fact that David magnifies the degree of difference between his dwelling in a 'house of cedar' and the 'curtains' (*yĕrî'â*) within which the ark dwells. 'Curtains' typically

---

14. This is, therefore, a self-consciously 'final form' reading of the text. The possibility of literary development is not therefore denied (cf. P. Kyle McCarter, *II Samuel: A New Translation with Introduction and Commentary* [Garden City: Doubleday, 1984], pp. 209–231), but neither are stages of possible development foregrounded. Such an approach is necessitated by Eslinger's approach, but it is also consistent with the recognition of the fact that the final narrator is attempting to shape our perceptions through the whole of the story. With Schniedewind, *Society and the Promise to David*, pp. 29ff., the general antiquity of the promise is to be maintained (cf. Antii Laato, 'Second Samuel 7 and Ancient Near Eastern Royal Ideology', *CBQ* 59 [1997], pp. 244–269) for evidence that relates the promise to various Akkadian sources), but this does not negate the need to understand the finished text.

15. Eslinger, *House of God*, p. 7.

refers to the elements that make up the Tabernacle (Exodus 26:1ff.), and refers to a tent in its entirety only in Jeremiah 4:20, though there the meaning is established through synonymous parallelism with *'ōhel* in the preceding line. It is certainly possible that David is simply seeking the approval of a court prophet to carry out his own plan, a plan that is ultimately political in its attempt to limit the freedom of Yahweh,[16] but no such motivation is attributed to David. Indeed, it is notable that, in contrast to Saul for whom statements of motivation are quite common (1 Samuel 13:11ff.; 14:24; 15:15; 18:8, 17, 21, 25, 28–29; 20:26, 30–31; 28:5; 31:4), we are rarely given narrative insights into David's motives apart from the two times when he refrained from killing Saul and nearly killed Nabal (1 Samuel 24 – 26). The motivation of David as king is always much more opaque than was the case for Saul, and even if only as the most loyal of court functionaries, Nathan has no reason to believe that there is a problem with David's plan.

It is David's plan, however, that will be subject to considerable review as Nathan now receives an actual word from Yahweh. Strictly speaking, the whole of verses 4–16 constitute a message that Yahweh gives Nathan, which Nathan is then to relay to David, a word that is said to come in the form of a nocturnal encounter with Yahweh, though it is also called a 'vision' in verse 17, which recounts Nathan's faithful report of the message to David. The message itself divides into three main sections. First, in verses 5–7, David's plan to build a house for Yahweh is declined. This actually represents a significant rebuttal for David, and taken without reference to the balance of the oracle could be construed as a complete rejection of the possibility of a temple.[17] Although the

---

16. So Donald F. Murray, *Divine Prerogative and Royal Pretension: Pragmatics, Poetics and Polemics in a Narrative Sequence about David (2 Samuel 5:17–7:29)* (Sheffield: Sheffield Academic Press, 1998), pp. 165–166.

17. This is one of the reasons why verse 13 (which has no exact parallel in Chronicles) is often considered suspect. Cf. McCarter, *II Samuel*, pp. 205–206. Eslinger, *House of God*, pp. 48ff., retains the verse and includes some spirited correspondence between himself and Antony F. Campbell as to its origin.

main focus in terms of covenant has typically been on the balance of the oracle,[18] the foundation for the later covenantal language is established here. Verses 8–11a are then marked off by the presence of a new introductory formula in verse 8 and focus on the elements of a historical recital of Yahweh's actions on David's behalf and a national promise. Covenantal forms are especially important here. The third section, verses 11b–16, is initially indicated by a third-person break from the surrounding first person and introduces the actual dynastic promise to David.[19] Running through all of this, of course, is the constant play on the word *bayit*, though this is not a feature examined in detail here.

Yahweh declines David's offer: 2 Samuel 7:5–7

It is notable that we do not receive a second-hand summary of Yahweh's message through Nathan, but rather have it narrated as if we are actually hearing the original message being spoken. This, of course, has the effect of highlighting the importance of the message,[20] as well as creating more immediacy since there is now no distance between the message and its announcement. But it also means that we retain Yahweh's words that are not a part of the message as such, but which nonetheless have an impact on its meaning. Most importantly, Yahweh directs Nathan to speak 'to my servant, to David'. The phrase itself is somewhat redundant, especially with the repetition of the preposition 'to' (*'el*) on both

---

18. Eg. Philip J. Calderone, *Dynastic Oracle and Suzerainty Treaty: 2 Samuel 7:8–16* (Manila: Loyola House of Studies, 1966).

19. A similar analysis is offered by Robert Polzin, *David and the Deuteronomist: A Literary History of the Deuteronomistic History*. Pt 3: *2 Samuel* (Bloomington: University of Indiana Press, 1993), pp. 71ff.; J. P. Fokkelman, *Narrative Art and Poetry in the Books of Samuel*. Vol. 3: *Throne and City* (Assen: van Gorcum, 1990), p. 221, divides verse 11 into three sections, but his 11c = 11b in this analysis. It is usually preferable to use *'atnāḥ* as the point of division within the verse into major sections.

20. Cf. Polzin, *David and the Deuteronomist*, pp. 71–72. Indirect discourse does, however, occur in verse 11b.

'my servant' ('*abdî*) and 'David'.[21] But the structure not only clari-
fies the question of the servant's identity; it also carries with it
considerable covenantal freightage. One of the standard features
of suzerainty treaties is that the great king speaks of vassals as 'my
servant', so even though this is a standard form of speech in
deuteronomistic literature we cannot simply regard this as a stock
element of style. Thus, in the second millennium BC treaty between
Mursilis and Duppi-Teshub, Mursilis consistently speaks of the
need for Duppi-Teshub to act loyally towards him, and appears to
require that when he dies, then Duppi-Teshub become 'vassal' (or
servant) to his son.[22]

Hence, even before the message itself begins, Yahweh's speech
has sought to generate a perlocutionary effect on Nathan, which is
to say that the oracle he is to deliver is to be understood in covenantal terms. The primary intent of Yahweh's words to Nathan is
that Nathan is to take a message to David, a directive illocution in
terms of Nathan, but in so doing a declarative illocution is used that
also makes a statement about David's relationship to Yahweh in
covenantal terms. Since this element is included in the information
passed on to readers, they are in a similar position to Nathan in their
awareness of David's position as one whom Yahweh will address
within the framework of a covenant. Gerbrandt also notes that the
only other figure to be described as 'my servant' with frequency in
the Deuteronomistic History is Moses, so the use of this title at this
point could also be a deliberate echo of Moses' status, and thus act
as a further pointer that a new stage is being initiated with David.[23]
But if something new was being initiated, it needed to be Yahweh as
suzerain who did so, not David, which seems to be why David is not
to build the temple.[24]

---

21. LXX removes the second '*el*, but this appears to be a smoothing over of
    style that misses the emphasis so generated.
22. Text in Bill T. Arnold and Bryan E. Beyer, *Readings from the Ancient Near
    East* (Grand Rapids: Baker, 2002), pp. 98–100.
23. Gerbrandt, *Kingship*, p. 170. Cf. McCarthy, 'II Samuel 7', p. 130.
24. Ronald F. Youngblood, '1 and 2 Samuel', in Frank E. Gaebelein (ed.),
    The Expositor's Bible Commentary (Grand Rapids: Zondervan, 1992),

Yahweh's actions on David's behalf: 2 Samuel 7:8–11a

The balance of verses 5–7 contains the reasons why David was not to build a temple and need not detain us here. However, significant covenantal forms occur in this passage and need to be considered. The illocutions here are also declarative, a form that is important because of the way in which it holds back from making a direct statement, which would need either a directive or assertive illocution. But once again, they are operative at two levels, addressing the specifics of David's relationship to Yahweh as king in the immediate context, while also addressing the longer-term covenantal elements.

Since verse 8 introduces a new stage in the discourse, it is not surprising to note the presence of a renewed introduction. What is somewhat surprising, though, is the virtual repetition of the phrase 'to my servant, to David' (*lĕ 'abdî lĕdāwîd*) from verse 5.[25] The effect of the repetition is not only to indicate that this is a new section of the discourse, but also to renew the associations with covenantal language that were raised previously. The elements in verses 5b–7 avoided direct covenantal language, so this multilevel illocution is required to enable Nathan and readers to know that such associations are being made. The importance of this becomes clear in verses 8b–9a. Here there is a brief recount of Yahweh's actions on behalf of David, narrating the way he took him from being a shepherd through to making him *nāgîd* (ruler) over Israel, whom Yahweh specifically calls 'my people'. Along the way Yahweh insists that he has been with David and has cut off his enemies from before him. Such a recount is, of course, a stock element in the prologue of suzerainty treaties, with the great king describing the benefits wrought for the vassal. Thus, this illocution also operates declaratively in that it simply states what it is that Yahweh has done for David. But this illocution, because of its various associations, also

---

vol. 3, p. 886; W. J. Dumbrell, *Covenant and Creation: A Theology of the Old Testament Covenants* (Carlisle: Paternoster, 1997), p. 148.

25. Since the prepositions *'el* and *lĕ* can function largely interchangeably at some points, there is no clear distinction in meaning between these two phrases.

indicates that Yahweh is David's suzerain, and that this suzerainty has been demonstrated through a period of history.

That Yahweh is acting as David's suzerain would also appear to be supported by the fact that the title *Yhwh ṣĕbā'ôt* (Lord of Hosts) is used. Although the title is translated in various ways, the general sense of the title is one of authority and power. But the association of this title with what appears to be new actions being initiated would also appear to be borne out by its distribution through the books of Samuel. The divine epithet occurs eleven times in the books of Samuel (1 Samuel 1:3, 11; 4:4; 15:2; 17:45; 2 Samuel 5:10; 6:2; 6:18; 7:8, 26, 29). This distribution is notable for the ways in which the term appears in clusters, and each time at the beginning of a new phase in Israel's life. In 1 Samuel 1 – 4 there is the record of how the family of Eli was removed and Samuel placed in authority, 1 Samuel 15 – 17 records the point of Saul's ultimate rejection, which is paralleled by the usage in 1 Samuel 17 where David is publicly acknowledged, while all the references in 2 Samuel are clustered into chapters 5–7, chapters that recount the processes by which David was to consolidate his power over the whole of the nation.

The point established by the narrative, though, is that these things happen at the initiation of *Yhwh ṣĕbā'ôt* and not at human initiative. The epithet is thus employed to make clear the points at which the new phases in Yahweh's interaction with Israel begin. Even more striking is the fact that the only two passages where God uses the epithet of himself are here and 1 Samuel 15:2 – in that case, the narrative recounts the point at which Saul is ultimately rejected, whereas here we have the promise to David, a promise that makes this chapter an exact counterbalance to 1 Samuel 15.

Attached to this historical prologue is a set of promises from Yahweh to David in verses 9b–10. These promises move from the specific situation of David to the nation as a whole, linking the nation's experience of Yahweh's blessing to the experience of David.[26] Such promises are also an allusion back to the promises to

---

26. The shift from converted imperfects to converted perfects signals this shift. H. W. Hertzberg, *I & II Samuel* (London: SCM, 1964), p. 285, is

Abraham in Genesis 15,[27] with their focus on the land and security within it. But there is also the unusual promise that Yahweh will grant David a 'great name', a promise that parallels the promise to Abraham in Genesis 12:2 and which itself stands in relief to the attempts of the builders at Babel to build a name for themselves. A great name in this context is probably to be understood as renown, and if so there is another echo of the suzerain–vassal relationship, since it would be recognized that the vassal cannot create a great name for himself and is entirely dependent upon the protection that the suzerain provides. Although the expression itself does not find exact parallels in the known suzerainty treaties, it is certainly consonant with them,[28] though the greater point of continuity is with the promises to Abraham.

This continuity is highlighted by the reference to the 'place' (*māqôm*) that will be given to the people, a place where they will know security. In spite of the views of some that *māqôm* should be seen as virtually equivalent to *'ereṣ*,[29] such a view seems improbable in that the promise to David must have a future element, and Israel is clearly in the land at this time. But neither can we restrict it only to the temple[30] since what is promised is a place for 'my people Israel', and it is their security that is in view. However, Murray has shown that the reference can be to a quality of life for the nation,[31] and this seems to be the most likely interpretation here. However, a link to the Abrahamic material still seems to be required, since it is ultimately a settled and secure life in the land to which the earlier

---

nervous about seeing these statements as promises in spite of this shift. But see the rebuttal of this view by Fokkelman, *Throne and City*, pp. 223–226.

27. Cf. Hans Joachim Stoebe, 'Erlebte Gegenwart – Verheissene Zukunft: Gedanken zu II Samuelis 7 und Genesis 15', *Theologische Zeitschrift* 53 (1997), pp. 133–134.

28. Calderone, *Dynastic Oracle*, pp. 45–46.

29. Youngblood, '1 and 2 Samuel', p. 889.

30. McCarter, *II Samuel*, pp. 202–203.

31. D. F. Murray, 'MWQM and the Future of Israel in 2 Samuel VII 10', *VT* 40.3 (1990), pp. 298–320.

promises look. Yahweh's speech indicates that this has not been their experience so far, but in giving David rest from his enemies (verse 11a, thus forming an inclusion with verse 1) the nation will experience similar rest and enjoyment of the land.

There are thus strong covenantal allusions running throughout this second section of Yahweh's speech. Once again, the speech acts themselves are declarative – they require no immediate response from David. But it is in the nature of declarative speech acts to leave room for consideration, and it is towards this that the perlocutionary force of Yahweh's speech is directed. By consciously adopting covenantal language, even without using the word *běrît*, Yahweh leads towards the conclusion that a covenant is indeed being established here, a covenant that is recognized by its use of forms of address, historical recital and promises to the vassal. What remains, however, is to move on to the conditions of covenant.

The dynastic promise: 2 Samuel 7:11b–16

A new phase in the speech is clearly indicated by the shift to third-person forms at verse 11b. As the text stands, this is most likely to be understood as indicating the rhetorical force of the announcement about to follow, the third-person forms being a deliberate contrast to that which surrounds them. What is to be noted is that Yahweh's language evokes announcements from earlier covenants within the Old Testament, notably the Abrahamic and Sinai covenants, and works them into a new announcement to David. Once again, Yahweh's speech acts are declarative, but have within them implications wider than just the bare statements themselves. The declaration itself is of vital importance – David shall not build a house for Yahweh but Yahweh shall build a house for him.

The nature of the house that Yahweh will build is indicated by the next statement, which is that a son of David's will succeed him on the throne, something that could not be regarded as certain following the example of Saul. Calderone points to a number of parallels between this promise and various covenant texts, especially Hittite ones.[32] But the covenantal allusions are

---

32. Calderone, *Dynastic Oracle*, pp. 50–51.

even stronger within the Old Testament itself, since we have reference to David's *zeraʿ* (seed), a term that not only has strong overtones from the Hittite treaties, but also to Abraham.[33] This is made apparent by the fact that the phrase *yēṣēʾ mimēʿēkā* (coming from you) occurs in verse 12 and Genesis 15:4. In Abraham's case, reference to a son to be born in the future and specifically from his own body made considerable sense since the basis of his complaint in Genesis 15 was precisely that he did not have a son of his own.

In contrast, David has had no trouble in fathering sons up to this point (2 Samuel 3:2–5; 5:13–16), so the phrase itself is redundant in terms of information, but is included precisely because of the need to link this promise to that of Abraham. At the same time, David is placed in a position of dependency on Yahweh, as befits a vassal, because although it would appear that he will have some choice over his successor, that son is yet to be born. Just as Abraham could not make Ishmael the acceptable figure for the promise he received, neither can David make any of his current sons the heir promised by Yahweh. Instead, he has to wait for the provision of that son.[34] It will be that son who will build the temple,[35] and thus indicate the status of Yahweh as suzerain over him as well, and, in return, Yahweh will establish a kingdom for him. Once again, this is the language of the suzerain who decrees who indeed can reign as king in subject realms, while this promise

---

33. Cf. the covenant with Aaron, Numbers 18:19, for a similar formulation.

34. That is why 2 Samuel 12:25 is so important: it confirms Solomon as the
   initial member of the line of David's seed, and thus the one eligible to
   build the temple. Such an observation also acts as further evidence that
   renders questionable the idea that 2 Samuel 9 – 20 and 1 Kings 1 – 2 form
   a 'Succession Narrative', since the narrative has now made clear that
   none of the older sons who are active in those chapters can actually
   succeed David.

35. Eslinger, *House of God*, pp. 57ff., sees an important distinction between
   David's desire to build a house in which Yahweh would dwell and a house
   for his name. But this seems overly subtle, and more likely represents a
   stylistic variation.

also parallels that to Abraham in Genesis 17:13 in which an 'enduring'[36] covenant was also promised for his seed (*zera'*).

Attached to this promise, though, are certain conditions that are to be understood in covenantal terms. The beginning of verse 14 has a clear echo of Exodus 19:4–6 with its adoption language, though a parallel can also be seen in Genesis 17:8b. What is made clear, though, is that there are conditions in this relationship, even if the exact sense of the 'human wounds' that are a part of it is disputed. Yahweh, as suzerain, acts as the father to the seed that would follow David, and in so doing retains the right of discipline when these descendants are not faithful to him. Nevertheless, a special relationship is established between Yahweh and David and, unlike the earlier relationship with Saul, Yahweh's *ḥesed* will not be removed from the line of David. This does not provide David with a blank cheque, since the exact form of the relationship between Yahweh and his descendants still needs to be resolved, but the use of a term with as much covenantal import as *ḥesed* is surely significant in establishing the fact that a covenant has been established. However, it would seem that even with these promises, there are hints that conditions apply,[37] and that Yahweh as suzerain still has the right of revocation. As Waltke argues, the promise for David endures, but disloyal sons can lose the benefits that the covenant offers, and David himself can still be punished for his own sin.[38]

---

36. Philip E. Satterthwaite, 'David in the Books of Samuel: A Messianic Expectation?' in Philip E. Satterthwaite, Richard R. Hess and Gordon J. Wenham (eds.), *The Lord's Anointed: Interpretation of Old Testament Messianic Texts* (Carlisle: Paternoster, 1995), p. 55, rightly notes that '*ōlām* does not necessarily have the sense of 'eternal', and indeed 1 Samuel 2:30 has already seen an '*ōlām* promise revoked by Yahweh.

37. See Knoppers, 'David's Relation to Moses', pp. 101–114, for the way the chronicler and Psalms work out the conditional and unconditional elements.

38. Bruce K. Waltke, 'The Phenomenon of Conditionality within Unconditional Covenants', in Avraham Gileadi (ed.), *Israel's Apostasy and Restoration: Essays in Honor of Roland K. Harrison* (Grand Rapids: Baker, 1988), pp. 131–132.

It is important to note, therefore, that throughout this speech, Yahweh's speech acts have been operating at two levels. At the primary level, Yahweh has rejected David's plan to build a temple, but promised instead to build a dynasty for David, within which one of David's descendants will build a temple for Yahweh. The declarative form employed thus leaves no doubt, and the perlocutionary effect is thus clear in terms of the impact on David. But by deliberately utilizing so many covenantal terms Yahweh also creates a second level of perlocutionary effect in that the promise to David in terms of his dynasty evokes a range of covenantal elements. These elements are an intentional component within Yahweh's speech and ensure that David is to understand what has been promised as a covenant. It is not a blank cheque for David, since discipline remains a possibility and even enduring covenants cannot automatically be assumed to have no limits, but it is clearly intended to lead David to the conclusion that, even though the word *běrît* has not been used, a covenant has been formed.

The narrator's speech acts

It is important to note that the narrator has final control over the shape and intention of a narrative,[39] since by the process of selecting material the narrator's point of view is presented to us. However, it is possible that a narrator may deliberately include material that represents a point of view different from that being presented by the narrative as a whole, and a skilful writer can thus allow conflicting points of view to be expressed while still seeking to integrate them into a coherent overall perspective. Traditionally, Old Testament criticism has regarded these different voices as indicative of sources to be studied, and though this may be an observation correct in itself, it does not address the

---

39. Cf. Meir Sternberg, *The Poetics of Biblical Narrative: Ideological Literature and the Drama of Reading* (Bloomington: Indiana University Press, 1985), pp. 41–56.

possibility of a meaning that is intended through the integration of such material. Thus, some recent studies have sought to demonstrate that the emphasis on pro- and anti-monarchical sources in I Samuel 8 – 12 may miss the point intended by the overall narrative voice.[40]

Fortunately, the general trend has been to assume that there is no disagreement between the intentions of Yahweh and those of the narrator. Eslinger, however, by his rejection of the role of the narrator and his insistence that the later reference to a covenant in 2 Samuel 23:5 indicates not only that David has fallen for Yahweh's rhetoric in 2 Samuel 7, but also that he needs to try to convince Yahweh of the justness of his claim of the existence of this covenant,[41] allows for the possibility of such a disjunction. Eslinger, of course, disavows an interest in such an issue, but since we have sought to demonstrate that Yahweh's speech acts in 2 Samuel 7:1–17 do indeed initiate a covenant, we need to ensure that these acts are consistent with the narrative voice of the whole of the books of Samuel.

In testing this issue it will be necessary to look for those points where the narrator intrudes into the text through direct comments as well as through consideration of structural matters. A key element to note here is that the narrator makes a very similar comment at two important structural points within 2 Samuel – both 2 Samuel 7:1 and 2 Samuel 22:1 refer to events that happened in David's life at the point when Yahweh had granted him security from his enemies. Although the phrasing of these two statements is not identical, they are certainly similar enough to be parallel to one another. Strikingly, both occur with central items in the chiasms (5:17 – 8:14 and 21 – 24) that bound the court narrative of

---

40. Lyle M. Eslinger, 'Viewpoints and Point of View in 1 Samuel 8–12', *JSOT* 26 (1983), pp. 61–76; V. Phillips Long, 'How Did Saul Become King? Literary Reading and Historical Reconstruction', in A. R. Millard, J. K. Hoffmeier and D. W. Baker (eds.), *Faith, Tradition and History: Old Testament Historiography in its Near Eastern Context* (Winona Lake: Eisenbrauns, 1994), pp. 271–284.

41. Eslinger, *House of God*, p. 91.

chapters 9–20,[42] and worship themes are present in both. As such, it seems that the narrator has signalled by the repetition of this information that these passages are to be read in the light of one another, as both show David responding to Yahweh's provision of security. In speech act terms, both statements are declarative, but as we have seen it is also important to note the intended perlocutionary effects that are provided. Obviously, because the narrator's own comments are relatively infrequent within the narrative of the books of Samuel, care must be exercised. But it is the very scarcity of comment that leads us to recognize the importance of these statements. At one level, they can be read as simply indicating when it was that David spoke, but at another they function as a means of leading the reader to see these passages as being related to one another. Thus, the one illocution by the narrator can have more than one perlocutionary outcome. For our purposes, it is the second level that is of importance, since the linking of these passages by the narrator indicates that they need to be read in the light of one another, and that each will to some extent shape the way in which the other is to be interpreted.[43]

Second Samuel 22 is thus a poem to be read in the light of 2 Samuel 7 as celebrating the goodness of Yahweh to David, one that also points to David as one who has depended upon Yahweh.

---

42. Cf. David G. Firth, 'Shining the Lamp: The Rhetoric of 2 Samuel 5–24', *TynBul* 51.2 (2001), pp. 203–224. Since the publication of that essay, I have come across similar analyses by H. J. Koorevaar, 'De Macrostructuur van het boek Samuël en die theologische implicaties daarvan', *AcT* 17.2 (1997), pp. 56–86; and H. H. Klement, *II Samuel 21–24: Context, Structure and Meaning in the Samuel Conclusion* (Frankfurt am Main: Peter Lang, 2000), pp. 61–68.

43. K. L. Noll, *The Faces of David* (Sheffield: Sheffield Academic Press, 1997), p. 134, traces the importance of this link to narrative time, and thus focuses only upon the proposed setting for the song. Following the same pattern as Eslinger, his approach is then to consider David's rhetoric within the song, though there are at least hints that he recognizes a larger intent on the part of the narrator, though he also works with a distinction between author and narrator that may be inappropriate for most Old Testament literature.

The David who speaks in this psalm knows that Yahweh has indeed acted for him. This, of course, leads into the poem of 23:1–7, David's so-called Last Words. The exact sense of this title need not detain us here, but it is clearly meant to indicate that these are words spoken by David near the end of his life, words that are able to look back over the whole of his reign. Thus, the narrator's intrusions with headings at 22:1 and 23:1 not only encourage us to read the whole of chapter 22 in the light of 2 Samuel 7, but also 23:1–7 as a mature reflection from a much later stage in David's life. Noll argues that this poem comes from a troubled mind, perhaps embittered because God has not acted as he had expected.[44] The poem is undoubtedly difficult, but it seems unnecessary to see it in such negative terms. Rather, it appears to be David's final recognition of the fact that authentic kingship in Israel is that which acts as a vassal to the suzerainty of Yahweh, a message that derives heightened authority from the presentation of David as a prophet in the opening lines.[45] But it is the allusions back to chapter 7 in verse 5 that are of most importance here, because there David specifically refers to an enduring covenant that Yahweh has made with his house.

Although the opening phrase of verse 5 (*kîlō'kēn*) is awkward to translate, whether we take it as a rhetorical question or asseverative, the ultimate sense remains the same – David is sure that his house (*bayit*), and not just David himself, exists in the relationship to Yahweh that was outlined in verses 3b–4.[46] The use of the word *bayit* in this context is surely significant since it refers back to the narrative of chapter 7 where *bayit* placed such a significant structural role. The word itself is relatively common,[47] but in none of its

---

44. Noll, *Faces of David*, p. 169.

45. Klement, *II Samuel 21–24*, pp. 215–218.

46. That it is David's 'house' and not just David himself who is in this relationship with Yahweh could undercut the idea raised by Walter Brueggemann, '2 Samuel 21–24: An Appendix of Deconstruction?' *CBQ* 50 (1988), pp. 383–397, that the closing chapters of 2 Samuel attempt to deconstruct the picture of the powerful David generated by 2 Samuel 5 – 8.

47. It has occurred some fifty-nine times since 2 Samuel 7.

uses since chapter 7 has it had the special sense it has there in terms of David except in Nathan's judgment statement of 2 Samuel 12:8–10.[48] At this point, therefore, we are assured that Nathan's judgment statement has been worked out, since David's house is now right with Yahweh, but the reference to David's house also causes readers to invoke the themes from 2 Samuel 7. This, in turn, is developed by David's reference to a *bayit 'ôlām* that Yahweh has set for him. The significance of this statement is that it too evokes reference to that which is enduring, again creating an allusion to 2 Samuel 7. The importance of this allusion is strengthened by the fact that the word *'ôlām* has only occurred twice since 2 Samuel 7 – in 2 Samuel 12:10 and 22:51. The reference in 12:10 is of interest because it is a part of Nathan's judgment oracle on David, which was also the last time David's *bayit* was mentioned with the special sense of 2 Samuel 7, and is perhaps a further linguistic indicator of the completion of David's punishment. But the reference in 2 Samuel 22:51 is even more important, since it combines a reference to Yahweh's *ḥesed* to his anointed (*māšîaḥ*), which is then defined in terms of David and his *zera'* and is said to be *'ad 'ôlām*.

Thus, the end of the first of David's poems also provides a cluster of linguistic links back to chapter 7 and simultaneously prepares us for his closing reflections in 23:1–7 through the deliberate use of covenantal terminology.[49] It is thus highly probable that the narrator of the books of Samuel considered the reference to a *běrît* in 2 Samuel 23:5 to be entirely appropriate, and that this covenant was to be found in 2 Samuel 7. The perlocution sought is thus one that wants to insist that the foundation for a Davidic covenant is found in 2 Samuel 7, a covenant on which both of David's closing poems reflect.

---

48. Curiously, there are ten references to the house of Saul since 2 Samuel 7 that do employ this special sense – 2 Samuel 9:1, 2, 3, 9; 12:8; 16:5, 8; 19:18; 21:1, 4.

49. This observation could support the suggestion that 2 Samuel 22, and not Psalm 18, is the original context for this psalm, though one could also argue that the presence of such material was suggestive to the narrator of verbal links to be exploited.

Conclusion

The speech acts of Yahweh, David and the narrator agree. In 2 Samuel 7 there is a collection of covenantal references that not only function at their declarative level of declining David's offer to build Yahweh a house, to which Yahweh offers to build David a house instead, but which also function to create an awareness of covenantal allusions that are developed throughout each stage of Yahweh's speech. Although the word *bĕrît* does not occur in the speech, a cluster of allusions are developed through form and content that point to the existence of such a covenant. In 2 Samuel 22:1 – 23:7 the narrator records two closing poems of David, both of which are linked back to 2 Samuel 7, also through a cluster of allusions in form and content. In these poems David is shown to be reflecting upon the importance of the promises to him in 2 Samuel 7:1–17, promises that he understands as being in the form of a covenant. But the narrator has provided readers with enough links to those chapters to indicate that these two poems are to be interpreted in the light of 2 Samuel 7:1–17, while also shedding more light back on to the earlier chapter. A dialogue between these two segments of the books of Samuel is thus opened up in which mutual clarification is gained. Through this dialogue, which represents a speech act on the part of the narrator, we discover that a covenant with David was indeed formed, and that even if it is not a formal covenant document, 2 Samuel 7:1–17 is indeed the record of the point at which that covenant was initiated.

© David G. Firth, 2005

4. A NEW-COVENANT SLOGAN IN THE OLD TESTAMENT

James Hely Hutchinson

It is well established that the formula 'I will be your God, and you will be my people' connotes covenant. In this chapter I shall argue that the formula 'Praise Yhwh, for he is good, for his *ḥesed* endures for ever' bears similar connotations. The two formulae are manifestly different in a number of ways, notably in terms of grammatical form and in terms of the person or people who utter them; and whereas the first formula features (with variants) throughout Scripture, beginning with the context of God's dealings with Abraham (Genesis 17:7–8) and ending with that of John's vision of the new creation (Revelation 21:3–4), the second formula is confined to the Old Testament – indeed, with one exception, it is restricted to the Writings, and principally to the books that open (Psalms) and close (Chronicles) this last part of the Hebrew canon. But we shall see that this second formula is closely associated with the idea of covenant, and bespeaks, in particular, the anticipation of *new*-covenant fulfilment.

Jeremiah 33:11

I propose to examine each of the instances of the formula and to do so in Hebrew-Bible order. We begin, then, with Jeremiah 33:11, which serves (significantly, as we shall note) as our 'base text', being not only the earliest case canonically (the only one we find outside the Writings) but also the earliest chronologically (the other cases of the formula featuring in books whose final form dates to a period subsequent to the writing of Jeremiah). Our verse falls within the section typically known as the 'Book of Consolation' (chs. 30–33),[1] which in turn is particularly noted for the high point at 31:31–34 (verses quoted and expounded at some length in Hebrews 8 – 10). Jeremiah 31:31 provides us with the only occurrence in the Old Testament of the expression 'new covenant' (although Jeremiah himself and other prophets use equivalent terms, notably 'eternal covenant' [Jeremiah 32:40; Ezekiel 16:60; 37:26] and 'covenant of peace' [Ezekiel 34:25; 37:26], and we should be careful to heed the strictures of James Barr who established incontrovertibly in the early 1960s that word and concept should not be confused).[2]

The issue immediately at hand, then, is whether Jeremiah 33:11 forms part of the prophecy concerning the *concept* of the new covenant. The unity of the section in question certainly points that way, with a host of phrases and terms occurring with striking density in the four chapters relative to the rest of the book, including *šûb šĕbût* (restore the fortunes of, which serves as an *inclusio* for the section [30:3; 33:26] and appears in five other texts[3] [including

---

1. Cf. J. A. Thompson, *The Book of Jeremiah* (NICOT; Grand Rapids: Eerdmans, 1980), p. 551; J. G. McConville, *Judgment and Promise: An Interpretation of the Book of Jeremiah* (Leicester: Apollos/Winona Lake: Eisenbrauns, 1993), p. 92.

2. 'In general it will surely be desirable, in order to avoid confusion, that we should not say "concept" where we mean "word", and that where we do say "concept" we should understand that we mean something other than a word' (*Biblical Words for Time* [London: SCM, 1962], p. 51); cf. his *The Semantics of Biblical Language* (Oxford: Oxford University Press, 1961), pp. 261ff.

3. Jeremiah 30:18; 31:23; 32:44; 33:7; 33:11.

the verse under consideration] but otherwise only four times in the whole of the rest of Jeremiah), *yāmîm bā'îm* (days are coming), *bêt yiśrāēl* (house of Israel), *bānâ* (build), *ḥesed* (which we shall leave untranslated for the moment), *qābaṣ* (gather). Of particular interest for our purposes is the word *běrît* (covenant), which features nine times in the Book of Consolation out of a total of twenty-four for Jeremiah as a whole, and the covenant formula 'I will be their God, and they will be my people' (and variants thereof; four occurrences in our section,[4] with only three others in the rest of Jeremiah).[5]

But a more important indicator than these lexical data is the observation that the Book of Consolation keeps replaying the same themes such that the last of the four chapters, 33 (with which we are concerned), 'adds little substantively new to the picture that [chs.] 30–32 have already painted'.[6] Just as there is no warrant for differentiating the *běrît ḥădāšâ* (new covenant) of 31:31 from the *běrît 'ôlām* (everlasting covenant) of 32:40, so also there are no grounds for divorcing the emphasis on the permanence of God's promises in 33:14–26 from the covenant spoken of as irrefragable in the preceding chapters (31:32; 31:35–37; 32:40) – even if the dimension of continuity with covenants previously established with Abraham (verses 22, 26) and David (verse 21) is highlighted in that passage at the end of chapter 33. As far as the immediate, preceding context of our verse is concerned, 33:8 leaves us in no doubt that the covenant on view in chapter 33 remains that of the preceding chapters: that verse speaks of the twofold solution to the problem of sin promised by Yhwh – internal transformation (cf. 31:32–33) and

---

4. Jeremiah 30:22; 31:1; 31:33; 32:38.

5. Jeremiah 7:23; 11:4; 24:7.

6. McConville, *Judgment and Promise*, p. 101. It is true, however, that verses 14–18, which are not found in the Septuagint, provide considerably more detail (regarding the Davidic king and the Levitical priests) than 30:9, 21 and 31:14 respectively. Regarding the difficult question of the possible priority of the Septuagint at 33:14–26, I am following Andrew Shead (in private correspondence) in regarding both recensions, the Massoretic Text and the Septuagint, as being the word of God addressed through Jeremiah (originally to different audiences).

forgiveness (cf. 31:34). In short, the promises of 33:11 form an integral part of the new covenant.

What are those promises? The verse sets forth a first promise, whose main verb has already appeared in verse 10 ('there shall be heard again') and that employs two formulae, followed by a second promise that explains (*kî* [for]) the first and contains a third formula:

1st promise	1st formula	[There shall be heard again] *the voice of mirth and the voice of gladness,* *the voice of the bridegroom and the voice of the bride,* the voice of those saying,
	2nd formula	*'Praise Yhwh of Hosts,* **for** *Yhwh is good,* **for** *his ḥesed is everlasting,'* bringing a thank-offering to the house of Yhwh,
2nd promise	3rd formula	**for** *'I will restore the fortunes* of the land as at first,' says Yhwh.

The first formula is peculiar to the book of Jeremiah and serves to draw our attention to the importance of the new covenant for reversing God's judgment meted out on the people in the shape of the Babylonian exile. 'The voice of mirth and the voice of gladness, the voice of the bridegroom and the voice of the bride' (7:34; 16:9; 25:10) will be heard again (33:10–11). Given that 25:9–11 binds together the disappearance of joyful voices, the devastation of the country and the domination of Babylon, it comes as no surprise that the renewed sound of joyful voices goes hand in hand with a restoration of the conditions that prevailed prior to the exile; indeed, the second promise of our verse speaks of fortunes being restored to their original state (*kĕbāri'šōnâ*), including in terms of the sacrificing of thank-offerings.[7]

---

7. *šûb šĕbût* must here mean more than simply to 'bring captives back' (contra the NIV's translation at 33:7); the idea of captives returning *is* on view in 32:37, but, tellingly, the expression *šûb šĕbût* does not feature in that verse.

But does 33:11 merely speak of the reinstatement of a prior state of affairs? The wider context of these four chapters also presents aspects of discontinuity between the old regime and the new, and the second formula in our verse seems to fall within the scope of such discontinuity. The slogan that will be found on the lips of joyful worshippers at the temple after the exile celebrates the goodness and enduring *ḥesed* of Yhwh – ideas that, in the light of these chapters, evoke the permanence of the new regime. Yhwh is 'good' (verse 11) because he fulfils his 'good word' (verse 14) regarding favourable circumstances that will not be reversed (verses 15–26). No longer (*lō'* . . . *ôd* [31:29–30]) will sons die on account of their fathers' sins; no longer (*lō'* . . . *ôd* [31:34]) will the knowledge of Yhwh be conveyed by the (indirect) mediation of a teacher; no longer (*lō'* . . . *ôd* [31:34]) will sins be remembered; no longer (31:38–40; *lō'* . . . *ôd lĕ 'ôlām* [31:40]) will the city be uprooted or torn down; never will David lack a man to sit on the throne, nor the Levitical priests lack a man to offer sacrifices (*lō' yikārēt* . . . *lō' yikārēt* [33:17–18]). According to 31:3, Yhwh's *ḥesed* springs from his love (*'aḥăbâ*) for the people, which is *'ôlām* (everlasting), just as the new covenant is a *bĕrît 'ôlām* (32:40).

The key term in our formula, *ḥesed*, is thus closely tied to God's love for his people, but, in line with the logic of 31:3, it cannot be identical to it. The NIV is forced to abandon its usual translation 'love' under the weight of this logic, opting for 'loving-kindness'. The ESV's usual translation 'steadfast love' suffers from the same tautology, which it implicitly recognizes at 31:3 with its translation 'I have loved you with an everlasting love; / therefore I have continued my *faithfulness* to you.' But if 'steadfast love' is wrong and 'faithfulness' right at 31:3, might that not also be the case at 33:11? I submit that the formula at 33:11 highlights Yhwh's everlasting faithfulness or loyalty to his new-covenant promises.[8]

---

8. I am taking a different line at this point from my colleague at the Institut Biblique de Nogent-sur-Marne, Sylvain Romerowski ('Que signifie le mot *ḥesed*?' *VT* 40 [1990], pp. 89–103), although on a number of other matters (regarding relationships between covenants) I am in his debt.

In sum, according to the word of Yhwh mediated through Jeremiah in the context of the first instance of our formula, the days that are coming will surpass a mere return to the status quo: on the other side of the exile lies a reversal of fortunes that cannot be undone; and, against this background, worshippers will recognize the enduring, unshakeable character of Yhwh's covenant loyalty and (accordingly) give him praise as they bring their thank-offerings to the temple.

Psalm 100:4c–5

For the next two cases of our formula, we turn to Book 4 of the psalter. Psalm 100 fits the bill of Jeremiah 33 precisely. Its super-scription designates it a *mizmôr lĕtôdâ*, a psalm for thanksgiving or thank-offering – the noun-cognate of the verb in the formula under discussion (*yādâ*) and the word used in Jeremiah 33:11 to refer to the sacrifice that post-exilic worshippers would offer at the temple. Indeed, given that here too the setting of the psalm is cultic, verse 4 issuing the call to worshippers to bring a *tôdâ* to the *temple*, 'thank-offering' is preferable to 'thanksgiving'.[9] The mood is one of joy, *śimḥâ* (verse 2) echoing (again) Jeremiah 33:11. And the reason for the call to joyful sacrificing at the temple is covenantal: according to verse 3, the worshippers are to recognize that Yhwh is not only their creator but also their shepherd (a motif present in Jeremiah 31),[10] they being 'his people', while the end of

---

9. Against most translations and commentaries. We would not, however, wish to be guilty of divorcing the act of offering this sacrifice (a subcat-egory of the 'sacrifice of peace-offerings'; cf. Leviticus 7:11–12) and the act of giving thanks to Yhwh! See the four categories of meaning for the noun given in BDB; also cf. K. Koch, 'Denn seine Güte währet ewiglich', *EvT* 12 (1961), p. 532 n. 3.

10. Cf. Exodus 15:13, 17 (a context that reflects Yhwh's loyalty to his promises in Genesis 15:13–16; note that Exodus 15:13 ties the shepherd-ing imagery to Yhwh's *ḥesed*).

verses 4 and 5 issue the call to praise Yhwh on account of his goodness and enduring *ḥesed* and *'ĕmûnâ*.[11]

The one major difference relative to Jeremiah's Book of Consolation is that the summons to worship Yhwh is addressed in verse 1 to 'all the earth'. Dating individual psalms is a hazardous affair, but the final form of the psalter as a whole is certainly post-exilic,[12] and, in the unfolding flow of that final form, I suggest that Books 4 and 5 are designed to respond to the despair of Book 3 – and in particular the despair at the end of Psalm 89, where the psalmist calls into question Yhwh's covenant loyalty (his promises to David) in the face of the loss of kingship entailed by the exile.[13] The psalter reveals that that response is not restricted to Israel:[14] it is anticipated that the slogan of Psalm 100 be found on the lips of Gentiles drawn from 'all the earth'.

Psalm 106:1

Psalm 106, our next psalm, reviews Israel's history from the per-spective of the problem caused by her unfaithfulness. It contains incident after incident in which Israel sinned against Yhwh fla-grantly (the episodes of the Golden Calf, the rebellion following the spies' reconnaissance of the land, Baal-Peor, and others), and

---

11. Given my translation 'covenant loyalty' for *ḥesed* for the cases of our formula, it might be objected that I am failing to distinguish between *ḥesed* and *'ĕmûnâ/'ĕmet*. Where context dictates the sense of 'faithfulness' for the former, and the latter is parallel to it, the two terms do indeed appear to be virtually synonymous; cf. G. R. Clark, *The Word Hesed in the Hebrew Bible* (JSOTSup 157; Sheffield: Sheffield Academic Press, 1993), pp. 259–261. Around a quarter of the 176 occurrences of *'ĕmûnâ/'ĕmet* are found in close proximity to *ḥesed*, the psalter accounting for the bulk of them.

12. Cf. Psalms 126, 137.

13. On the question of the prominent role played by Psalm 89 in the struc-tural unfolding of the psalter, I follow G. H. Wilson, *The Editing of the Hebrew Psalter* (Chico: Scholars Press, 1985), pp. 212–214.

14. A theme not restricted to Books 4 and 5: see, for example, Psalms 67, 87.

it wrestles with the question of the implications of such sin for the people's relationship with Yhwh. We note from the psalm that Yhwh punishes such sin to the extent of having many of the sinners put to death. But we also observe that he holds back from pouring out the full measure of his anger, implying that the people are not obliterated altogether: thus Moses (verse 23 [the Golden Calf incident of Exodus 32 – 34]) and Phinehas (verse 30 [the Baal-Peor incident of Numbers 25]) act as mediators who alleviate the degree of punishment inflicted on the people. The concluding summary of the psalm is given in verses 43–46:

> Many times he delivered them,
>   but they were rebellious in their purposes
>   and were brought low through their iniquity.
>
> Nevertheless, he looked upon their distress,
>   when he heard their cry.
> For their sake he remembered his covenant,
>   and relented according to the abundance of his steadfast love.
> He caused them to be pitied
>   by all those who held them captive.[15]

In other words, the bottom line is that, even when sin was at its height in Israel's history, Yhwh's covenant loyalty stood firm. The covenant referred to in verse 45 is the Abrahamic, whose unconditional nature has been the subject of rejoicing in the preceding psalm (with which Psalm 106 is twinned)[16] as well as forming the basis of Moses' intercession following the idolatry of the Golden Calf incident (Psalm 106:23 reflects Exodus 32:12–14 and Deuteronomy 9:25–27, where the promises to the patriarchs are on view). Yhwh never loses sight, we learn, of his intention to bring

---

15. ESV. The word underlying 'steadfast love' is ḥesed.

16. For discussion of the phenomenon of 'twinning' in the psalter, see W. Zimmerli, 'Zwillingspsalmen', in J. Schreiner (ed.), *Wort, Lied und Gottespruch: Beiträge zu Psalmen und Propheten: Festschrift für J. Ziegler* (Würzburg: Echter Verlag, 1972), pp. 105–113.

the Abrahamic promises to realization, which means that he can never abandon his people altogether; and it is this reality that gives hope to the exiles and (specifically) gives rise to the exiles' prayer in verse 47 ('Save us . . . and gather us from among the nations, / that we may give thanks to your holy name').

What may we say, then, about the slogan in verse 1? The temple-setting is absent (unusually for the formula), for the people are in exile; but the new-covenant theology is clearly present in the psalm. 'We have sinned,' the exiles confess in verse 6; yet, since Yhwh's *ḥesed* endures forever, the exile will not spell the end. At no stage has Yhwh turned his back on the promises he made to Abraham. The prayer of verse 47 is firmly anchored in the truth that those promises remain valid, and so (in line with Jeremiah 33) it is envisaged that the people will find their way back to the land and there praise Yhwh's name. Herein lies Book 4's fundamental answer to the despair of Book 3: contrary to the psalmist's deduction from the loss of kingship entailed by the exile (Psalm 89), God's covenant loyalty remains unshakeable.

Psalm 107:1

The next occurrence of the formula is found at the beginning of the next psalm, which is also the beginning of the psalter's fifth book. The link with Psalm 106 is not restricted to the way in which the two psalms open: the reader is immediately struck in verses 2–3 of Psalm 107 by the answer to the exiles' prayer from 106:47. Now redeemed and gathered, the former exiles are here to reflect on Yhwh's covenant loyalty: *ḥesed* features five times in addition to verse 1, four of these as part of the refrain that structures the psalm[17] ('Let them praise Yhwh for his *ḥesed*, / for his wonderful deeds for the children of men') and the fifth being in the closing verse where we learn that those who are wise should understand Yhwh's *ḥasdê*. Do we find a temple-setting here? The last two occurrences of the psalm's refrain are elucidated with a second

---

17. Verses 8, 15, 21, 31.

line of jussives (verses 22 and 32), and it is verse 22 that does indeed inform us that the returnees are to sacrifice thank-offerings (*tôdâ* again) with joy[18] – exactly in line with Jeremiah 33 and Psalm 100. Once again, it is entirely appropriate to describe the formula of verse 1 as a slogan that bespeaks new-covenant fulfilment.

Psalm 118:1, 29

The next cases of the formula, the first and last verses of Psalm 118, occur in a setting that, again, conforms well to the prophecy of Jeremiah 33:11. An individual has been delivered from death at the hands of the nations (verses 5–21), and this act of salvation operated by Yhwh has implications for the people as a whole (verses 2–4, 22–27). Indeed, the people are gathered at the temple, probably[19] offering a sacrifice and expressing their joy (the verb cognate with *śimḥâ* features in verse 24) that the rejected stone has become the key foundation stone.

Although the psalm poses a number of difficulties of interpretation, much light is thrown on it by its role in the unfolding literary structure of Book 5. The preceding psalm, the shortest in the psalter, reminds us of Psalm 100 with its summons to all nations to recognize Yhwh's *ḥesed* and *'ĕmet*.[20] Moving back, Psalm 116 closes with the psalmist declaring that he will offer a *tôdâ* in the temple (verses 17–19) – and this in response to Yhwh's act of delivering him from death (verses 3, 8–9). Further links with Psalm 118 may be discerned in Psalm 115, which presents the sequence 'Israel . . . house of Aaron . . . those who fear Yhwh' (verses 9–11; cf. Psalm 118:2–4). In common with Psalm 117, Psalm 115 also ascribes praise to Yhwh for his *ḥesed* and *'ĕmet*. In fact, Psalm 118 is often considered to be the climax of the group known as the 'Egyptian

---

18. The word here is *rinnâ* rather than *śimḥâ*, but the mood is essentially the same as that on view in the texts we have already examined.

19. Verse 27 is tricky. See the discussion in F. D. Kidner, *Psalms 73 – 150* (TOTC; Leicester: IVP, 1975), pp. 415–416.

20. See n. 11 above.

Hallel' that stretches back to Psalm 113 and incorporates the reference in Psalm 114 to the exodus from Egypt.[21] Is it not fair to say, in the light of the post-exilic setting of Book 5,[22] that the formula which frames Psalm 118 is the appropriate response to the new exodus? The psalm's links with Exodus 15 (in verses 14–16, 21, 28)[23] provide additional support for this idea of a post-new-exodus thanksgiving. If we find the perspective of Jeremiah 33 once again confirmed, we must nonetheless recognize that the slogan is found on the lips of 'those who fear Yhwh' (Psalm 118:4), which surely includes representatives of the nations (cf. Psalm 117:1) – a dimension we have noted in relation to Psalm 100 but that is not found in Jeremiah's Book of Consolation.

Psalm 136:1

The last example of the formula in the psalter appears in Psalm 136:1 (with its last three words recurring, as a reverberating refrain, in every verse). The basis of the praise is set forth in the psalm in terms of Yhwh's acts in creation and providence and, supremely (in its central core, verses 10–22), in his redeeming of his people

---

21. Although this grouping may owe as much to Jewish tradition as to the inherent unity that the six psalms exhibit, see the various links between the psalms identified by M. Berder, *'La pierre rejetée par les bâtisseurs': Psaume 118, 22–23 et son emploi dans les traditions juives et dans le Nouveau Testament* (*EBib*, n.s. 31; Gabalda: Paris, 1996), pp. 92–95.

22. Psalm 107, discussed briefly above, serves a programmatic function for the fifth book as a whole, the return from exile being depicted by means of a range of themes that recur in subsequent psalms (new exodus, deliverance from death, journey to Zion, forgiveness of sins etc.). As F. Delitzsch argues in relation to Psalm 113, 'In all likelihood . . . the psalmist writes under the vivid impression of the deliverance from Babylon. Ver. 9 reminds us of Isa liv. 1, lxvi. 7f. The "barren woman" is the Jerusalem of the Exile' (*Biblical Commentary on the Psalms* [tr. D. Eaton; London: Hodder & Stoughton, 1889], vol. 3, p. 186).

23. Exodus 15:2a, 6, 12.

from Egypt and his leading them through to the land. We should note the shift from the use of the third person ('Israel') to first person ('us', 'our') that occurs in verses 23–24 ('It is he who remembered *us* in *our* low estate . . . / and rescued *us* from our foes'): while the deliverance spoken of in these two verses matches that of the preceding section, with *zākar* (remember) in verse 23 probably bearing covenantal connotations that evoke Yhwh's acting upon his promises to Abraham (cf. Exodus 2:24),[24] here the objects of Yhwh's deliverance are evidently a new generation.

May we go so far as to speak (again) of that generation as having experienced a new exodus? The links with preceding psalms (all the way back to Psalm 120, but especially back to Psalm 132) provide some support for this notion and also move us into the realm of temple-worship, as we have come to expect of the context of our slogan. That Psalm 135 is twinned with Psalm 136 is uncontroversial: verses 10–12 of the former (which speak of the exodus and subsequent movement to Canaan) figure (with some variants) in verses 17–22 of the latter, while an element of our slogan features in verse 3a of Psalm 135 ('Praise Yhwh, for Yhwh is good'). It is a particularly prominent feature of Psalm 135 that the praise to be ascribed to Yhwh (by 'the house of Israel . . . the house of Aaron . . . the house of Levi . . . those who fear Yhwh' – a sequence similar to that noted above for Psalms 115 and 118) takes place in the temple: the importance of this location is highlighted by the way in which the psalm opens and closes (verses 1–2, 21). This psalm is tightly bound not only to Psalm 136 but also to Psalm 134, as the strong echoes of the opening verse of the latter psalm in Psalm 135:1–2 will readily show. Again, we note (in Psalm 134) the summons to Yhwh's servants to bless Yhwh in the *temple*.

These links between Psalms 134, 135 and 136 cannot be viewed in isolation from the group of fifteen 'Songs of the Ascents' (so their superscriptions) of which Psalm 134 is the last. This group speaks of a journey (or perhaps a series of journeys) from Meshech

---

24. Cf. A. M. Harman, *Commentary on the Psalms* (Mentor; Fearn: Christian Focus, 1998), pp. 417, 426.

and Kedar (Psalm 120:5) to Jerusalem (e.g. Psalm 122). Within this group Psalm 132 stands out by virtue of its length and provides us with one of Book 5's most explicit answers to the despair of Book 3. On the one hand, the promise that the Davidic kingship would be established forever depended on David's sons' keeping of Yhwh's covenant (verse 12); on the other hand, Yhwh has not forsaken Zion nor the temple as his dwelling-place, for he will make a horn to sprout for David (verse 17), clothing Zion's priests with salvation and enabling her saints to shout for joy (verses 9, 16). Yhwh's covenant loyalty remains intact: the people will be restored to Zion under a Davidic king, with joyful worship at the temple duly re-established.

If we step into the shoes of the original recipients of the psalter, returnees at Jerusalem, we can affirm that they have, from one perspective, enjoyed a new exodus, and they once again worship Yhwh at the (second) temple; but I submit that the function of these psalms in final shape of Book 5 is to motivate the people to look for a more glorious return to Jerusalem and the fulfilment of the covenant blessings of Psalm 132. It is appropriate for them to praise Yhwh, for he is good, for his covenant loyalty is eternally dependable; but the full realization of Yhwh's covenant programme lies in the future and hinges on the emergence of David's 'horn'. Once again, the literary context of the formula we are examining (in this case in Psalm 136) drives us to affirm that the slogan moves in the sphere of a foreshadowing of new-covenant fulfilment. To be sure, Yhwh has remembered his people and brought them back from Babylon (some of them, at any rate! [Psalm 136:23]); and yet, even following this return from exile, the people still need to call on Yhwh to remember (act upon [Psalm 132:1]) his covenant promises to David.

Ezra 3:11

As we turn to Ezra 3:11, we find confirmation of the pattern of ideas that the texts in Jeremiah and the psalter have built up for us. From the opening verse of Ezra, the question of the fulfilment of Jeremianic prophecy is on view ('in order that the word of Yhwh through the mouth of Jeremiah might be fulfilled'). The historical context is clear: 50,000 exiles have returned to Jerusalem under Zerubbabel and Joshua (ch. 2), and the work of reconstructing the temple has begun (ch. 3). A full-orbed fulfilment of the promises found in Jeremiah's Book of Consolation remains a long way off: the return has so far been on a small scale; the city's reconstruction essentially lies in the future; and, at this stage, even the rebuilding of the temple will meet with opposition before it is finally completed (cf. chs. 4–6).

Many, indeed, are moved to weep 'with a loud voice' (3:12) as they compare the foundations of the new temple with what they recall of Solomon's temple. And yet there is nothing incongruous about the appearance of the slogan at 3:11, nor the joy that accompanies this praise of Yhwh (3:12–13), for the beginnings of the new temple point to Yhwh's faithfulness to his promises, or at least to a substantial improvement in the people's circumstances that presages the fulfilment of the new covenant (even if the reader of the closing chapters of Ezra and of Nehemiah is only too conscious that the heart-transformation prophesied by Jeremiah has yet to be realized, to say nothing of the absence of a Davidic king).

1 Chronicles 16:34

The last group of occurrences of the formula feature in the final book of the Old Testament, Chronicles. At first blush, they pose a problem for the thesis I am propounding, for the six instances of the formula in question appear to have been recorded as part of the narrative of events that took place during the reigns (chiefly) of David and Solomon – long before the exile. Particularly problematic is the first case, that of 1 Chronicles 16:34, for here the slogan seems to correspond to Psalm 106:1 but is apparently found on the lips of Levites appointed by David! Is our earlier assumption, that Psalm 106 is spoken by exiles, therefore incorrect, as several commentators (including Gerald Wilson[25] and

---

25. Wilson, *Hebrew Psalter*, pp. 184–185.

Alec Motyer[26]) maintain? For several reasons, I suggest that the chronicler is quoting the psalter and not vice versa.

First, there is only one captivity in relation to which the language of Yhwh having 'pity' on his people (Psalm 106:46–47) is used; namely the Babylonian exile.[27] Secondly, the psalm in 1 Chronicles 16 corresponds to parts of Psalms 105 and 96 as well as of Psalm 106: other things being equal, it is easier to account for this in terms of the chronicler's activity of selecting from the psalter to draw up a composite psalm than in terms of the psalter's dependence on 1 Chronicles 16. Thirdly, several lexical, morphological and syntactical discrepancies between 1 Chronicles 16 and the corresponding psalms are readily explained by the chronicler's reworking of material and by his theological emphases. For example, where Psalm 105:6 addresses *zera' 'abrāhām* (the seed of Abraham), we find in 1 Chronicles 16:13 *zera' yiśrāēl* (the seed of Israel), in keeping with the chronicler's emphasis on *kol yiśrāēl*.[28] Or again, instances of imperatives feature in Chronicles where the psalter has third-person perfectives (a phenomenon not found in reverse),[29] as exemplified by 1 Chronicles 16:15 where the *people are called upon to remember* the Abrahamic covenant, whereas in Psalm 105:8 we learn that *Yhwh remembered* it. We come across another example of second person (in Chronicles) in place of third person (in the psalter) four verses later: *bihyôtĕkem* (when *you* were, 1 Chronicles 16:19) where Psalm 105:12 has *bihyôtām* (when *they* were). A fourth

---

26. J. A. Motyer, 'The Psalms', in D. A. Carson, R. T. France, J. A. Motyer and G. J. Wenham (eds.), *New Bible Commentary: 21st Century Edition* (4th ed.; Leicester: IVP, 1994), p. 557.

27. See 1 Kings 8:50; 2 Chronicles 30:9; Jeremiah 42:12; cf. Harman, *Psalms*, p. 351.

28. Cf. H. G. M. Williamson, *1 and 2 Chronicles* (NCBC; Grand Rapids: Eerdmans/London: Marshall, Morgan & Scott, 1982), p. 129; R. L. Pratt, Jr, *1 and 2 Chronicles* (Mentor; Fearn: Christian Focus, 1998), pp. 15–16.

29. Although we do find an imperative in Psalm 96:10 (*'mrû*), where the chronicler has a jussive (*wy'mrû*, 1 Chronicles 16:31), and another imperative in Psalm 106:48 (*hllû*), where the chronicler has an infinitive absolute functioning as an imperative (*whll*, 1 Chronicles 16:36).

reason, which ties in with these instances, lies with the chronicler's overall purpose; namely 'to interpret to the restored community in Jerusalem the history of Israel as an eternal covenant between God and David which demanded an obedient response to the divine law'.[30] As far as chapter 16 in particular is concerned, 'it is probable that [the Chronicler] would be inviting [his contemporaries] to renew their faith in the God who, having answered the prayers and aspirations expressed in these verses so abundantly in the days of David and Solomon, could be relied upon to do so again despite all appearances in a later day'.[31]

Williamson's analysis fits well both with the chronicler's omission of much material in Psalms 105 and 106 that is not germane to his purposes[32] and with the chronicler's preference for imperatives: his readers, the returnees at Jerusalem,[33] are to praise Yhwh for his historic faithfulness to his promises by way of anticipating his future (new) covenant loyalty. That, then, is the sense of the slogan as found in 1 Chronicles 16:34.

It may be objected that, if the chronicler is quoting the psalter, verses 8–36 are unlikely to constitute the precise words of the Levites of David's day. Yet the chronicler's account does not require that they be taken this way; even if his editing of Psalm 106:48 (*'mrû*) at verse 36b (*wy'mrû*) is designed to show that the historical narrative resumes at this point and that the people of David's day say 'Amen' to the preceding (composite) psalm (and the Massoretic punctuation tells against this reading), we should recall that 'historical reportage is often more akin to painting than

30. B. S. Childs, *Introduction to the Old Testament as Scripture* (Philadelphia: Fortress, 1979), p. 644.

31. Williamson, *1 and 2 Chronicles*, p. 128. Cf. Pratt, *1 and 2 Chronicles*, p. 144.

32. The long historical review with which the psalmist is concerned in the part of Psalm 105 that has no parallel in Chronicles would not have tied in well with the chronicler's emphasis in the immediate context on the arrival of the ark of the covenant in Jerusalem; similarly, Psalm 106's preoccupation with the people's inveterate sinning is not that of the chronicler; hence the latter's omission of all but the beginning and end of the psalm.

33. Cf. 1 Chronicles 9.

photography' and that the psalm of 1 Chronicles 16 does not purport to be a verbatim transcript of the Levites' words.[34] Understanding the psalm both as providing a faithful historical portrait and as a summons addressed to the post-exilic community, we find that the slogan in 1 Chronicles 16:34 fits the bill of the occurrences we have already examined: it connotes confidence in the prospective realization of Yhwh's covenant purposes in a post-exilic era (note that the following chapter sets forth Yhwh's promises to David, including with regard to an eternally established throne, 1 Chronicles 17:14), and the context is one of rejoicing (1 Chronicles 15:25–29; 16:31) and of offering sacrifices at the tabernacle (1 Chronicles 16:1–7).

It follows from our interpretation that the prayer of the following verse, 1 Chronicles 16:35, presupposes a future, more glorious return than the one the chronicler's contemporaries have already enjoyed, and this perspective would appear to tie in well with the way in which the book ends (2 Chronicles 36:22–23): the Old Testament concludes by evoking Jeremianic prophecy regarding the end of the exile (2 Chronicles 36:21–22), suggesting that the real return to Jerusalem lies beyond the post-exilic community's experience. Once again, we learn that we are required to look for the fulfilment of our base text, Jeremiah 33:11, in a period later than that of the return under Zerubbabel. W. J. Dumbrell puts it this way:

> Understanding that the exile was open-ended (Dan. 9), and that the projections of Isaiah 40–55 were still to come, the Chronicler proclaims that the kingdom of God will come, the second exodus will occur . . . Bolstering a tired community, the Chronicler assures his people that God will never withdraw from his Abrahamic commitments, that the Promised Land will once again be Israel's, and that a theocracy will be established. Whatever the present disappointments, they can be endured if a theology of hope can be maintained. Thus, the Chronicler emerges as a theologian of eschatological enthusiasm. He belongs to the

---

34. V. Philips Long, *The Art of Biblical History* (FCI 5; Grand Rapids: Zondervan/Leicester: Apollos, 1994), p. 85.

prophetic movement – one that would never give up on Israel's hope. Notwithstanding the disappointing conclusion to the Ezra-Nehemiah period, the reforms had set covenantal directions, and such directions would guide the future hope of Israel.[35]

1 Chronicles 16:41

First Chronicles 16:41 underlines verse 34 and provides 'an indication of the type of psalmody most characteristic of the worship as led by the Levitical guilds';[36] in relation to the chronicler's agenda, this additional highlighting of the faithfulness of Yhwh to his covenant promises is intended to fuel the returnees' expectations of future divine covenant loyalty.

2 Chronicles 5:13; 7:3; 7:6

The instances of the formula found in 2 Chronicles 5:13, 7:3 and 7:6 call for comments virtually identical to those we have made with respect to the cases in 1 Chronicles 16. The key contextual features we have come to associate with the slogan are present: the offering of sacrifices at the temple (5:6; 7:1; 7:4; 7:7), rejoicing (7:10), Yhwh's keeping of covenant promises as evidenced by a climactic moment of redemptive history, in this case the arrival of Yhwh's glory in the temple (6:4–6, 10, 14 [note the incidence of *ḥesed*]; cf. 6:41 [note the use of *ṭôb*, 'good'], 7:10 [*ṭôb* and *ṭôbâ*, 'goodness']). Chapter 6, sandwiched between occurrences of our slogan, is particularly illuminating: the emphasis in Solomon's prayer of dedication on the future accomplishment of the Davidic covenant is strengthened in the chronicler's account (relative to that of 1 Kings 8) by the striking way in which it ends. Verses 41–42 draw on two texts that are significant for

---

35. W. J. Dumbrell, *The Search for Order: Biblical Eschatology in Focus* (Grand Rapids: Baker, 1994), pp. 151–152.

36. Williamson, *1 and 2 Chronicles*, p. 132.

their treatment, from a post-exilic perspective,[37] of the promises made to David.

The first is Psalm 132:1, 8–10; we have discussed this psalm briefly above, although we should note that here in Chronicles the saints are to rejoice *baṭṭôb* (in the goodness) – a change in the direction of our formula. The second is Isaiah 55:3 where *ḥasdê dāwîd* evokes, both here and in Isaiah, Yhwh's dependability vis-à-vis David and not vice versa (cf. 2 Chronicles 6:17).[38] Once again, the implication is that the chronicler is shaping his material in such a way as to inspire in his contemporaries confidence that Yhwh will honour his covenant commitments; the three cases of the slogan in these chapters (added relative to the author's *Vorlage*) play an important part in serving this purpose. It appears, then, that the Davidic promises, reaffirmed in the post-exilic era, are coterminous with Jeremiah's promise of a new covenant; certainly, the chronicler's use of the formula is of a piece with that of the books of Jeremiah, Ezra and the psalter.

---

37. It is, however, my conviction that the Isaiah prophecy was made before the exile, Isaiah being given prophetic insight during the eighth century into the prospective post-exilic setting.

38. H. G. M. Williamson has settled the debate relating to the Isaiah text (' "The Sure Mercies of David": Subjective or Objective Genitive?' *JSS* 23 [1978], pp. 31–49); one could also appeal to Acts 13:33–37. The debate is more complex with respect to the phrase in 2 Chronicles, notwithstanding the probability that the chronicler is citing Isaiah. The most compelling argument in favour of a subjective genitive at 2 Chronicles 6:42b lies in the way in which Psalm 132 (which is, after all, on view in verses 41–42a) opens with a prayer that Yhwh remember David's godly deeds (see e.g. the second argument put forward by R. Dillard, *2 Chronicles* [WBC 15; Waco: Word, 1987], pp. 51–52). But verses 11ff. allude to the divine promises made by Yhwh in favour of David. Nor should the various echoes of Psalm 89 in Psalm 132 be overlooked (see W. A. VanGemeren, 'Psalms', in F. E. Gaebelein [ed.], *The Expositor's Bible Commentary* [Grand Rapids: Zondervan, 1991], vol. 5, pp. 803–809), for the perplexity in Psalm 89 turns on the absence of the *ḥasdê* that Yhwh had promised to David (note especially verse 50).

2 Chronicles 20:21

One text remains, however; namely 2 Chronicles 20:21. The chapter recounts the deliverance of Judah from the hands of the Moabites and Ammonites during the reign of Jehoshaphat. The context is anomalous inasmuch as the slogan is uttered on the battlefield in the wilderness of Tekoa (verse 20) – clearly outside a temple-setting! That said, verse 19 specifies that it is the Levites who voice the praise of Yhwh, as is true of all the other cases of the slogan in Chronicles (and of the Ezra 3 text). Further, following the routing of their enemies, the people do return to Jerusalem, and in particular to the temple, with joy and to musical accompaniment (echoing, again, other texts of the formula;[39] verses 27–28).

Of even greater significance is the expression of trust in Yhwh's covenant loyalty: we should note the reference to the Abrahamic promises in verse 7 and the way in which, in verses 8–9, Jehoshaphat's prayer harks back to Solomon's prayer of dedication for the temple in 2 Chronicles 6 – the context for three of the instances of the formula in Chronicles, as we have already observed. This last case is thus no exception but lines up well with the contextual features we have by now come to regard as axiomatic for our formula; and, with this section (20:1–30) not featuring in 1 Kings, we may (again) be confident that the chronicler has (characteristically) added it to his account of the kings of Judah with a view to engendering greater trust on the part of his readership in Yhwh's covenant intentions (in this case, the fulfilment of the Abrahamic promises). The slogan, 'which the Chronicler intends as illustrative of the praise offered'[40] in the historical context of Jehoshaphat's day, has peculiar applicability to his own post-exilic day, as words to be taken on the lips of those who look forward to the realization of the new covenant.

---

39. The first two instruments mentioned appear in 1 Chronicles 15:16; 15:28; 16:5; 2 Chronicles 5:12; the third instrument features in Ezra 3:10; 1 Chronicles 15:24; 15:28; 16:6; 16:42; 2 Chronicles 5:12; 5:13.

40. Williamson, *1 and 2 Chronicles*, p. 299.

Conclusion

It has not been our primary aim to define the new covenant, although we have had cause along the way to note how closely aligned it appears to be with the promises made to Abraham and to David; and we have also noted that the new covenant provides for a permanent solution to the problem of the exile – a solution that is not fulfilled in the immediate post-exilic period. Nor has it been our chief aim to provide tight definitions of the terms found in our formula, although it has been striking to note that 'loyalty' or 'faithfulness' has consistently proven to be an appropriate rendering of *ḥesed* in these covenantal contexts. But two remarks may be made by way of conclusion.

First, questions of degrees of continuity and discontinuity between the new covenant and covenants set up before the exile – which remain a source of division among Christians, especially between (Reformed) covenant-theologians on the one hand and dispensationalists on the other – may be fruitfully studied in the books of Psalms and Chronicles. The frequency with which the slogan is found in these books suggests that they provide fertile terrain (possibly hitherto unexploited) for examining relationships between covenants; certainly, in both books the question of the status of the Davidic covenant following the exile is given considerable prominence.

Secondly, our slogan provides much nourishment for the soul of the Christian reader of the Old Testament. For if, in canonical terms, the texts we have examined lie at the threshold of the New Testament, we have also seen that, in theological terms, they propel us forward to the revelation and epoch of the New Testament, since they force us to direct our sights to the locus and timing of their fulfilment. We have found that the formula, associated with the joyful offering of sacrifices at the second temple, anticipates the fulfilment of the new covenant with confidence long before the incarnation of Christ. The Christian believer is in the privileged position of being able to take the slogan on to her lips with even greater assurance that new-covenant conditions will one day be fully and finally brought about, for she can look back to the enthronement of David's 'horn' at Calvary and in the resurrection-ascension-session that followed (John 12; Acts 2:29–36); as one of 'those who fear Yhwh' in the 'last days', she forms part of the spiritual temple, offering spiritual sacrifices to God by virtue of her faith in Jesus Christ (1 Peter 2:4). What was realistic, given Yhwh's goodness as a consistent promise-keeper, for the post-exilic returnee at Jerusalem is all the more realistic for the twenty-first-century believer: conscious that she deserves a condemnation far greater than the exile, yet already participating in new-covenant blessings that will soon be consummated, she is driven to praise God wholeheartedly and with much rejoicing, for he is indeed 'good, for his covenant loyalty endures forever'.[41]

---

41. I wish to thank Danny Mullins and Anthony Petterson for their comments on earlier versions of this chapter.

5. COMMUNITY, KINGDOM AND CROSS: JESUS' VIEW OF COVENANT

Kim Huat Tan

This chapter attempts to bring together the key themes of Jesus' ministry and organizes them under a head. The themes are those of the community, the cross and the kingship of Yahweh. The glue that binds them together – if we are not to wrench Jesus from his Jewish and biblical roots, or to regard him simply as an antiquarian hippy or teacher, walking about and observing birds and foxes just to make pithy sayings out of them – must be the covenant. This may appear to be a foolhardy step to take since the output of research on Jesus and the covenant is meagre. But recently, two substantial pieces of work have sought to understand Jesus' ministry from the vantage point of the covenant.[1] So there are encouraging signs that my announced undertaking may be on the right track.

---

1. T. Holmén, *Jesus and Jewish Covenant Thinking* (Leiden: Brill, 2001); N. T. Wright, *Jesus and the Victory of God* (Minneapolis: Fortress, 1996). Constraints of space do not allow me to interact in detail with these works but it would be clear to readers familiar with these works where I demur from their results, especially that of the former.

If ever there were an impediment to such an undertaking, it would be that the noun *diathēkē* (covenant) appears only once in the extant sayings of Jesus and this is found in three parallel accounts of the cup-saying, spoken at the Last Supper (Matthew 26:28 || Mark 14:24 || Luke 22:20).[2] The verb *diatithēmi* (to confer?), if admissible, occurs only twice but in the same logion connected with the Last Supper in Luke 22:29.[3] So for all intents and purposes, we can say that the explicit use of the noun or the verb is found only in the Last Supper traditions. However, it must be pointed out that word-statistics should not be the final arbiter for assessing significance unless one's understanding of how important a thing is is limited only to the pages of a concordance.

That this should be taken seriously is well illustrated by the traditions connected with Hillel. In these traditions there is no explicit reference to God. Are we to conclude that Hillel spoke as a Jewish atheist or had no concern whatsoever for the God of Israel?[4] Indeed, Sanders has demonstrated that the covenant remained central for Jewish belief and praxis of the Second Temple period even though the term was not frequently found.[5] Like glue, the covenant theme was often invisible but it served the all-important function of binding and holding things together. Consequently, we

---

2. The word occurs thirty-three times in the entire NT. In the Gospels there is one other occurrence, found in Luke 1:72. In this passage Luke portrays Zechariah as connecting the new overture of Yahweh through the birth of John the Baptist with the covenant.

3. The word occurs seven times altogether in the NT. All the uses of the verb in the NT occur in connection with the making of a covenant (or possibly a testament; see Hebrews 9:16–17).

4. See D. C. Allison, 'The Continuity between Jesus and John', *JSHJ* 1 (2003), p. 9.

5. E. P. Sanders, *Paul and Palestinian Judaism* (London: SCM, 1977). While Sanders' demonstration of the centrality of the covenant has often been regarded as the watershed in NT studies, earlier and just as significant attempts were also made: A. Jaubert, *La Notion d'Alliance dans le Judaïsme aux Abords de l'Ère chrétienne* (Paris: Du Seuil, 1963); and G. W. Buchanan, *The Consequences of the Covenant* (Leiden: Brill, 1970).

must be attentive to the workings of the *concept*, or how certain issues are necessarily entailed or intimately associated with it such that when they are discussed, the concept may safely be assumed to be presupposed.

Looking for the implicit in the explicit: covenant connections

The method and results of Holmén's work show typically the difficulties confronting a researcher in this area. If the Last Supper narrative be discounted, the probe for Jesus' attitude towards the covenant can only be done by inference; that is, by considering Jesus' attitude towards matters the practice of which was regarded by contemporaneous Jews as showing loyalty to the covenant.[6]

However, the Last Supper traditions are too significant to be ignored in this probe. Thus, they will be evaluated and faced boldly without, of course, discounting the need for a wider base of enquiry. This wider base of enquiry must look for indications of covenantal concern. I propose that such indications are found in discussions on community boundaries and how the story of God and Israel is thought to proceed in order for it to reach its divinely intended climax; that is, the narrative presupposed by the term 'the kingdom of God'. We must begin with how the covenant is understood in the OT.

Community as the entailment of covenant

The first thing to note is that the concept of a covenant inexorably demands the attendant concept of a community. The covenant is, above all, relational.[7] Those in covenantal relationship with Yahweh are regarded as his people. Who these people are and what they must do to remain as such are demonstrated through rites, praxis

---

6. Holmén, *Jesus*, p. 37.

7. Cf. E. W. Nicholson, *God and His People: Covenant and Theology in the Old Testament* (Oxford: Clarendon, 1986); G. E. Mendenhall and G. A. Herion, 'Covenant', *ABD*, vol. 1, pp. 1179–1180.

and symbols.[8] But these are not the foci. They serve only the function of maintaining the relationship between Yahweh and his people, and in this regard they demarcate and preserve community.[9] These practices and concrete *realia* are therefore the identity markers, not to be understood in the abstract, but concretely in relation to identity in a community. It is thus not surprising that in the prophetic description of a covenant to be restored or made anew the constituting of a community follows it cheek by jowl (Isaiah 55:1–13; 59:15b–21; 61:1–9; Jeremiah 31:31–33; Ezekiel 16:59–63; Hosea 2:14–23).[10]

Thus, it becomes understandable why covenant terminology, scarce in Second Temple Jewish literature, appears so frequently in the writings of the Qumran community.[11] This community was sectarian and the members, by understanding themselves as the one true community of Yahweh, were defining themselves over against other Jewish groups and laid claim to being the inheritors of the covenant heritage. Joining this community amounted to being a member of the new covenant (*CD* 6.19a; 8.21b; 19.33b–34a; 20.12).[12]

The upshot of all this is that there is an ecclesiological dimension to the covenant.[13] The covenant is not just about rules and

---

8. See N. T. Wright, *The New Testament and the People of God* (London: SPCK, 1992), pp. 123–126.

9. So also E. J. Christiansen, *The Covenant in Judaism and Paul: A Study of Ritual Boundaries as Identity Markers* (Leiden: Brill, 1995), pp. 6–7.

10. See K. H. Tan, *The Zion Traditions and the Aims of Jesus* (Cambridge: Cambridge University Press, 1997), pp. 207–209. Cf. W. J. Dumbrell who groups such passages under the heading of New Covenant theology in his *Covenant and Creation* (Exeter: Paternoster, 1984), pp. 169–200.

11. Cf. M. A. Knibb, *The Qumran Community* (Cambridge: Cambridge University Press, 1987), p. 84; M. A. Elliott, *The Survivors of Israel: A Reconsideration of the Theology of Pre-Christian Judaism* (Grand Rapids: Eerdmans, 2000), pp. 245–307.

12. Cf. Sanders' similar conclusion in his *Paul and Palestinian Judaism*, p. 241.

13. See the overall thesis of Christiansen, *Covenant in Judaism and Paul*.

regulations. Its existence presupposes a relationship constitutive of identity. In short, the very concept itself entails a people.

The hope for the kingdom as the climax of the covenantal story

Hays and Wright have ably argued for the fundamental importance of story for a community's self-understanding.[14] Basing this chapter on their insights, I want to propose that for the Jews of Jesus' day, this story may be understood as none other than the covenant story, a story of promise and fulfilment, a story often regarded as open-ended and awaiting the climax to come. In other words, it is the story of the return of Yahweh to Jerusalem to be king and fulfil the promises made through the prophets.[15]

The notion that at the climax of the covenant Yahweh will act powerfully to vindicate himself and rescue his people is frequently found in the prophets, but it is most clearly evidenced in Deutero-Isaiah. In Isaiah 52:7 the return of Yahweh to Zion is regarded as good news, and that return is announced with the words 'Your God reigns!' This ushers in a situation in which Israel is restored to her land. In the conception of Deutero-Isaiah, the regathering of the people comes about in order that they may be placed in a renewed relationship with Yahweh (Isaiah 55:3–13; 59:15b–21). That this should be the case is not surprising, as it was the people's failure to be faithful covenantal partners that occasioned their exile in the first place. The declaration of God's reign is therefore tied up with the return of the people from exile and their participating as beneficiaries of a covenant ratification ceremony. This covenant is understood as eternal (i.e. unbreakable), and issuing in salvific conditions for the restored people (Isaiah 59:15b–21; 61:4–9). The return of Yahweh to reign in Jerusalem may then be construed as

---

14. R. B. Hays, *The Faith of Jesus Christ: An Investigation of the Narrative Substructure of Galatians 3.1–4.11* (Chico: Scholars Press, 1983); Wright, *People of God*. Cf. the recent collection of essays in B. W. Longenecker (ed.), *Narrative Dynamics in Paul: A Critical Assessment* (Louisville: Westminster/John Knox, 2002).

15. Cf. the thesis in my *Zion Traditions*; Wright, *Victory of God*, p. 203; and his earlier work, *People of God*, pp. 268–279.

the eschatological phase of the covenantal relationship between Yahweh and his people.[16] Such a pattern of thought is also attested at Qumran.[17] In a most interesting text, the renewal of the covenant is explicitly connected with the establishment of the kingdom by the prince of the congregation. I am referring to 1QSb 5.20–21:

> Of the Instructor. To bless the prince of the congregation who [. . .] [. . .] his [. . .] And he will renew the covenant of the [Com]munity for him, to establish the kingdom of his people for eve[r, to judge the poor with justice] . . .

The *Rule of the Blessings* (1QSb) contains the benedictions to be given by the *maśkîl* (instructor) to different Qumran sectaries when the sons of darkness are finally eliminated; that is, when the long-expected denouement of the Qumran community has come. Consequently, the word *'ôlām* (for ever) occurs many times[18] and often in relation to the word *běrît* (covenant),[19] signalling that while the thought of the document is nuanced eschatologically, it is also at the same time anchored in the story of God and Israel. The blessing in column 5 is reserved for the prince of the congregation. Charlesworth and Stuckenbruck understand the subject of the action in 5.21 to be God.[20] If they are correct, the situation

---

16. See the discussion in J. Gray, *The Biblical Doctrine of the Reign of God* (Edinburgh: T. & T. Clark, 1979), pp. 161–181.

17. See the lucid exposition of S. J. Hafemann, 'The Spirit of the New Covenant, the Law, and the Temple of God's Presence: Five Theses on Qumran Self-Understanding and the Contours of Paul's Thought', in J. Ådna, S. J. Hafemann and O. Hofius (eds.), *Evangelium – Schriftauslegung – Kirche: Festschrift für Peter Stuhlmacher zum 65. Geburtstag* (Göttingen: Vandenhoeck & Ruprecht, 1997), pp. 173–174. Cf. the magisterial survey of Sanders, *Paul and Palestinian Judaism*, pp. 239–328.

18. 1QSb 1.3 (twice), 6, 26, 28; 2.25, 28; 3.4, 5, 7, 21, 26(?); 4.3(?); 26; 5.23, 25.

19. 1QSb 1.3; 2.25; 3.26(?); 5.23. Other passages where the word *běrît* occurs are 3.23; 5.21.

20. J. H. Charlesworth and L. T. Stuckenbruck, 'Blessings (1QSb)', in

envisaged is that of Yahweh's renewing his covenant through the
prince of the congregation as the intermediary. This would then
lead to the setting up of Yahweh's kingdom, which would also be
given to his people. The connection of *malkût* (kingdom) with *'ām*
(people) in line 21 probably has as its background the Sinaitic
covenant where Israel, the covenant partner, was to be known also
as a kingdom (Exodus 19:5–6).

Thus, it may safely be claimed that, in its Jewish context, the
kingdom theme arose from and was understood within the framework of the story of Yahweh and his people in which the
covenant played a critical role. As Gray observes, 'the consummation of the purpose of her God . . . was for Israel inconceivable
without the fulfilment of her hopes in the Covenant and its historical prelude and its sequel in the occupation of the land and the
election of Zion as the seat of God and of David and his
House'.[21] An eschatological outlook was often connected with the
covenant because the time when the covenantal relationship with
Yahweh would no longer be subjected to the vagaries of history
and human weakness has yet to arrive and was eagerly expected.
The upshot of all this is that Jewish eschatology should not be
severed from the concept of the covenant. This would hardly bear
mentioning if it were not for the mysterious neglect of it in NT
scholarship.[22]

J. H. Charlesworth (ed.), *The Dead Sea Scrolls: Hebrew, Aramaic, and Greek
Texts with English Translations*. Vol. 1: *Rule of the Community and Related
Documents* (Tübingen: Mohr-Siebeck/Louisville: Westminster/John
Knox, 1994), p. 129.

21. Gray, *Reign of God*, p. 182.

22. Even the recent work by J. P. Meier, *A Marginal Jew. Rethinking the Historical
Jesus: Mentor, Message and Miracles* (New York: Doubleday, 1994), which
although it has a lengthy discussion on Jesus' message of the kingdom of
God, does not discuss the possibility of covenantal connections (vol. 2,
pp. 237–506). The same may be said for many books on the theme 'Jesus
and the kingdom'.

Kingdom and community in Jesus' ministry

In the light of the above discussion, the pericopes featuring Jesus' redrawing of the boundaries of community as a consequence of his kingdom proclamation may be regarded as having important connections with covenantal thought. But there is more than meets the eye, in that the manner in which Jesus engaged this reveals his understanding of what exactly constituted covenant identity markers, and how this might clash with current Jewish concepts.

The parable of the good Samaritan

We shall start with the parable of the good Samaritan. This is one of the very few parables printed in red in the *Five Gospels* of the Jesus Seminar in America.[23] Much of the scholarship on this parable has focused on the question of form; that is, whether it is an example story or a comparative *māšāl*.[24] While it certainly will help the task of interpretation if the form could be determined, we have also to bear in mind the following. First, such classification of forms is ours, and not that of first-century Jews. Secondly, Gerhardsson warns us, after many years of studying the parables, that the extant parables were formulated without deliberate categorization.[25] In other words, forms did not seem to be the main consideration for the progenitor, tradent or the evangelist.

However, it is the frame of the parable of the Good Samaritan that draws much scepticism. The usual arguments used to support the assertion that this frame is Lukan are the following: Luke tends to generalize the parables and this parable has been generalized into an example story, and so its original setting has been lost; secondly,

---

23. Indicating Jesus said exactly this: see R. Funk and R. W. Hoover (eds.), *The Five Gospels: The Search for the Authentic Words of Jesus* (New York: Macmillan, 1993), pp. 323–324.

24. E.g. J. D. Crossan, 'Parable and Example in the Teaching of Jesus', *Semeia* 1 (1974), pp. 63–104; and B. Witherington III, *Jesus the Sage: The Pilgrimage of Wisdom* (Edinburgh: T. & T. Clark, 1994), pp. 192–193.

25. B. Gerhardsson, 'If we Do Not Cut the Parables out of their Frames', *NTS* 37 (1991), pp. 323–324.

the subject matter of the frame sounds suspiciously like the discussion of Jesus and another lawyer in Mark 12:28–31 ‖ Matthew 22:34–40.[26] Calling the parable an example story[27] certainly helps to bolster these two arguments. Nevertheless, there are good grounds for assuming that the frame of the parable is authentic and has always been joined with the parable.

First, the arguments usually cited cannot stand up to scrutiny. Indeed, the argument that Luke tends to generalize is a generalization in itself. Why should it be that if Luke did this with the parable of the persistent widow in Luke 18, it should be assumed that he was certainly doing the same with the parable of the good Samaritan? Furthermore, the perceived similarities between Mark 12:28–31 and Luke 10:25–37 have been overdone. In the former passage the answer citing the love command as the greatest was given by Jesus; in the latter, the lawyer provided that answer as the one means to eternal life. Again, in the former passage no debate was envisaged and the lawyer's answer was commended by Jesus; the same cannot be said for the latter passage.[28] There are just too many discrepancies between the two pericopes for the hypothesis to be cogent. Indeed, it seems to me that for Jesus to have engaged himself in discussion on the great commands on different occasions and with different thrusts should be regarded as the best explanation of the phenomenon we now have.[29]

Secondly, if Gerhardsson is right, free-floating parables are not found in the Jesus traditions, with the possible exception of the parable of the rich man and Lazarus.[30] The evidence provided by

---

26. Witherington, *Jesus the Sage*, p. 193. Cf. J. Nolland, *Luke 9:21–18:34* (WBC 35B; Dallas: Word, 1993), p. 580.

27. E.g. J. Jülicher, *Die Gleichnisreden Jesu* (2nd ed.; Tübingen: Mohr, 1899), vol. 1, p. 114; R. Bultmann, *The History of the Synoptic Tradition* (2nd ed.; Oxford: Blackwell, 1968), p. 178.

28. See C. A. Evans, *Mark 8.27–16.20* (WBC 34B; Nashville: Nelson, 2001), p. 262.

29. See T. W. Manson, *The Sayings of Jesus: As Recorded in the Gospels according to St. Matthew and St. Luke* (London: SCM, 1950), pp. 259–260.

30. Gerhardsson, 'Parables', pp. 325–326.

the Synoptic Gospels points in the direction of contextually anchored parables. This being the case, the settings provided by the evangelists are to be taken seriously, as they are the earliest witnesses to what the parables could have meant.[31] These settings provide moorings in an otherwise tumultuous hermeneutical sea. The belief that many parables are 'naked narratives with indeterminate messages'[32] therefore depends on considerations *not found in the Gospels*, but arises, most probably, from the *agendas* of certain schools of interpretation.[33] Indeed, Gerhardsson avers that the parables were given to illuminate aspects of Jesus' kingdom message.[34]

Thirdly, the frame and the parable cohere well structurally, at least in terms of rabbinic teaching methods. Blomberg argues that they conform to the approach known as *yelammedenu rabbenu*, which has a four-part structure:[35]

1. Question on a scriptural text (verses 25–27).
2. A second text given to illuminate (verse 28).
3. The exposition (in this case, the parable).
4. The final remarks (verse 37).[36]

Even if we regard this as unconvincing, the point that the frame coheres well with the parable still stands. The parable is framed by

31. Ibid., p. 322.
32. Ibid., p. 333.
33. This may be the desire to give the parables autonomy, treating them as naked texts and divorcing them from the particularity of history, especially that of Jesus of Nazareth. This fits in well with the postmodern agenda and the anti-establishment agenda too.
34. Gerhardsson, 'Parables', p. 329.
35. C. L. Blomberg, *Interpreting the Parables* (Leicester: Apollos, 1990), p. 231.
36. On the possibility of Jesus' using rabbinic methods, see B. Gerhardsson, *Memory and Manuscript* (Uppsala: Gleerup, 1961); R. Riesenfeld, *The Gospel Tradition* (Oxford: Blackwell, 1970); R. Riesner, *Jesus als Lehrer* (Tübingen: Mohr, 1981); and most recently, S. Byrskog, *Jesus the Only Teacher: Didactic Authority and Transmission in Ancient Israel, Ancient Judaism and the Matthean Community* (Stockholm: Almqvist & Wiksell, 1994).

a double *inclusio*, provided by the questions on the identity of the neighbour (verses 29, 36) and the injunctions to perform (verses 28, 37). The objection that there is a discrepancy between the lawyer's second question ('who is my neighbour?') and Jesus' answer in query form ('who has been a neighbour?') misses the profound subtlety of Jesus' message, which I hope to demonstrate later.

Fourthly, there is a very high degree of historical plausibility to the frame.[37] The frame has the command to love the neighbour as its focus and we know that the love command is one key aspect of the teaching of Jesus, whether this is to be directed to one's enemies or otherwise.[38] Moreover, the question asked by the lawyer coheres well with the first-century Jewish context. It is about 'inheriting eternal life' and this means not our modern popular notion of going to heaven when one dies but the thoroughly Jewish concept of the inheritance of the age to come. Furthermore, the lawyer's seeking to be justified (*thelōn dikaiōsai heautōn*) need not be construed as an attempt to contradict Jesus and defend himself[39] but as a genuine desire to be counted among those who would be justified; that is, accepted by Yahweh as belonging to the people who would inherit the age to come.[40]

---

37. This is now known as the criterion of historical plausibility and some prominent scholars who defend a version of it are J. Jeremias, *The Theology of the New Testament*. Vol. 1: *The Proclamation of Jesus* (London: SCM, 1971); G. Theissen and D. Winter, *The Quest for the Plausible Jesus: The Question of Criteria* (Lousville: Westminster/John Knox, 2002); and Wright, *Victory of God*.

38. On the love command, see J. Piper, *Love Your Enemies* (Cambridge: Cambridge University Press, 1979). Cf. R. Neudecker, '"And You Shall Love Your Neighbour as Yourself – I am the Lord" (Lev 19,18) in Jewish Interpretation', *Bib* 73 (1992), pp. 512–514.

39. So J. A. Fitzmyer, *The Gospel according to Luke* (New York: Doubleday, 1985), vol. 2, p. 886.

40. S. Keesmaat utilizes a similar idea in her 'Strange Neighbours and Risky Care (Matthew 18.21–35; Luke 14.7–14; Luke 10.25–37)', in R. Longenecker (ed.), *The Challenge of Jesus' Parables* (Grand Rapids:

Thus, the lawyer's two questions are linked up with the notion of the eschatological coming of the kingdom of God. Such questions may be regarded as prompted by and dovetailing with the key theme of Jesus' preaching. More importantly, the lawyer's two questions arose from the presupposition that the Shema[41] is the key confession of Israel in which her covenantal status is summed up. These horizons of meaning were thoroughly first-century Jewish concerns.

Finally, in the light of the preceding discussion, it would be highly improbable that the frame as we have it is a Lukan invention for introducing the parable. As Marshall points out, the parable must have been occasioned by a question or an event, the subject matter of which would be the love command.[42] If this is the case, and since such a setting has a certain amount of specificity to it, a legitimate question may be asked about how such a frame could have been lost if that found in Luke is not it. If we do not buy into the scholarly categorization of the parable as an example story,[43] we are on the high road of making sense of the meaning of this parable in its original context.

If the frame belonged originally to the parable, what should not be missed is the covenantal horizon of the discussion between Jesus and the lawyer. The pericope begins with a question that is thoroughly Jewish. How is one assured of eternal life; that is, the life of the age to come? The reply of Jesus draws the questioner back to Torah, the charter of the covenant. Life is a gift of being in covenantal relationship with Yahweh but the Torah defines what it means to be in that relationship (Leviticus 18:5; Deuteronomy 6:2; 30:6). So, if there is one way to gain the life of the age to come, this would be found in the Torah, and thus, Jesus' question. The answer

---

Eerdmans, 2000), pp. 276–277, which is also found in Wright, *Victory of God*, pp. 305–307. But some of her proposals appear to me to be too fanciful; e.g. resurrection.

41. Comprising Deuteronomy 6:4–9; 11:13–21; Numbers 15:37–41. See rabbinic discussions in *m. Ber.* 1.1–3.5; *m. Šabb.* 8.3.

42. I. H. Marshall, *The Gospel of Luke* (Exeter: Paternoster, 1978), pp. 445–446.

43. Cf. Nolland, *Luke 9:21–18:34*, p. 591; Wright, *Victory of God*, p. 306.

given by the lawyer connects the whole discussion to the Shema. This shows how the Shema has attained the status of something like a creed and is thought to sum up the Torah (*Epistle of Aristeas* 106; Josephus, *Jewish Antiquities* 4.212; Philo, *On the Special Laws* 4.141; *b. Ber.* 47b).[44] Having the status of a creed, the Shema also sums up what it means to be a member of the community that is in relationship with Yahweh (cf. Wisdom of Solomon 11–15; *Sibylline Oracles* 3:8–45; Josephus, *Jewish Antiquities* 5.1, 27, 112; Philo, *On the Decalogue* 65).[45] In the Lukan passage the primary praxis of the Shema (to love Yahweh), is connected with the love for one's neighbour.[46] That the two may be linked in Jewish theology is not surprising since the neighbour is defined as a member of the covenant community (cf. *Testament of Issachar* 5.2; 7.6; *Testament of Dan* 5.3; Philo, *On the Decalogue* 109–110; *Sifra* 19.18).[47] Viewed from

44. Cf. E. E. Urbach, 'Self-Isolation or Self-Affirmation in Judaism in the First Three Centuries', in E. P. Sanders (ed.), *Jewish and Christian Self-Definition* (London: SCM, 1981), vol. 2, p. 273. For rabbinic preoccupation with the interpretation of the Shema, see B. Gerhardsson, *The Testing of God's Son (Matt 4.1–11 and parr.)* (Uppsala: Gleerup, 1966), pp. 71–76; and his recent 'The Shema' in Early Christianity', in F. van Segbroeck et al. (eds.), *The Four Gospels* (Leuven: Leuven University Press, 1992), vol. 1, pp. 276–278. The Nash Papyrus (first or second century BC) is indicative of this: the Shema is found with the Decalogue on the same sheet. See W. F. Albright, 'A Biblical Fragment from the Maccabean Age: The Nash Papyrus', *JBL* 56 (1937), pp. 145–176.

45. Cf. J. D. G. Dunn, *The Partings of the Ways between Christianity and Judaism and their Significance for the Character of Christianity* (London: SCM, 1991), pp. 19–21.

46. Cf. the tradition in Mark 12:28–34. Insightful comments on how the Shema is linked up with the two commands that in turn sum up the Decalogue are found in D. C. Allison, 'Mark 12.28–31 and the Decalogue', in C. A. Evans and W. R. Stegner (eds.), *The Gospels and the Scriptures of Israel* (Sheffield: Sheffield Academic Press, 1994), pp. 270–278. Cf. also E. Nielsen, *The Ten Commandments in New Perspective* (London: SCM, 1968).

47. The context of Leviticus 19:18 presupposes this and *rēa'* should most probably be interpreted as a fellow Israelite. This concept is appropriated

such a vantage point, it may be argued that the sum of what covenantal responsibilities entailed may be found essentially in the Shema. Properly understanding the Shema and properly undertaking its primary praxis would lead one to inherit the life of the age to come.

Bauckham has recently argued that the parable was told to resolve potential conflicts in the injunctions of Torah in order to emphasize that the love command should take precedence over purity laws.[48] If he is correct, Jesus' interpretation of Torah comes to the fore in the parable. That, in my opinion, is only partially correct. If the whole parable wishes to establish a halakhic point, we should expect it to make clear the victim's death and not describe his condition with the ambiguous *hemithanē* (half-dead).[49] Contracting impurity that disqualifies one for priestly duty can happen only if a corpse is touched (Leviticus 21:1–2; Ezekiel 44:25–27). Of course, in the imaginary world of the parable, the presumption that the victim was dead may be posited of the priest but the point is that, for Jesus, the whole discussion appears to revolve around a different issue and certainly not a halakhic one. Appealing to rabbinic discussions on the corpse of obligation serves actually to destroy the case, as it was deemed obligatory to bury a corpse, even for the high priest and the Nazarite, Israel's two most consecrated men (*m. Naz.* 7.1; cf. 6.5).[50]

---

and further illuminated in *y. Ned.*[*yerushalmi Nedarim*] 9:4. Cf. J. Milgrom, *Leviticus17–22* (Anchor Bible; New York: Doubleday, 2000), pp. 1654–1656. Sirach 12:1–7 and 1QS [*Community Rule*] 1:9–10 give evidence that love cannot be extended to enemies or sinners.

48. R. J. Bauckham, 'The Scrupulous Priest and the Good Samaritan: Jesus' Parabolic Interpretation of the Law of Moses', *NTS* 44 (1998), pp. 475–489.

49. Cf. A. J. Hultgren, *The Parables of Jesus: A Commentary* (Grand Rapids: Eerdmans, 2000), p. 96; Nolland, *Luke 9:21–18:34*, p. 593. See also the philological discussion in T. Kazen, *Jesus and Purity Halakhah: Was Jesus Indifferent to Impurity?* (Stockholm: Almqvist & Wiksell, 2002), pp. 191–193.

50. Thus, there is absolutely no debate! Dead or alive, the priest cannot plead ritual impurity as an excuse for not helping! Bauckham is aware of this

Secondly, it would make more sense for Jesus to speak of a different Jewish priest helping the victim, as this would certainly demonstrate the point Bauckham is arguing for.[51] Why is there a reference to a Samaritan instead? Bauckham's answer is that he is mentioned for shock value[52] and to bolster the point that the love command takes precedence over purity laws, because the one key difference between the religion of the Jews and that of the Samaritans was the temple and its cult.[53] The cultic horizon should certainly be kept in view but I want to argue that the parable is best understood in covenantal terms, because the question that prompted this parable connects the obtaining of the life of the age to come with performance of the primary praxis of the Shema.

I start by taking the cue from Crossan that the focal point of the parable is not the good deed itself but *the goodness of the Samaritan*,[54] but I shall situate it in the context provided by the frame as attested in Luke. If all Jesus wanted to do was to be provocative, a Gentile would be a better choice; but this was not the case, because Jesus was not teaching that by simply loving others a person could gain the life of the age to come.[55] That, in the terms of the covenant, was a heresy. Instead, the love for the neighbour must be understood in a covenantal context in which the one true God was confessed as Yahweh. This same confession was made by Samaritans even if they disagreed with the Jews over many points of law, especially those that were connected with the cult. But in contrast to the

----

objection but does not see it as destroying his case. After a lengthy discussion, which does not produce a shred of evidence that there was debate over its obligatoriness, he writes, 'we *may hazard a reasonable guess* that it was [controversial]' ('Scrupulous Priest', p. 484; my emphasis).

51. Bauckham is aware of this but he judges such a way of telling the parable to be 'tediously obvious'; see his 'Scrupulous Priest', p. 485.

52. Samaritans were regarded as enemies and put in the same category as the Philistines and Edomites (Sirach 50.25–26).

53. Bauckham, 'Scrupulous Priest', pp. 486–487.

54. Crossan, 'Parable and Example', p. 75 (his emphasis).

55. Pace Hultgren, *Parables of Jesus*, p. 98.

Jewish priest and Levite, the Samaritan in the parable demonstrates that he has understood the true essence of adherence to the Shema by the actions he performs. Thus, the provocative point of the parable is that it is the Samaritan, the one whom Jewish polemics often regarded as being outside the covenant (Sirach 50.25–26; *b. Sanh.* 57a; *Gen. Rab.* 81:3 [on Genesis 35:4]),[56] who is portrayed as the true confessor of the Shema through his loving the person in need. The key representatives of Israel's religion and cult – priest and Levite – have failed to do that.

Jesus' parable thus answered the lawyer's questions in many ways. First, the true confession of the Shema is demonstrated effectively through the love of neighbour and such true confession leads one to the life of the age to come (both Jesus and the lawyer agree over this point). The giving of the parable was meant to clarify the identity of the neighbour and what loving a neighbour meant. Second, Jesus' question at the end of the pericope was subtly designed to lead the lawyer to call the Samaritan 'neighbour' by focusing on the identity of the 'neighbour'. This answered the lawyer's question of who his 'neighbour' was. The Samaritan was to be regarded as 'neighbour' because he too believed in the Shema and practised its primary praxis even if he followed a different cultic system. Being a true confessor of the Shema he belonged to the covenant community.

If my analysis is on target, there is some form of repristination going on in Jesus' teaching. Jesus used the cue provided by the lawyer to hark back to the situation at the founding of the nation (Deuteronomy 6:4–5) in which the Samaritan and the Jewish split was irrelevant. *Endzeit* (end time) equals *Urzeit* (original time) may be one chief characteristic of Jesus' teaching. But Jesus did not stop there. He went on to exhort the lawyer to do likewise and this leads to my third point.

---

56. For such indications, see J. Jeremias, *Jerusalem in the Time of Jesus: An Investigation into Economic and Social Conditions during the New Testament Period* (Philadelphia: Fortress, 1969), pp. 352–358; C. A. Evans, 'Samaritans', in C. A. Evans and S. E. Porter (eds.), *Dictionary of New Testament Backgrounds* (Downers Grove: IVP, 2000), pp. 1059–1060.

To do likewise meant for the lawyer that he was to follow the Samaritan's example in order to answer his own questions. The Samaritan proved that he was the true adherent of the Shema *by being a neighbour* to the man in need, whose identity is purposely left undefined. So the neighbour was no longer defined by a fellow Israelite or even by one who belonged to the covenant community but by the person in need. The love between people in covenant with God must extend outwards beyond the community. If this is correct, we have here a potential link between Jesus and Paul: both taught the pre-eminence of love and showed openness to the outsider.[57]

Doubtless, many queries about covenantal status may be raised here regarding Jesus' exposition of the Shema. But what should not be missed is that, according to this parable, the children of the Shema or the members of the covenant transcend race and cult.[58] To name the Samaritan as the faithful son of the covenant amounts to challenging the received understanding on the identity of the true members of the covenant community. One can hardly find in the literature of the Second Temple period a parallel to Jesus' deployment of the Shema for such a purpose. Indeed, while there is evidence for the concept of a Jewish remnant *within* Israel, there is none for that which says that the Samaritans form part of the true community of Yahweh. This amounts to nothing less than a redefinition of the covenant community. Who then belongs to the family of Yahweh if Jewish descent does not guarantee that?

We may draw a line from here to the pericopes that speak of the displacement of many in Israel in favour of people who were not

---

57. Cf. the proposals of A. J. M. Wedderburn, 'Paul and Jesus: Similarity and Continuity', *NTS* 34 (1988), pp. 161–180.

58. Viewing the parable as dealing with the connection between a true confession of the Shema and a community's boundaries (i.e. monotheism and election) is scarcely done in the history of scholarship. The most recent contribution, which gives what is typical (i.e. 'an exemplary behaviour story'), is made by Hultgren, *Parables of Jesus*, 2000, pp. 93–101. But see Wright, *Victory of God*, pp. 305–307, which in many ways is similar to what is argued here.

regarded as belonging to it when the eschaton arrived. Here we think of passages such as Matthew 8:11–12 || Luke 13:28–30 and Luke 4:24–27. Such passages are usually regarded as being composed post-Easter,[59] but this should be called into question since there is a coherence of ideas between such passages and the parable of the good Samaritan. There is therefore significant indication in the Jesus traditions that membership in the covenant was not what many Jews thought it to be.[60]

The Twelve

The result of the preceding discussion can now be safely combined with the data provided by passages that speak of the calling and the role of the Twelve to strengthen my case further. The setting apart of twelve followers by Jesus is regarded by the majority of scholars as authentic and there is a consensus that this was a symbolic act, pointing to the reconstitution of Israel.[61] The Twelve are described as the little flock connected with the kingdom in Luke 12:32. This recalls the many OT passages that speak of Israel, especially the remnant, as the flock of Yahweh (Jeremiah 23:1–4; Ezekiel 34; cf.

---

59. The typical arguments are found in Funk and Hoover, *Five Gospels*, pp. 280, 348. On the difficulties connected with the interpretation of the former passage, see D. C. Allison and W. D. Davies, *A Critical and Exegetical Commentary on the Gospel according to Saint Matthew* (Edinburgh: T. & T. Clark, 1991), vol. 2, pp. 27–29. For the latter, see J. A. Fitzmyer, *The Gospel according to Luke* (New York: Doubleday, 1981), vol. 1, p. 526; for a more confident assessment, see Marshall, *Gospel of Luke*, p. 180. See, on the theme of judgment in the Jesus traditions, the recent work of S. Bryan, *Jesus and Israel's Traditions of Judgment and Restoration* (Cambridge: Cambridge University Press, 2002).

60. Already in Second Temple Jewish literature the concept of covenantal dualism is found; i.e. not everyone who is born a Jew is in the covenant. See the treatment of Elliott, *Survivors of Israel*, pp. 309–353.

61. See the recent magisterial treatment of J. P. Meier, leaving no stone unturned, in his *A Marginal Jew: Rethinking the Historical Jesus*. Vol. 3: *Companions and Competitors* (New York: Doubleday, 2001), pp. 125–163. Cf. W. Horbury, 'The Twelve and the Phylarchs', *NTS* 32 (1986), pp. 503–527.

Isaiah 41:14).[62] The Twelve are also promised thrones and will judge Israel in the age to come (Matthew 19:28; Luke 22:29–30). This is, at least, symbolic language for the coming into being of a community that plays the role of the vindicated remnant.[63] In short, the existence of the Twelve formed the warp and woof of Jesus' ministry. It was not an afterthought or an aside but was linked to it as of necessity.[64] The OT background explains why this is the case. Jesus' gathering of a community symbolized by the Twelve mirrors the situation envisaged in many prophetic passages where Yahweh is portrayed as regathering the survivors of Israel in order to make a covenant with them.

The upshot of all the above observations is that Jesus may be regarded as not just simply regathering Israel but also as redefining it somewhat. Thus, it can be stated that Jesus was very much taken up with questions of covenantal identity or, to be more precise, how covenantal identity was best evidenced.

The kingdom theme

When the key theme of Jesus' ministry, the kingdom of God, is examined, our case receives further support. However, the phrase *hē basileia tou theou* (the kingdom of God) may be defined, it is clear that it includes elements of God's mighty act to judge and save and his inaugurating a state of affairs congruent with his being the sole ruler of the universe. As it was argued earlier, this kingdom theme in its Jewish context arose from, and was understood within, the framework of the story of Yahweh and his people in which the covenant played a critical role.[65]

Jesus' pronouncement that the kingdom of God has arrived in his ministry is conceivably dependent upon such a background.

---

62. Cf. G. R. Beasley-Murray, *Jesus and the Kingdom of God* (Exeter: Paternoster, 1986), p. 186.

63. We may find a parallel to this in 4Q521 2.ii.7, where Yahweh is said to honour the *ḥāsîdîm* (pious ones) upon the throne of an eternal kingdom.

64. Cf. Meier, *Companions and Competitors*, p. 137.

65. Cf. Wright, *Victory of God*, p. 203; and his earlier work *People of God*, pp. 268–279. See also Dumbrell, *Covenant and Creation*, p. 206.

Consequently, it is not surprising that with the proclamation of the dawn of the kingdom comes also the call of disciples, mirroring the regathering of the people of God. In addition to this, there are also many indications in the Jesus traditions that Jesus understood his ministry to be the climax of the covenant story of God and his people.[66] This is clearly seen in the parable of the wicked tenants[67] and in the nuptial images associated with Jesus' teaching. In Mark 2:18–20 Jesus defends his disciples' non-fasting by appealing to the presence of a wedding.[68] Fasts were practised not just because they were instituted for religious festivals but also as a way to show a repentant attitude before Yahweh so that he would act to rescue Israel from her plight (cf. Isaiah 59:20).[69] The Pharisees were not busybodies nor majoring on minutiae, as they were looking for the consolation of Israel.[70] The lack of fasting by someone who announced that the kingdom was at hand therefore created a perplexing puzzle for them, which prompted the question. Jesus' answer claimed that a wedding was taking place. It is seldom noticed that such nuptial images speak of Yahweh's covenantal relationship with Israel and that, in the prophetic corpus, talk of Yahweh's (re)marriage with Israel signifies the climactic phase of her restoration (Isaiah 50:1; 54:4–5; 62:4–5; Hosea 2:16–23; cf. Jeremiah 3:8;). Indeed, it is cogent to argue that to speak of a wedding in connection with kingdom proclamation would inexorably lead Jewish listeners to think of the covenant between Yahweh and Israel.

Finally, it may be added that my earlier discussion on the good Samaritan fits into this scheme of thought. There is explicit

---

66. So, Wright, *Victory of God*, passim; and M. de Jonge, *God's Final Envoy: Early Christology and Jesus' Own View of His Mission* (Grand Rapids: Eerdmans, 1998).

67. See further K. Snodgrass, *The Parable of the Wicked Tenants: An Inquiry into Parable Interpretation* (Tübingen: Mohr, 1983).

68. The *Five Gospels* printed the saying in verse 19 in pink (indicating Jesus said something close to this).

69. Cf. Holmén, *Jesus*, pp. 129–133; and Wright, *Victory of God*, p. 433.

70. See Wright, *People of God*, pp. 185–203.

evidence for the connection between the confession of the Shema
and the confession of Yahweh as king. Although this evidence is
late, the concept most probably has roots harking back to the time
before Jesus. In *Genesis Rabbah* 65.21 (on Genesis 27:22), the text
says, 'this is the voice that silences both celestial and terrestrial
beings . . . When Israel say, "Hear O Israel," the angels are silent
and then drop their wings. And what do they proclaim? "Blessed
be the name of his glorious kingdom for all eternity." '[71] The interesting point about this passage is the prominence given to the
Shema[72] and its linkage with the kingdom of Yahweh. Israel's true
confession of the Shema establishes firmly her relationship with
Yahweh and demonstrates her fidelity. This takes precedence over
the affairs of the world and the praise of the heavenly minstrels.
Consequently, when Israel confesses the Shema, the world and the
heavenly minstrels are silenced. The proclamation of the eternal
reign of Yahweh is then sounded. What, then, is the logic here?
Whenever Israel may be said truly to confess the Shema, Yahweh's
eternal reign is manifested. The kingdom does not come without
connection to Israel's covenant.[73]

The Last Supper: community, kingdom, cross and covenant

It is when we come to the Last Supper traditions that we see the
coming together of the themes of community, kingdom, covenant
and Jesus' death. That this should be the case need not surprise us
in that, according to the Synoptic records, this event is presented
as the crowning explanation of the intention of Jesus and his

---

71. H. Freedman, *The Midrash Rabbah* (London: Soncino, 1977), vol. 1, pp.
    597–598.
72. The opening words are metonymic for the whole creed. See Gerhardsson,
    Testing of God's Son, pp. 71–76; 'Shema' in Early Christianity', p. 277.
73. Cf. the results of J. Marcus in a different connection in his 'Authority to
    Forgive Sins Upon the Earth: The *Shema* in the Gospel of Mark', in
    C. A. Evans and W. R. Stegner (eds.), *The Gospels and the Scriptures of Israel*
    (Sheffield: Sheffield Academic Press, 1994), pp. 196–211.

understanding of his role and place in the ongoing story of God and Israel. In these traditions we see the unique contribution of Jesus to the concept of the covenant. But before all this can be clinched we have to perform a ground-clearing exercise.

The historicity and nature of the event

In an earlier work I defended the authenticity of this incident and refuted the notion that this supper was last only in the sense that the church, in retrospect, understood it to be so and hence, elevated it to a pre-eminent status.[74] I also argued that Luke 13:31–33 provides us with evidence that Jesus did expect to die and regarded that death as part and parcel of his vocation, perhaps even its crowning event. Given all this, the sayings uttered at the Last Supper become highly significant, for they show definitively what Jesus thought his ministry was all about.[75] In the intervening years nothing in the scholarly literature has caused me to change my mind. The recent objections mounted by the scholars of the Jesus Seminar (namely that the account is not attested in the *Didache* and the cup-saying is too scandalous to be credible in that it violated the Levitical ban on drinking blood) are not new and they have been ably answered by Klawans in a recent article.[76]

If the Last Supper traditions are substantially authentic, what can we say about their meaning and significance? A word's

---

74. Tan, *Zion Traditions*, pp. 198–200.

75. Ibid., pp. 57–80. Cf. B. F. Meyer, 'Recondite Hermeneutics and the Last Supper Rite', in J. Ådna, S. J. Hafemann and O. Hofius (eds.), *Evangelium – Schriftauslegung – Kirche: Festschrift für Peter Stuhlmacher zum 65. Geburtstag* (Göttingen: Vandenhoeck & Ruprecht, 1997), pp. 296–309.

76. J. Klawans, 'Interpreting the Last Supper: Sacrifice, Spiritualization, and Anti-Sacrifice', *NTS* 48 (2002), pp. 1–17, where he defuses the main objection raised by the Jesus Seminar against the authenticity of the tradition. Klawans' answer is that there was no literal eating of flesh and drinking of blood in the tradition and the language used is metaphorical. Unfortunately, he does not consider the all-important connection the tradition makes with the Sinaitic covenant and the significance of its being the crowning symbolic act of Jesus.

meaning comes from its function within a sentence and the sentence's function within, for want of a better word, a story.[77] The pronouncements of Jesus during the meal must be understood within two stories in order for their full meaning to be discerned. The first is his own story – that of his life and ministry – and the second is the ongoing story of God and the people of Israel because the cup-saying speaks of a covenant to be ratified. Furthermore, if we juxtapose these traditions with the parable of the good Samaritan, it may be inferred that Jesus showed himself to be the true confessor of the Shema by loving his disciples to the very end. At the most hazardous point of his life, he expressed that what he had done, and would be doing, was for them. Such love was also explained as being linked with a covenant.

All this takes on greater significance if we construe the Last Supper as being patterned after the Passover feast. We are aware of the chronological problem associated with the event but this can be circumvented since all that is needed is a demonstration that the supper was *held as though it were* a Passover meal. Constraints of space and time prevent me from demonstrating this at length and I shall be relying on the work of other scholars.[78] The significance of the meal, then, is that Jesus, in the last great symbolic demonstration

---

77. For a good statement of such relationships, see S. Maitland, *A Big Enough God: Artful Theology* (London: Mowbray, 1995), pp. 141–142. Cf. also J. R. Searle, *Intentionality: An Essay in the Philosophy of Mind* (Cambridge: Cambridge University Press, 1983). For a magisterial treatment of such issues, see A. C. Thiselton, *The Two Horizons* (Exeter: Paternoster, 1980).

78. There is therefore no need to decide between the Johannine and Synoptic traditions over the matter of dating. For such a line of argumentation, see F. J. Leenhardt, 'This is My Body', in O. Cullmann and F. J. Leenhardt, *Essays on the Lord's Supper* (London: Lutterworth, 1958), pp. 39–40; Wright, *Victory of God*, pp. 555–557; and R. T. France, *The Gospel of Mark* (NIGTC; Grand Rapids: Eerdmans/Carlisle: Paternoster, 2002), pp. 559–563. The classic study arguing that the Last Supper was a Passover *seder* is J. Jeremias, *The Eucharistic Words of Jesus* (London: SCM, 1966). For a recent work on this, see P. M. Casey, *Aramaic Sources of Mark's Gospel* (Cambridge: Cambridge University Press, 1998), pp. 219–252.

of the meaning of his vocation, fused together the story of the
Exodus and his story, the Sinaitic covenant with the covenant he
was instituting.[79] Just as the Exodus event and the Sinaitic covenant
led to the creation of a people, so also could the Last Supper be
understood as the foundational interpretation of an impending
event that would lead to the creation of the new people of God.
All this dovetails nicely with the oft-recurring biblical nexus of
deliverance–covenant–people. But what really is this covenant that
Jesus understood himself as inaugurating? To answer this, we need
to take a closer look at the cup-saying. Indeed, the full significance of the bread-saying can be understood only in the light of the
cup-saying.

The covenant theme

There are two strands of tradition relating to the cup-saying of the
Last Supper: the Markan strand, where only the word 'covenant' is
mentioned; and the Lukan–Pauline strand, where the adjective
'new' is attached to the word, and thus, offering us evidence that
some Christian circles did understand Jesus' death as inaugurating
the new covenant. But what really was the precise voice of Jesus?

Tradition criticism of the cup-saying is notoriously difficult.
However, I have argued in an earlier work that the two traditions
should not be prised apart woodenly on the basis of whether or not
the word 'new' is dominical.[80] The OT prophetic literature and other
Jewish literature from the Second Temple period did not strive for
terminological precision when describing the covenant to be ratified
in the last days. As the covenant between Yahweh and Israel was
understood to be breached, the prophets looked for a remedy and to
a time when Yahweh would act to repair that breach and eradicate
the conditions leading to covenant-breaching. In other words, they
were looking for an event that would mark the climax of the
covenant story of Yahweh and his people. Consequently, it is understandable why although in Jeremiah 31:31 the prophet refers to a
new covenant, in Jeremiah 32:40 and 50:3, he also expects the

---

79. So, Wright, *Victory of God*, p. 554.
80. Tan, *Zion Traditions*, pp. 203–215.

coming of an everlasting covenant. This latter terminology is also found in Isaiah 55:3, 61:8 and Ezekiel 16:60. Interestingly, in 1QS 5.4–5 the Qumran community calls itself a 'community of the everlasting covenant' and this is done cheek by jowl the stating of the importance of a circumcised heart. This community also believed that the new covenant had been inaugurated with them (*CD* 6.19a; 8.21b; 19.33b–34a; 20.12). All this offers evidence that the prominent Jeremiah and Ezekiel passages (Jeremiah 24:7; 31:31–33; 32:38–40; Ezekiel 11:19–20; 18:31; 36:26–27) may be fused together, including Deuteronomy 30:6–10, to refer to one event: the ratification of a covenant at the *eschaton*, which will remedy the obduracy of the heart. Even if the adjective *ḥādāš* (new) is scarcely attached to the noun *bĕrît* (covenant) in all the extant Jewish literature written before AD 70 except in Jeremiah 31:31 and the Qumran scrolls,[81] this need not mean that the concept of the new covenant was unimportant but only that different terms were used to describe what many Jews understood to be the same event.

Covenant, community and cross

It is precarious then to differentiate between the Markan strand and the Lukan–Pauline strand based just on the word 'new': the same expectation may be expressed through different terms depending on the context and thrust. What is important, then, is not the derivation of the exact form of the cup-saying but understanding it against the background story presupposed.

First, it suggests that what Moses originally ratified was regarded as ineffective when it concerned the covenant status of Jesus' disciples; otherwise there would be no need for a covenant ratification through Jesus' blood.[82] While it is unclear whether the

---

81. *CD* 6.19; 8.21b ‖ 19.33b–34a; 20 ‖ 12; and possibly 1QpHab 1.16–20a and 4Q504 2.5. Regarding how Qumran understood itself as the community of the new covenant, where repristination was the chief emphasis, see Hafemann, 'Spirit of the New Covenant', pp. 173–174; and Tan, *Zion Traditions*, pp. 210–215.

82. Of course, different explanations for this state of affairs were given by different Jewish groups in the Second Temple period.

covenant to be ratified was construed to be *replacing* that which was ratified at Mount Sinai or *renewing* it, it is nevertheless clear that a new covenant-making act was regarded as being needed. This implies that the covenant status of many Jews in Jesus' day would have been called into question. Thus, we have a line back to the traditions that portray Jesus (and John the Baptist)[83] as questioning the boundaries of covenantal membership as they were perceived then. The true community of Yahweh in the view of Jesus cannot simply be equated with the nation.

The positive corollary of the above point is that a covenant renewal being fused in meaning with the story of the exodus amounts to saying that this is the covenant that would create the new people of God, linked to a new exodus.[84] Indeed, many scholars have pointed out that Jesus' sayings and actions in that incident were not just interpretative but were also an act of bestowal and hence constitutive in nature.[85] Those who gathered at that table became beneficiaries of Jesus' self-giving in order that they might be constituted as Yahweh's eschatologically restored people. The ecclesiological aspect of the Last Supper narrative thus stands out.

What is astonishing about this covenant is that, according to Jesus, it would be effected only through his sacrificial death.[86] Why is this covenant linked with the cross? This is an immensely important subject that warrants a book-length treatment, which

---

83. Cf. D. C. Allison, 'Jesus and the Covenant: A Response to E. P. Sanders', *JSNT* 29 (1987), pp. 57–78, the arguments of which are repeated in his 'Continuity between Jesus and John', pp. 16–19; and R. L. Webb, *John the Baptizer and Prophet: A Socio-Historical Study* (Sheffield: JSOT Press, 1991), pp. 173–178.

84. Such a thought is also attested in the post-exilic era. See Zechariah 9:11.

85. Among many, see Jeremias, *Eucharistic Words*, p. 109; and recently, Meyer, 'Recondite Hermeneutics', p. 308.

86. B. D. Chilton's attempt to reinterpret it to mean the sacrifice of an animal smacks of special pleading. See his *The Temple of Jesus: His Sacrificial Program within a Cultural History of Sacrifice* (University Park: Pennsylvania State University Press, 1992), pp. 152–154.

I cannot provide here. But I can offer a sketch of the key proposals.[87]

If it takes Jesus' death to inaugurate this covenant and thus bring about the climax of the covenant story, who Jesus thought he was becomes an urgent question. Passages on the eternal or new covenant do not envisage a blood sacrifice for inauguration to be effected. The passage in Zechariah 9:9–11 (as tantalizing as it may be since it was enacted by Jesus in his entry to Jerusalem) is no exception, since the covenant in verse 11 refers to the Sinaitic, the basis for Yahweh's emancipatory action.[88] In a covenant relationship two entities are represented. Did Jesus think of himself as representing the people before Yahweh or vice versa? If he represents the human side of the covenantal relationship, he might then be regarded as the faithful Israelite who followed Yahweh's will unswervingly, even to the point of death.[89] But how does this inaugurate a covenant? In the Jewish context, that death could perhaps be understood as moving the compassion of Yahweh to act mercifully to deliver Israel (cf. the Maccabean literature).[90] But such Maccabean passages presupposed an *extra muros* conflict and not an *intra muros*, which is found predominantly in the Jesus traditions. Furthermore, such Maccabean deaths were never regarded as inaugurating an eschatological covenant.

---

87. For a good survey on recent work on the death of Jesus, see S. McKnight, 'Jesus and His Death: Some Recent Scholarship', *CurBS* 9 (2001), pp. 185–228.

88. D. L. Petersen, *Zechariah 9–14 and Malachi: A Commentary* (OTL; London: SCM, 1995), p. 60.

89. Cf. P. Doble, *The Paradox of Salvation: Luke's Theology of the Cross* (Cambridge: Cambridge University Press, 1996); de Jonge, *God's Final Envoy*; J. B. Green, *The Death of Jesus: Tradition and Interpretation in the Passion Narrative* (Tübingen: Mohr, 1988), pp. 316–317.

90. Namely 2 Maccabees 6:18–31; 2 Maccabees 7 (especially 7:37–38); 4 Maccabees 5 – 18. For discussion on the significance of these writings for understanding Jesus' death, see M. N. Bockmuehl, *This Jesus: Martyr, Lord, Messiah* (Edinburgh: T. & T. Clark, 1994), p. 90; Wright, *Victory of God*, pp. 582–583.

The other possibility is to regard Jesus as appropriating the rather ambiguous motif enshrined in the first two Servant Songs of Isaiah (Isaiah 42:6 and 49:8), where the Servant is said to be given as a *běrît 'ām*.[91] What exactly this means is disputed,[92] but it is just possible that the Servant is portrayed as the embodiment of the covenant.[93] If Jesus appropriated this idea, he would have viewed himself as the mediator between Yahweh and his people through his sacrifice. If we dare bite the bullet, Jesus may be said to be the covenant in the flesh! However, whether or not Jesus made use of the template provided by the Servant Songs for his self-understanding remains a highly disputed subject in NT scholarship.[94]

Is it possible that Jesus was acting out the character of Yahweh in this covenant inauguration as he had frequently done in different ways prior to this event? In the covenant story Yahweh was seen as faithful, gracious and giving. Could Jesus be saying that, at the climax of this story, the faithful, gracious and giving nature of Yahweh was expressed through sacrifice? Consequently, the primary action in ratifying this covenant was a definitive sacrificial action, linked with Yahweh, and expressed through the life and ministry of Jesus. Jesus acted out the kingdom, he enacted the return of Yahweh to Zion, and he made concrete the love of Yahweh, through self-sacrifice, in the making of the eschatological covenant. In this regard, it may be argued that interpretations which seek to understand Jesus' idea of his death as that of offering

---

91. In Isaiah 49 this covenant is almost certainly linked with the return from exile (verse 9).

92. See the succinct summary of the issues (mainly on how the genitive is to be construed) in K. Baltzer, *Deutero-Isaiah* (Minneapolis: Fortress, 2001), pp. 131–132.

93. W. Brueggemann, *Isaiah 40–66* (Louisville: Westminster/John Knox, 1998), pp. 113–114; J. A. Motyer, *Isaiah: An Introduction and Commentary* (Leicester: IVP, 1999), p. 261.

94. Cf. the essays in William H. Bellinger (ed.), *Jesus and the Suffering Servant: Isaiah 53 and Christian Origins* (Harrisburg: Trinity Press International, 1998).

a sacrifice to Yahweh on behalf of the nation[95] or his dying the death of a martyr in order to avert the wrath of God as in the Maccabean literature[96] are slightly wide of the mark.

Instead, Jesus' death must be understood within a story, the story of gracious covenant-making and its being breached, a story of Yahweh's reaching out to Israel to bring about a definitive covenantal relationship that cannot be breached. In this climax of the story, the love of Yahweh is demonstrated through the sacrifice of Jesus to inaugurate this covenant and bring about the restoration of Israel. Once this dimension to the Last Supper accounts is rejected, it is very difficult to see how the early church could insist that the death of Jesus showed the faithful and gracious love of Yahweh. Of course, I recognize that the proposals sketched above need not be regarded as mutually exclusive. But the last possibility that I have adumbrated should be considered seriously.

Covenant, kingdom and cross
Finally, it remains to be asked whether there is a connection between Jesus' preaching of the kingdom and the Last Supper. We may indeed presume that these are linked because the contrary would mean that Jesus abandoned his central message at the most crucial point of his ministry. This presumption receives confirmation in Mark 14:25 and Luke 22:29; that is, if we regard their connection with the Last Supper accounts as authentic.[97]

---

95. Defended ably by Wright, *Victory of God*; and S. McKnight, *A New Vision for Israel: The Teachings of Jesus in National Context* (Grand Rapids: Eerdmans, 1999).

96. Cf. H. Schürmann, *Jesu – Gestalt und Geheimnis: Gesammelte Beiträge* (Paderborn: Bonifatius, 1994); Bockmuehl, *This Jesus*; and Wright, *Victory of God*.

97. See the treatment of the authenticity of the Markan passage by Meier, *Mentor, Message and Miracles*, pp. 303–309. He supports the priority of the Markan version over that of Luke 22:18; but cf. Beasley-Murray, *Kingdom of God*, pp. 261–263, who supports the Lukan. Luke 22:29–30 is ably defended by H. Schürmann, *Jesu Abschiedsrede, Lk 22, 21–38:3: Teil einer*

The source-critical question surrounding these two logia bristles with difficulty: Mark 14:25 has a parallel in Luke 22:18, while Luke 22:29–30[98] has a partial parallel in Matthew 19:28. Regarding the first logion, whether the priority should be given to Mark or to Luke does not affect our results adversely, since both passages are connected with the Last Supper. The same cannot be said for Luke 22:29–30. It is not clear whether Luke 22:29 + 30a is to be assigned to 'L' or Q. If Q, then Luke 22:28–30 may be construed as one Q unit and its linkage to the Last Supper becomes highly questionable in view of Matthew 19:28.[99] However, if it is to be assigned to L, we may possibly conjecture that it was originally linked to the Last Supper traditions[100] and Luke includes the Q logion – in this case Luke 22:30b ‖ Matthew 19:28 – as a supplement and combines it with Mark 10:41–45 or a source similar to it.[101] However, there are also other possible permutations, rendering the source-critical problem more complex.[102] Thus, while there are very good grounds to regard Luke 22:29 as traditional and plausibly authentic,[103] its present placement does not command the same confidence.[104] But Luke 22:29 offers evidence of an explicit link

quellenkritischen Untersuchung des lukanischen Abendmahlsberichtes, Lk 22, 7–38 (Neutestamentliche Abhandlungen; Münster: Aschendorffsche, 1957), pp. 37–62.

98. Strangely, Luke 22:29 does not receive treatment in Holmén, *Jesus*.

99. Cf. D. C. Allison and W. D. Davies, *A Critical and Exegetical Commentary on the Gospel according to Saint Matthew* (ICC; Edinburgh: T. & T. Clark, 1997), vol. 3, p. 55; and J. Nolland, *Luke 18.35–24.53* (WBC 35C; Dallas: Word, 1993), p. 1063.

100. So Schürmann, *Jesu Abschiedsrede*, pp. 37–62.

101. Cf. Nolland, *Luke 18.35–24.53*, pp. 1062–1063.

102. Such as Luke 22:29, 30a being regarded as a traditional unit secondarily added, or it is only verse 29 that is from tradition which Luke redactionally expands with verse 30a, or that Luke 22:29, 30a is Lukan etc.

103. Cf. E. P. Sanders, *Jesus and Judaism* (London: SCM, 1977), p. 99; Beasley-Murray, *Kingdom of God*, p. 277; Fitzmyer, *Gospel according to Luke*, p. 1414.

104. Cf. Dupont who argues that although Luke 22:29, 30a is a discrete unit, it has been secondarily introduced into the narrative at this point. See his

between *basileia* (kingdom) and *diatithēmi*. Judging from how the word is used in Luke-Acts and the rest of the NT,[105] *diatithēmi* may be said to be the verbal equivalent of the noun *diathēkē*.[106] If it could be demonstrated that it was originally linked to the Last Supper traditions, the potential for our study would be great. Mark 14:25 does not have this word or its cognate but speaks of the certainty of Jesus' drinking wine with the disciples, presumably at the consummation of the kingdom. Supposing that they are both authentic and that they were originally linked with the Last Supper narrative, what results accrue for us?

Mark 14:25 might possibly be interpreted as referring either to Jesus' abstinence from banqueting[107] or to his expectation of post-mortem survival and confidence in the certain consummation of the kingdom of God.[108] Such ideas are propounded in much of the secondary literature.[109] I want to propose that there is more to its meaning and this makes Jesus' role central in the consummation of the kingdom.[110] It is true that Jesus intended to state his belief in

---

'Le logion des douze trônes (Mt 19,28; Lc 22,28–30)', *Bib* 45 (1964), pp. 395–396.

105. Acts 3:25; Hebrews 8:10; 9:16, 17; 10:16.

106. In the LXX, the combination of *diatithesthai* and *diathēkē* is often used to translate that of *bĕrît* and *kārat*. E.g. Genesis 15:18; 21:27, 32; Deuteronomy 5:2; 2 Kings 10:19 etc. The verb is also used to translate *kārat* in covenantal contexts; see especially Exodus 24:8, the key covenantal narrative!

107. The classic case for this is presented by Jeremias, *Eucharistic Words*, pp. 207–209.

108. Cf. M. de Jonge, 'Mark 14.25 among Jesus' Words about the Kingdom of God', in W. L. Petersen, J. S. Vos and H. J. de Jonge (eds.), *Sayings of Jesus: Canonical and Non-Canonical. Essays in Honour of Tjitze Baarda* (Leiden: Brill, 1997), pp. 123–135, especially p. 130; Evans, *Mark 8.26–16.20*, p. 395; Meier, *Mentor, Message and Miracles*, p. 308.

109. For a succinct presentation, especially the interpretation of *kainon*, see Evans, *Mark 8.26–16.20*, pp. 395–396.

110. Pace M. de Jonge, 'Jesus' Role in the Final Breakthrough of God's Kingdom', in H. Lichtenberger (ed.), *Geschichte – Tradition – Reflexion*.

the certainty of the consummation of the kingdom in this logion but this was done for the purpose of answering an implicit objection that his death rendered his whole mission futile. In effect, Jesus was saying that his death, far from being an unfortunate event, was related to the very inauguration of the eschatological covenant that would give the definitive impetus for the kingdom to be consummated. This links up with many sayings in the Jesus traditions that attest to Jesus' predicting – and consequently, charging with meaning – his impending death.[111] Reading the Markan narrative in this way gives a smoother transition from the themes of the Last Supper to the logion about the consummation of the kingdom.

Regarding Luke 22:29, Nolland argues that, since the royal destiny of Jesus is oriented to the future, the horizon of Jesus' impending death should not be drawn into the interpretation of the logion. Moreover, the twice-occurring *diatithēmi* in the logion should be translated as 'confer'.[112] This is hardly cogent, as the key incident before this logion was given in Luke's Gospel as the Last Supper, and, even more damaging, the verse that precedes speaks of a *peirasmos* (trial, temptation)! Surely, in the Lukan context the death of Jesus is in view and is intended to be the hermeneutical key to the meaning of the logion. What Nolland misses is the intimate connection of Jesus' death with the consummation of the kingdom. Furthermore, *diatithēmi* should be translated not as 'confer'[113] or 'vest'[114] but with verbs that mention the covenant idea[115] as the other Lukan usage in Acts 3:25 makes clear.[116] This is true also for the entire NT and the vast majority of its occurrences in the LXX.

Festschrift für Martin Hengel zum 70. Geburtstag. Band 3: Frühes Christentum (Tübingen: Mohr-Siebeck, 1996), pp. 265–286.

111. Cf. B. F. Meyer, *The Aims of Jesus* (London: SCM, 1979), p. 218.

112. Nolland, *Luke 18.35–24.53*, p. 1066.

113. Cf. NIV.

114. Cf. REB.

115. Among the English transations I have come across, only the New World Translation gives such a rendering!

116. Cf. the judicious discussion in Marshall, *Gospel of Luke*, pp. 817–818.

In the logion under consideration, Jesus speaks of a covenant-ing action between Yahweh and himself that involves kingship. This covenanted kingship is extended to the Twelve, not in the sense of their setting up another kingdom but of their participat-ing in his reign.[117] The logion that follows in verse 30 confirms this: the disciples will eat and drink at Jesus' table in his kingdom. Eating and drinking here signify participation[118] and recall the sig-nificant actions performed at the Last Supper. The Twelve here stands for restored Israel. Therefore, the total impact of the logion is that Israel is renewed and in this form shares in the kingdom mediated through Jesus of Nazareth, the vicegerent of Yahweh. Thus, death would not stall such a programme. This trend of thought is similar to that of Mark 14:25.

Even if I am wrong to postulate that Mark 14:25 and Luke 22:29 were originally connected to the Last Supper narrative, it can still be argued that there is evidence to show that kingdom and covenant are connected in at least one saying of the authentic Jesus traditions. But if my postulation is right, these two themes may also be regarded as connected to the cross. Thus, the death of Jesus, so eloquently interpreted by the Last Supper, was regarded as neces-sary for the climax of the covenantal story and the consummation of the kingdom of God.

Conclusions

Where has all this discussion taken us? If we take into account that the very concept of a covenant entails an ecclesiology and a the-ology, which in turn sets in motion a story that has a climax which is awaited, we cannot escape the notion that Jesus' ministry was intimately connected with the covenant, even though the term *diathēkē* occurs only once in the extant Jesus traditions. Almost all scholars would accept that the key aspects of Jesus' ministry

---

117.   Cf. Beasley-Murray, *Kingdom of God*, p. 277.

118.   See Isaiah 25:6; Amos 9:13–14; Hosea 2:22; and Joel 2:24–26; 3:18. Cf.
        2 Baruch 29:5 and *1 Enoch* 10:19.

concern the formation of a community and the proclamation of the kingdom of God. These come together implicitly with the covenant theme in Jewish thought. However, what is implicit is made explicit in the Last Supper traditions, which we judge to be authentic and intended by Jesus to be the crowning explanation of what his ministry signified and the role he had in the ongoing covenantal story of Yahweh and his people. The themes of community, kingdom and covenant come together profoundly at the Last Supper.

But the surprising twist to all this is that it is through Jesus' death that there can be assurance that the kingdom will be consummated, the restored community will come into being, and the eschatological covenant — or possibly, the new covenant — will be inaugurated. This twist is best understood not from the national angle nor the Maccabean but that of the story of the covenant. In this story Yahweh acts faithfully and sacrificially to bring about the climax to the story despite the vagaries of history and the intransigence of human subjects. Is the covenant not the glue that holds together the key aspects of Jesus' ministry?

6. LUKE AND THE NEW COVENANT: ZECHARIAH'S PROPHECY AS A TEST CASE

Alistair I. Wilson

Introduction

The text of Luke 22:20, according to most English translations and the adopted text of the standard critical editions of the Greek NT, indicates that, in the context of his final meal with his disciples, Jesus took a cup of wine and said, 'This cup is the new covenant in my blood'. The phrase 'the new covenant' (*hē kainē diathēkē*) appears to be an echo of the only occurrence of the precise Hebrew phrase *bĕrît ḥădāšâ* in the OT, found in Jeremiah 31:31 (LXX 38:31, where the Greek noun and the adjective are in the reverse order: *diathēkē kainē*).[1] This chapter will consider whether this allusion is inconsequential or whether it points to a

---

1. The standard commentaries are fairly unanimous in recognizing this allusion, although they vary in the significance they attach to the echo. See, for example, D. L. Bock, *Luke 9:51–24:53* (BECNT; Grand Rapids: Baker, 1996), p. 1727; J. A. Fitzmyer, *The Gospel according to Luke X–XXIV* (AB; New York: Doubleday, 1985), p. 1402; J. B. Green, *The Gospel of Luke*

greater significance of New Covenant theology within Luke's
writings.

Tracing 'New Covenant' influences: methodological issues

At the outset we can say that there are no other portions of Luke's
writings (in either the Gospel or Acts) which clearly cite the Greek
text of Jeremiah 31 (38):31–34. Thus, if we are convinced that
only direct citation is valid evidence of influence then we can
stop here! However, it seems to me that this approach would
unduly restrict our opportunity to see the impact of this portion
of the OT (and other related portions) on Luke's writing. Towards
the end of his recent book,[2] which pays particular attention to the
account in Genesis of Abraham and Isaac on Mount Moriah,
Walter Moberly undertakes a study of Matthew's Gospel in which
he sets out to 'consider how the substantive issues of human life
in relation to God as raised in Genesis 22 are raised in the New
Testament also'. This, he goes on to clarify, is 'an exercise quite
distinct from studying the specific New Testament usage of
Genesis 22'.[3] Moberly seems to wish to distance himself from
studies that attempt to trace intertextual connections between a
NT text and an OT text for two reasons. Firstly, 'one cannot be
other than largely agnostic on the historical question of what traditions were not only known by Matthew but also deliberately used
by him . . . We simply do not know.'[4] Secondly, he wishes to ensure
that the Gospel narrative is read 'as meaningful in its own right'.[5]
This seems to me to be a productive approach to explore further,
though it is clearly rather more subjective than an approach based

---

(NICNT; Grand Rapids: Eerdmans, 1997), p. 763; I. H. Marshall, *The
Gospel of Luke* (NIGTC; Carlisle: Paternoster, 1978), p. 806.

2. W. Moberly, *The Bible, Theology and Faith* (Cambridge: Cambridge
University Press, 2000).

3. Ibid., p. 184.

4. Ibid., p. 186.

5. Ibid., p. 187.

on explicit citations of the OT. Thus I will aim to read portions of Luke's narrative with a view to 'the substantive issues' that reflect the concerns of Jeremiah 31:31–34 without seeking to claim that any given portion of Luke is an 'echo' or 'midrash' or whatever of Jeremiah's words. There are, I believe, several reasons for adopting this approach with the Gospel of Luke.

Firstly, it is widely acknowledged that the concept of the New Covenant is developed in OT passages where the exact phrase is not present. (I will identify some of these shortly.) Thus, it is essential that any NT development of New Covenant theology be identified in conceptual terms rather than solely by linguistic echoes.

Secondly, it is clear that the concept of the 'New Covenant' is of considerable significance for NT theology (not least, in the writings of Paul),[6] yet explicit citations of the OT texts (whether Jeremiah 31:31–34 itself or other passages associated with the New Covenant) are rare.[7] We might just mention in passing the significance of the New Covenant motif within the writings associated with the Qumran community (1QpHab 2.1–4; 1Q28b; 1Q34; CD 6.19; 8.21; 19.34; 20.12) as an illustration of the impact of this scriptural theme on a Jewish religious community in the first century.

Thirdly, it is widely recognized that Luke at times adopts a 'Septuagintal' style, which suggests that 'Luke is not introducing a *new* story, but continuing an old one, whose real "beginning" is the LXX.'[8] While this cannot be used as an argument for the presence of New Covenant themes as such, it does point to an understated use of the OT, which might lead us to expect that any such themes would be integrated into Luke's narrative with some subtlety.

---

6. See S. J. Hafemann, *Paul, Moses and the History of Israel* (Peabody: Hendrickson, 1995); W. S. Campbell, 'Covenant and New Covenant', in *DPL*, pp. 179–183.

7. The most notable citation and discussion of Jeremiah 31:31–34 is found in Hebrews 8:8–12 and 10:16–17. See S. Moyise, *The Old Testament in the New: An Introduction* (London: Continuum, 2001), pp. 103–104. See also Romans 11:26.

8. Green, *Gospel of Luke*, p. 52.

Fourthly, Luke's infancy narrative is undoubtedly riddled with allusions to the OT, particularly in the various hymnic/prophetic passages, without including explicitly identified quotations.[9] P. Williamson comments, 'although the "new covenant" is mentioned explicitly only at the institution of the Lord's Supper, the Gospels are pregnant with associated ideas'.[10] However, Williamson does not identify any specific examples in Luke's Gospel and he suggests that Matthew places more emphasis on fulfilment than the other Gospels. It is my hope that I can provide some specific evidence for the truth of Williamson's comment with respect to Luke.

'New Covenant' and 'covenant' in Luke's Gospel

Despite the fundamental significance of the concept of 'covenant' throughout the OT, and throughout the NT in general, the Greek term *diathēkē* occurs only four times in the canonical Gospels (Matthew 26:28; Mark 14:24; Luke 1:72; 22:20). Three of these occurrences appear in the Synoptic evangelists' accounts of Jesus' final meal with his disciples and particularly in his interpretative words over a cup of wine. Matthew and Mark are agreed that Jesus said *touto estin to haima mou tēs diathēkēs* (this is my blood of the covenant; although they vary slightly in recording the words that immediately follow).[11] Luke, however, records Jesus' words as *touto*

---

9. See particularly in R. E. Brown, *The Birth of the Messiah* (ABRL; 2nd ed.; New York: Doubleday, 1993), pp. 386–389, the chart that identifies allusions in Zechariah's prophecy.

10. P. Williamson, 'Covenant', in D. Alexander and B. S. Rosner (eds.), *New Dictionary of Biblical Theology* (Leicester: IVP, 2000), pp. 419–429 (p. 427).

11. Mark (14:24) and Matthew (26:28) agree in recording that Jesus spoke of 'my blood of the covenant', which seems most naturally to echo Exodus 24:8; Matthew: 'for many'; 'for the forgiveness of sins'; Mark: 'for many'. Luke refers to the meal as 'this Passover' and so there can be little doubt that the reference to Exodus (though an earlier section, chs. 12–13) is still present. If it is assumed for the moment that the Two-Source hypothesis

to potērion hē kainē diathēkē en tō haimati mou ('this cup is the new covenant in my blood').[12] The fact that Luke alone preserves a form of words which unambiguously recalls the words of Jeremiah 31:31–34 immediately suggests that Luke may have a particular interest in that concept and that particular sensitivity to the related themes may prove fruitful when reading Luke's Gospel.

The fourth occurrence of the term *diathēkē*, however, is unique to Luke and is found in the midst of Zechariah's prophecy on the occasion of the naming (and circumcision) of his son (1:72). While this linguistic fact alone does not justify sweeping conclusions, the character of these two occurrences of this Greek term suggests that there may be some benefit in giving more sustained attention to this text with respect to possible resonances with the New Covenant. In this study I intend to consider (1) the relationship between the 'covenant' of Zechariah's prophecy and the 'New Covenant', and (2) the significance of the phrase 'forgiveness of sins' as a crucial element of the New Covenant promise of Jeremiah 31:31–34 and a distinctive emphasis within Luke's narrative. That is, I will ask whether selected aspects of Luke's narrative suggest that he has more than a passing interest in the 'new covenant' of Jeremiah and whether his minimal formal reference

---

is essentially correct, then it is interesting that Luke departs from the wording of Mark at this point.

12. The presence of the term 'new covenant' in Luke is itself a matter of dispute. Although there is plenty of support for the text from the main Alexandrian texts (notably Sinaiticus [ℵ] and Vaticanus [B]), the absence of Luke 22:19b–20 from the Western text (notably Codex Bezae [D]) has led to some scholars, following the wording of Westcott and Hort (see B. M. Metzger, *A Textual Commentary on the Greek New Testament* [New York: UBS, 1975], pp. 191–193), identifying this text as an example of a 'Western non-interpolation'. Some would admit that MS evidence 'clearly attests the presence of *kainē*' in Luke but believe that this gives it only 'weak, late attestation' (S. Lehne, *The New Covenant in Hebrews* [JSNTSup 44; Sheffield: JSOT Press, 1990], p. 84). See the thorough discussions in Metzger, *Textual Commentary*, pp. 173–177; and J. Jeremias, *The Eucharistic Words of Jesus* (London: SCM, 1966), pp. 138–159.

to the new covenant in 22:20 is, in fact, simply a pointer to an underlying theological significance.[13]

'New Covenant' in the OT

The foundational passage for understanding the concept of the 'New Covenant' is Jeremiah 31:31–34, particularly because it is here alone that the Hebrew expression *běrît ḥădāšâ* is used. This very linguistic fact means that the phrase itself is somewhat less useful in defining its significance; context must provide content to the phrase. The uniqueness of the phrase does, however, make it a highly distinctive means of referring to the passage in which it is found. To be read alongside this passage there is a remarkably similar passage in Jeremiah 32:37–41 that speaks, not of a 'new covenant' but of an 'everlasting covenant'.[14] There are, however, several other passages that relate to this theme conceptually, although they do not use the precise phraseology. Notable are Jeremiah 30 – 33 (cf. 33:4–11); Ezekiel 34; 36 – 37 (cf. 36:24–26); Isaiah 40 – 55 (cf. Isaiah 42:6).[15]

There can be little doubt that Jeremiah's prophecy indicates the superiority ('not like') of the New Covenant over 'the covenant which I made with their fathers in the day I took them by the hand to bring them out of the land of Egypt' (31:32, NASB, rev. ed., 1995). This latter phrase appears to identify the previous covenant unambiguously as the Sinai covenant.[16] Yet it is not clear that the

---

13. I have restricted myself in this chapter to consideration of Luke's Gospel, but a similar approach could also be taken to Luke's second volume, the Acts of the Apostles. Notably, I have identified several passages where the forgiveness is identified as the particular benefit of faith in Jesus Christ in Acts: 2:38; 5:31; 10:43; 13:38; 26:18.

14. See the comparison in G. von Rad, *Old Testament Theology* (London: SCM, 1965), vol. 2, pp. 214–217.

15. See J. G. McConville, *běrît*, *NIDOTTE*, vol. 1, pp. 747–755 (especially p. 752).

16. G. Van Groningen argues that other references to the covenant in Jeremiah suggest that the covenant refers more broadly to 'Yahweh's covenant with Abraham, Moses, Israel, and David' (*Messianic Revelation in*

superiority relates to the content of the covenants. In fact, it is generally recognized that, in O. P. Robertson's words, 'the newness of the new covenant must not stand in absolute contradiction to the previous covenants. A factor of continuity must be recognised.'[17] Such continuity is seen, for example, in the initiative of YHWH in establishing both covenants ('I will make'/'I made') and the continued significance of YHWH's instruction (*tôrâ*; although the writing materials employed will be different).[18] So what, then, distinguishes the New Covenant described by Jeremiah from the Sinai covenant?

McComiskey identifies four distinctive characteristics of the New Covenant as presented in Jeremiah 31:31–34:[19]

1. 'Obedience will be facilitated by a change in the nature of those who are included in the covenant.'
2. 'A divine–human relationship will be established.'
3. 'The participants in the covenant will have a new relationship with God.'
4. 'God will no longer remember the sins of his people.'

McComiskey's first point is surely on target. The fatal flaw in the earlier covenant relationship was not the covenant that God made

---

the Old Testament [Grand Rapids: Baker, 1990], p. 721). Yet the explicit association with the exodus from Egypt seems to connect the previous covenant to Sinai in particular.

17. O. P. Robertson, *The Christ of the Covenants* (Phillipsburg: Presbyterian & Reformed, 1980), p. 281. So also Van Groningen: 'the main elements of Yahweh's covenant with Abraham, Moses, Israel, and David remain in force in Jeremiah's proclamations' (*Messianic Revelation*, p. 721).

18. Cf. G. L. Keown, P. J. Scalise and T. G. Smothers, *Jeremiah 26–52* (WBC; Dallas: Word, 1995), p. 134.

19. T. E. McComiskey, *The Covenants of Promise* (Leicester: IVP, 1985), pp. 84–89. Somewhat different analyses are found in W. A. VanGemeren, *Interpreting the Prophetic Word* (Grand Rapids: Zondervan, 1990), pp. 316–317; P. R. House, *Old Testament Theology* (Downers Grove: IVP, 1998), p. 318; and C. H. H. Scobie, *The Ways of Our God* (Grand Rapids: Eerdmans, 2003), pp. 484–485.

but the rebellion of the people ('which they broke') and the crucial difference between this covenant and that which went before is the way in which the problem of human failure is dealt with. The emphasis on the 'everlasting' character of this covenant appears to emphasize precisely that it is not susceptible to the breach perpetrated in the past.[20]

His second and third points are more contentious, however. With respect to the establishment of a divine–human relationship, Jeremiah's prophecy indicates that God had previously established a relationship with his people ('I was a husband/master to them'), which is described in terms of care and protection.[21] Yet it is clear

---

20. Robertson, *Christ*, p. 285; House, *Theology*, p. 319. In discussing this passage, J. Goldingay suggests that Jeremiah's words indicate that by a great future display of grace God's rebellious people will be won over to faithfulness: 'Yhwh's compassion, restoration, forgiveness and cleansing will be the wonders that inspire a change in the people's lives' (*Old Testament Theology*. Vol. 1: *Israel's Gospel* [Downers Grove: IVP, 2003], p. 714). This view, however, seems to me to fail to recognize the greatness of the act and the tenderness of the care YHWH had *already* shown towards his people, but with no such 'inspired' response from the people. Goldingay appears to take the view that all God can do is to demonstrate his love in more and more striking ways and hope for a positive response. This seems to be his view of the significance of the cross, also. Thus, recognizing only a very partial response to Christ's death, he laments, 'Perhaps there is nothing else God can do' (p. 715). Jeremiah's prophecy appears to take a more realistic view of human hardness and to indicate that God will accomplish something within his chosen people that will enable them to choose what they would otherwise never choose. Von Rad is much more in tune with Jeremiah when he writes, 'If God is again gracious to him, how can [someone] in any way stand before him as man without once again coming to grief because of his heart's opposition to God? The answer which Jeremiah received to this question was the promise that God would himself change the human heart and so bring about perfect obedience' (*Theology*, vol. 2, p. 217).

21. Although the use of *ba'al* may appear to suggest a rather overbearing relationship, W. T. Koopmans argues on the basis of the broader biblical

that Jeremiah does suggest a new *quality* of relationship and the *inclusiveness* of the relationship is also apparently emphasized by means of reference to the two parts of the divided kingdom (verse 31) and by the emphasis on 'each' and 'from the least to the greatest' (verse 34).

It is the final point relating to forgiveness of sin that I want to focus on in this chapter. In fact, I must take issue with McComiskey from the start as he emphasizes the 'forgetting of sin' aspect of the New Covenant as that which is most distinctive (the language in Jeremiah 31:34 almost perfectly reverses the promise of judgment in Jeremiah 14:10).[22] In fact, this note is generally muted in the OT and almost entirely absent from the NT, the only occurrences of the verb being the citations of Jeremiah 31 in Hebrews 8:12 and 10:17. It seems much more likely to me that there is a measure of parallelism in the last two phrases in Jeremiah 31:34 and that 'forgiveness of sin' should be regarded as the major promise rather than 'forgetting of sin'.[23]

---

testimony to the image of God as a faithful husband to his people that the use of this term in Jeremiah 31:32 'must not be mistaken to convey a sense of harshness'. See W. T. Koopmans, *ba'al*, in *NIDOTTE*, vol. 1, pp. 681–683 (here p. 682). This is confirmed in this context by God's further explanatory note 'when I took them by the hand'. This phrase (including minor variations) is found seldom in the OT. In Isaiah 45:1 YHWH describes Cyrus as the one 'I have taken by the right hand' (NASB), while in Isaiah 51:18, YHWH laments that there is not one of the reared sons of Jerusalem who will take her by her hand. Interestingly, in the NT it is found only in Hebrews 8:9 in a citation of this portion of Jeremiah, but the act of taking someone by the hand (implying personal involvement and tenderness) is ascribed to Jesus in six texts: Matthew 9:25; Mark 1:31; 5:41; 8:23; 9:27; Luke 8:54. The fact that most of these occurrences are found outside Luke's Gospel indicates that there is probably no attempt by Luke to recall the language of Jeremiah's prophecy.

22. Cf. similar language used in the Psalms and Isaiah, either in a *plea* that God would forget sin, or more rarely in a *promise* that he will: Psalms 25:7 (plea); 79:8 (plea); Isaiah 43:25 (promise); 64:9 (plea).

23. Cf. Isaiah 43:25, where the promise 'I will not remember your sins' stands in parallel with 'I am he who blots out your transgressions'. See J. P. J. Olivier,

In passing, and in addition to these characteristics, we must surely add that the New Covenant is an *eschatological* covenant. The phrase 'the days are coming' (*yāmîm bā'îm*) signals this eschatological character, but so too does the fact that most of the circumstances envisaged have simply not been realities in Israel's experience up to the time of Jeremiah's prophecy.[24] This is to say, the New Covenant is evidence that YHWH is breaking into the experience of his people in an unprecedented manner. This should be taken into account when considering the way in which possible examples of New Covenant theology in Luke should be evaluated.

When we consider other OT passages associated with the concept of the New Covenant, we find less emphasis on the forgiveness of sins. For example, in Jeremiah 32:40 and 50:5 there is reference to an 'everlasting covenant', yet there is no explicit promise of forgiveness of sins in these texts.[25] This fact should make us wary of identifying forgiveness of sins as the *only* or *major* benefit of the New Covenant, but we may still regard it as a *significant* benefit associated with the New Covenant. What is more, the text of Jeremiah 31:31–34, which the NT recalls as the foundation of New Covenant theology, reaches its climax in the declaration of complete forgiveness.

Thus, as we prepare to consider a portion of Luke's Gospel, we may state that Jeremiah 31:31–34 suggests that the New Covenant is not substantially different in character from previous covenants, but that God now will act in a new way to protect the covenant from the faithlessness of his people, to include the widest range of people within the covenant relationship and to bring forgiveness to all those who stand within this covenant relationship.

---

sālaḥ, in *NIDOTTE*, vol. 3, pp. 259–264, for the use of this key term and other related vocabulary.

24. This is particularly evident in the reference to a united people composed of the house of Israel and the house of Judah. See Van Groningen, *Messianic Revelation*, pp. 721–722.

25. Jeremiah 36:3 presents the forgiveness of sins as a possibility contingent on repentance, but there is no reference to the New Covenant.

Zechariah's prophecy

Having looked briefly at the conceptual background, we turn
now to Zechariah's prophecy in Luke 1:67–79, known commonly as the *Benedictus*.[26] Numerous contested issues relating to
the literary history of this text are fully treated in the works of
R. E. Brown and S. Farris,[27] but which are not my concern here.
For the purposes of this chapter I will assume that the canonical text accurately reflects Luke's theological intention. That is,
regardless of the specific details of the literary history of the
prophecy, the composition as it is found in the canonical text is
intended to be read as a unit and accurately represents what
Luke wishes to say.

Zechariah's words, like Mary's before him (1:46–55), serve, in
literary terms, to slow the narrative down from a fairly quick pace
in order to allow reflection on the significance of the events that
have been taking place.[28] These extended declarations of praise
provide theological interpretation of God's acts in history and
thus provide the reader of the Gospel with a key to understanding
what is taking place. These poetic compositions are therefore very
significant and worthy of careful attention. Thus the drama that
has been in motion since the very beginning of Luke's narrative
and Zechariah's encounter with the angel Gabriel, and which has
just come to a climax in the shockingly unexpected twist in the
naming ceremony, is given a theological interpretation in this
poetic speech.

The prophecy is associated with the presence (and no doubt
the activity) of the Holy Spirit.[29] This is, of course, a distinctive

---

26. The traditional title is derived from the first word of the prophecy as
    found in the Latin Vulgate translation.
27. See Brown, *Birth*, pp. 346–355; and S. Farris, *The Hymns of Luke's Infancy
    Narratives* (JSNTSup 9; Sheffield: JSOT, 1985), pp. 1–98.
28. So Green, *Gospel of Luke*, p. 112.
29. Compare the earlier experience of Mary and Elizabeth. Mary's song is not
    explicitly linked to the presence of the Holy Spirit, but the wider context
    testifies to his activity. Simeon and Anna in Luke 2 are also characterized

emphasis of Luke's writings.[30] The Spirit is the one who declares
and brings about God's new purposes (cf. Luke 4:18).[31] The role of
the Holy Spirit is not directly associated with the concept of the
New Covenant in Jeremiah 31:31–34, but there is reference to the
Spirit in Ezekiel 36:26–27, which reflects similar concerns. There
YHWH declares that he will act in the experience of his hard-
hearted people to enable them to respond to him as they ought.[32]
Thus, we might anticipate that the role of the Spirit would be
important to an author steeped in the full scope of 'New Covenant
theology' in the OT Scriptures.

Zechariah's prophecy appears at first glance to be a 'song' of
praise to God in response to the birth of his son. Thus, this passage
completes a threefold pattern of divine promise of a son, birth of
a son and praise.[33] In fact, however, Zechariah's words seem to
reflect on a much greater set of events than simply the joyful occasion of John's birth, a set of events that gives particular significance
to the birth of this child. The prophecy is formed from two clearly
distinct sections: Section 1 (68–75) is a 'Benediction'[34] that con-
siders God's dealings with his people, using aorist verbs. Section 2
(76–79), is introduced by means of the direct address to the child
John, and is characterized by future verb forms. Zechariah's direct
address to his son John forms the transition point between the two
sections. Although these two sections are clearly identifiable, it is
unnecessary to argue that they were not originally intended to be

---

by the presence and enabling of the Holy Spirit. See also Acts 2:17–18;
11:27; 13:1; 19:6; 21:9.

30. See particularly M. M. B. Turner, *Power from on High: The Spirit in Israel's
Restoration and Witness in Luke–Acts* (JPTSup 9; Sheffield: Sheffield
Academic Press, 1996).

31. J. B. Green, *The Theology of the Gospel of Luke* (Cambridge: Cambridge
University Press, 1995), pp. 41–47.

32. W. Hildebrandt, *An Old Testament Theology of the Spirit of God* (Peabody:
Hendrickson, 1995), pp. 65, 94–96.

33. Green, NICNT, *Gospel of Luke*, p. 112. Compare the similar pattern relating to Jesus.

34. Ibid., p. 113. The *běrākâ* form is found in several places in the NT.

placed together.[35] In fact, the reflection in the first section on past covenant faithfulness on the part of YHWH appears to be an appropriate prelude to the note of anticipation in the second section. The use of the important term *episkeptomai* (to visit) in verses 68 and 78 appears to form an *inclusio* around the prophecy.[36] If this is the case, then it is a further argument for the essential unity of the composition.

As with Mary's song, there are numerous allusions to OT passages throughout this passage. These are identified routinely in the standard commentaries and monographs,[37] so that there is no need to identify them all again here. Our concern is whether there is evidence of an awareness of or emphasis on the concept of the New Covenant, and several features of Zechariah's song suggest some reflection of New Covenant theology (exemplified by Jeremiah 31:31–34).

In particular there is reference to the covenant promises to the people of God. This is the dominant note of the first part of the prophecy. Zechariah blesses the covenant God ('the Lord God of Israel', verse 68; cf. 1:16) for his faithfulness. This reference to Israel, combined with the reference to 'his people' in the second part of the verse, emphasizes Luke's presentation of the ensuing events as the fulfilment of the purposes of the one, true God for his one, true people (cf. 7:16).[38] God's purposes for his 'people' are also highlighted in 1:77. In this first section of the prophecy, Zechariah blesses God for two stated reasons: because he has 'visited' (*epeskepsato*; cf. Exodus 4:31; Luke 7:16) and accomplished 'redemption' for his people; and because he has raised up a 'horn of salvation' in the house of David. In fact, Green suggests

---

35. See the discussion in Brown, *Birth*, p. 381. Although Brown takes a less radical view than some, he still regards verses 76–77 as a 'Lukan insertion' into an existing 'canticle'.

36. So Nolland, *Luke1–9:20* (WBC; Dallas: Word, 1989), p. 83. Discussion of the significance of this term follows shortly.

37. Brown's chart, *Birth*, pp. 386–389, is particularly helpful.

38. J. Jervell, *The Theology of the Acts of the Apostles* (Cambridge: Cambridge University Press, 1996), pp. 18–25.

plausibly that these two statements should be understood as two perspectives on a single act of God. In its OT context, the term 'visited' would most naturally apply to YHWH's extraordinary act of liberation in the exodus (Exodus 4:31),[39] but the causal link (*hoti*) between Zechariah's blessing of God and God's activity suggests that it is in Zechariah's own day that this redemption has been accomplished. That is, the aorist tenses do not refer to events in history but are used prophetically of a set of circumstances that has been newly brought about, yet which may be interpreted in the light of the historic events of OT history. The most natural referent would be the birth of John, although perhaps, within the structure of Luke's narrative, Zechariah's words are also intended to allude to the various aspects of the announcement of Jesus' birth. The faithfulness of Israel's God is further explained in terms of his raising up a 'horn of salvation' (verse 69, the first reference to the key term 'salvation', *sotēria*, in the passage).

This image of strength (cf. particularly the use of this image in Hannah's prayer, 1 Samuel 2:10) is here related to 'the house of David' (Psalms 132:16–17; Ezekiel 29:21), which suggests an echo of YHWH's covenant with David, expressed in 2 Samuel 7:12–13. This is remarkable because John was, in R. E. Brown's words, 'scarcely a Davidic savior'.[40] This apparent incongruity suggests that Zechariah is drawing our attention to some act of God, other than the birth of John, which fulfils his covenant promise to David. As Fitzmyer points out, the reference to God's covenant with David in the angel's words to Mary in 1:32–35 provides the wider context in which to interpret Zechariah's remark.[41]

---

39. Green, *Gospel of Luke*, p. 116. See BDAG, s.v. *episkeptomai*, which places these occurrences of the verb under the gloss 'make an appearance to help'. Although the noun *lytrōsis* is not used in connection with the events of the exodus, the cognate verb *lytroō* is employed in the LXX in Exodus 6:6. Note also the connection between covenant and redemption in Psalm 111:9.

40. Brown, *Birth*, p. 377. Similarly, J. A. Fitzmyer, *The Gospel according to Luke I–IX* (AB; New York: Doubleday, 1981), p. 383.

41. Fitzmyer, *Luke I–IX*, p. 383.

Thus, although Zechariah will relate the 'covenant' of verse 72 to Abraham, we have in fact a broad perspective on covenant faithfulness in the first part of Zechariah's prophecy. Israel's God has been faithful to all his promises. This is reinforced by means of the reference to the prophets in general rather than any particular prophet. There is a sense of a culmination of prophetic promises.

The covenant themes continue in verse 71, which begins with the second of three references to salvation (*sotēria*) within the prophecy. The words echo Psalms 106:10, a psalm that celebrates the exodus, and thus again provides reinforcement to the view that the exodus is a major interpretative key to this prophecy.[42] The references to 'enemies' and 'those who hate us' might suggest that Zechariah interprets YHWH's acts in political terms here, although I. H. Marshall believes that 'it may be doubtful how far the political language earlier in the hymn is to be pressed'.[43]

Verse 72 is composed of two infinitives that indicate the result of God's action.[44] The first infinitive indicates that God has acted 'to show mercy'. The second, that he determined 'to remember his holy covenant'. Fitzmyer is surely correct in claiming that the combination of 'mercy' and 'covenant' points to YHWH's *ḥesed* (covenant love/faithfulness/mercy).[45] Thus, all that has taken place in Zechariah's experience is intended to demonstrate the covenant faithfulness of the God of Israel.

This 'covenant' is immediately explained, in verse 73, to be 'the oath (*orkon*) which he swore to our father Abraham'. This must be a reference to the promise that YHWH makes to Abram in Genesis 12:1–4; 15:18–19; 17:1–4 (and Isaac and Jacob, Genesis 26:1–5;

---

42. See the comments earlier on 'redemption' and 'covenant' in this psalm.

43. I. H. Marshall, *Luke: Historian and Theologian*, p. 99.

44. Brown, *Birth*, pp. 371–372, asserts that the non-articular infinitives indicate result rather than purpose.

45. F. I. Anderson, 'Yahweh, the Kind and Sensitive God', in P. T. O'Brien and D. Peterson (eds.), *God Who Is Rich In Mercy* (Homebush West: Lancer, 1986), pp. 41–88.

28:13–15; Psalm 105:8); that is, to the foundational covenant of the OT.[46] Lagrange draws attention to Leviticus 26:42, where God promises to remember his covenant when his people confess their sins. He comments, 'It seems, then, that 72a means to forgive the sins of the fathers.'[47]

It is important to note that Zechariah's words concerning 'the oath which he swore to our father Abraham' have been entirely positive so far. In no way has he raised any concerns about the effectiveness of the earlier covenant. But already it is possible to see that there are echoes of the state of affairs envisaged in Jeremiah 31:31–34, even although there has been no explicit reference to that text.

Verse 76 marks the second part of Zechariah's prophecy as he directly addresses his infant son. John is recognized as a very significant figure, 'the prophet of the Most High' (ESV), but, nonetheless, a preparatory figure. The echo of Isaiah 40 indicates clearly (as do the more redactional uses of this portion of OT Scripture in the other Synoptic Gospels) that John's role is to prepare for the Lord. That is, he is to announce the eschatological coming of YHWH to his people.

Verse 77 indicates the purpose of John's future ministry by means of an 'epexegetical infinitive' of purpose, which develops the prior infinitive of purpose in 1:76,[48] and a prepositional phrase: *tou dounai gnōsin sotērias tō laō autou en aphesei hamartiōn autōn* (to give knowledge of salvation to his people in/by forgiveness of their sins). This verse includes the third occurrence of the key Lukan term 'salvation', but two other terms are introduced, which are particularly significant with respect to possible echoes of Jeremiah 31: 'knowledge' and 'forgiveness'.

Several commentators make passing reference to Jeremiah 31:34 when commenting on this verse, but none develop their brief

---

46. Liefeld identifies the oath with Genesis 22:16–18, 'where the Lord promised Abraham not only that his descendants' enemies would be subdued but also that universal blessing would result from his obedience' (W. L. Liefeld, 'Luke' [EBC; Grand Rapids: Zondervan, 1984], vol. 8, p. 840).

47. 'Il semble donc que 72a signifie pardoner les péchés des pères' (M.-J. Lagrange, *Évangile selon Saint Luc* [Paris: Gabalda, 1948], p. 60).

48. D. L. Bock, Luke 1:1–9:50 (BECNT; Grand Rapids: Baker, 1994), p. 189.

notes.[49] The noun 'forgiveness' (*aphesis*)[50] occurs five times in Luke's Gospel[51] and a further five times in Acts.[52] Brown claims that verse 77 is a 'Lucan composition',[53] whereas R. Webb comments less provocatively that 'forgiveness of sins' is 'a Lukan emphasis'.[54] Webb recognizes that this fact might lead to the conclusion that a Christian concept was read back into the ministry of John, but suggests that the typical association of 'forgiveness of sins' with 'the name of Jesus' (cf. Acts 2:38) or 'belief in Jesus' (Acts 10:43) makes this unlikely.[55] Although Luke does not employ a particular OT phrase here, Nolland, drawing attention to Jeremiah 31:34, is correct to note that 'the idea is clear enough'.[56]

One might argue that there is nothing particularly remarkable in Zechariah's words, because forgiveness was something that God had made accessible to all through the sacrificial system. For example, Exodus 34:7 declares YHWH to be the one who 'forgives iniquity, transgression and sin'. If this is the case, however, then it is surely all the more remarkable that as Zechariah rejoices in God's new acts of grace towards his people, he highlight's forgiveness of sins as the result of these new events.

Forgiveness of sins in Luke-Acts

Having considered possible New Covenant references in Zechariah's prophecy, I will now make a few comments on the

---

49. See, for example, Green, *Gospel of Luke*, p. 114; Petrus J. Gräbe, *Der neue Bund in der frühchristlichen Literatur: unter Berücksichtigung der alttestamentlich-jüdischen Voraussetzung* (FB 96; Würzburg: Echter Verlag, 2001), p. 79. Also NASB margin references.

50. *NIDNTT*, vol. 1, pp. 697–703.

51. Luke 1:77; 3:3; 4:18 (twice); 24:47.

52. Acts 2:38; 5:31; 10:43; 13:38; 26:18.

53. Brown, *Birth*, p. 390 n. 36.

54. R. L. Webb, *John the Baptizer and Prophet* (Sheffield: JSOT Press, 1991), p. 171.

55. Ibid., pp. 171–172.

56. Nolland, *Luke 1–9:20*, p. 89.

place of forgiveness, a significant aspect of the New Covenant, in Luke's Gospel. If this is a theme of particular importance to Luke, then it may increase the likelihood that a reference to forgiveness in the context of discussion of covenant reflects an awareness of the emphases of Jeremiah's New Covenant prophecy.

Fitzmyer argues that Luke not only describes instances where Jesus offers forgiveness of sins, but actually regards this phrase as an appropriate summary of the total significance of Jesus: 'When Luke looks back at the Christ-event, another way in which he sums up its effect is "the forgiveness of sins".'[57] There are numerous references to forgiveness in Luke's Gospel:[58] 1:77 (L); 3:3 (Mark); 5:20–24 (Mark); 6:37 (partly L); 7:42–49 (L); 11:4 (Q?); 12:10 (Mark); 17:3–4 (Q); 23:34 (L); 24:47 (L).[59] It is worth noting that, while it cannot be said that Luke's emphasis on forgiveness is unique when compared with the other Synoptic Gospels, it is nonetheless clear that Jesus' declaration of forgiveness is understood by Luke to be a central aspect of his ministry.

For example, Luke's account of Jesus' teaching in the synagogue at Nazareth, which sets the tone for Jesus' ministry in Luke's carefully structured narrative, includes two occurrences of the term *aphesis* (both in 4:18), which are understood in the sense of freedom or release. While there seem to be clear echoes of the exodus and the jubilee in this passage, I. H. Marshall suggests that the reader may be expected to detect a reference to forgiveness of sins here.[60] This is particularly likely as the term has already been used in the stock phrase 'forgiveness of sins' in 1:77. Further, in the account of the healing of the paralytic (Luke 5:17–26, which is common to all three Synoptics and which appears early in the narratives of Mark and Luke), Jesus' statement of forgiveness is the contentious act that leads to the dramatic tension between the

---

57. Fitzmyer, *Luke I–IX*, p. 223.

58. I assume Markan priority and fairly loose definitions of Q, M and L (including the possibility that they represent a combination of various written and/or oral sources) in my allocation of material.

59. Cf. several references in Acts: 2:38; 5:31; 8:22; 13:38; 26:18.

60. Marshall, *Luke*, pp. 182–184.

religious leaders and Jesus. Luke and Mark both include the longer explanation of the problem: 'who can forgive sins except God alone?' That is to say, the availability of forgiveness is not in question; what is controversial is Jesus' claim that he has authority to forgive. In fact, the repetition of the various phrases that express forgiveness of sins (20, 21, 23, 24) heightens the reader's awareness of the centrality of this issue in coming to terms with who Jesus is.

Another passage that emphasizes forgiveness, this time unique to Luke, is the account of the unnamed woman who anoints Jesus' feet with ointment and the following dialogue with Simon the Pharisee (Luke 7:36–50). Here, again, forgiveness dominates the passage. Jesus tells a parabolic story in which forgiveness is described as the cancellation of financial debt (thus drawing on a notable strain of OT usage). Then in verse 47 Jesus declares that the woman's love reveals the extent of her experience of forgiveness. This need not have been controversial, as we have just noticed, but then Jesus proceeds to make a direct proclamation of forgiveness that draws a response from those who hear similar to that of the Jewish authorities who watch Jesus' encounter with the paralytic.

Also relevant is the series of parables in Luke 15 that emphasize 'lostness' and 'foundness'. Although the language of forgiveness is not employed in this passage, scholars are agreed that the wider context of acceptance of sinners who repent (15:2, 7, 10) suggest that the Father's acceptance of his wandering son, without condemnation for the catalogue of sinful acts of which his elder brother, at least, is all too well aware, is an image of forgiveness.[61] V. Taylor suggests that 'here we have a warmer conception of forgiveness than anywhere else in the New Testament, and one which merges into a picture of reconciliation, but the essential characteristics of forgiveness are here plainly present'.[62]

Similarly, Scobie notes that 'Luke shows a special interest in the themes of repentance, forgiveness and conversion, nowhere more so than in Luke 15'.[63] This collection of parables is surely a

---

61. Ibid.: 'the theme is the pardoning love of God for the sinner' (p. 139).
62. V. Taylor, *Forgiveness and Reconciliation* (London: Macmillan, 1941), p. 22.
63. Scobie, *Ways*, p. 718.

particularly strong example of a text that deserves to be read along the lines of Moberly's approach. In fact, it might be suggested that it provides one of the most striking illustrations of what 'not remembering sins' might mean.

Likewise, the parable of the Pharisee and the tax collector (18:9–14) does not use the language of forgiveness; but the cry of a self-conscious sinner for atonement in the arena of God's provision for the sin of his people suggests that forgiveness is the appropriate conceptual background to this account. That the tax collector returns home 'justified' suggests that he received the forgiveness he sought.

N. T Wright on 'the forgiveness of sins'

In *Jesus and the Victory of* God Wright states boldly, 'Forgiveness of sins is another way of saying "return from exile".'[64] Wright's argument is that the prophets to whom we have made reference (Jeremiah, Ezekiel, Isaiah) 'saw Israel's exile precisely as a result of, or the punishment for, her sins'. Thus, return from exile indicates, according to Wright, that sins are no longer being punished. Drawing on Jeremiah 31:31–34 and particularly Jeremiah 33:4–11, he states the point again: 'Forgiveness, in other words, is not simply one miscellaneous blessing which will accompany covenant renewal. Since covenant renewal means the reversal of exile, and since exile was the punishment for sin, covenant renewal/return from exile *means* that Israel's sins have been forgiven – and vice versa.'[65]

This view is controversial and has received considerable attention. I want to look briefly at two passages that are unique to Luke and that raise questions concerning Wright's interpretation.

The first text is Luke 23:34. This is a remarkable (if admittedly textually disputed)[66] text in that it is a prayer of Jesus on behalf of

---

64. N. T. Wright, *Jesus and the Victory of God* (London: SPCK, 1996), p. 268.
65. Ibid., p. 269.
66. See the discussion in Metzger, *Textual Commentary*, p. 180.

those who crucified him: 'Father, forgive them (*aphes autois*), for
they do not know what they are doing.' To whom does 'them'
refer. According to Green, 'In this co-text, the "them" for whom
Jesus intercedes includes both Jews and Romans – that is, those
who have found concord in their opposition to Jesus.'[67] Brown
argues that the last-named antecedent for this pronoun is the
'chief priests and the rulers of the people' in 23:13. Yet, verse 32
clearly indicates that Jesus would die as one of a group of crim-
inals condemned by the Roman authority. Those who carry out
the orders of Pilate are most naturally Romans. It is also questionable whether Luke believes that the Jewish leaders are so lacking in
knowledge of what is taking place. Wright does not refer to this
text in his major book on Jesus. Perhaps he regarded the textual
foundation as too precarious. However, if the text reflects Jesus'
words, then he must at least include Romans as those who would
receive 'forgiveness of sins'. This prayer is clearly meaningless for
Roman soldiers according to Wright's very Jewish interpretation.

The second text is Luke 24:45–49. In this narrative, the risen
Jesus commissions his followers to take the message of repentance
with respect to forgiveness of sins to all the nations ('and to preach
in his name repentance with reference to forgiveness of sins (*eis
aphesin hamartiōn*) to all the nations, beginning from Jerusalem',
verse 47). As this message is specifically addressed to the nations,
which must include Gentiles, it is hard to see how it can bear the
significance of return from exile. Wright does in fact recognize this
difficulty, as he explains in a footnote: 'Of course, once the gospel
goes out to the gentile world the specifically Jewish context and
echoes become progressively fainter; but, here as elsewhere, we
must take it that "restoration eschatology" was the original matrix
of the idea, and that a detached, dehistoricized or privatized application came later.'[68] In fact, this text appears to reflect the kind of
New Covenant theology we have been considering. We might note
in passing that Jesus' instructions are derived from the Scriptures,

---

67. Green, *Gospel of Luke*, p. 820. So R. E. Brown, *The Death of the Messiah*
    (New York: Doubleday, 1994), vol. 2, p. 973.
68. Wright, *Jesus*, p. 273 n. 121.

although no specific text is cited. The message is centred on forgiveness and it is to be proclaimed to all nations, suggesting a gathering of a single, multi-ethnic 'people of God'.

Conclusion

The absence of direct quotations of Jeremiah 31:31–34 from Luke's Gospel does not require that we conclude that there is an absence of New Covenant theology. The one reasonably clear allusion to Jeremiah's prophecy which is found in Luke 22:20 suggests that Luke may have been more influenced by this strand of theology than first appearances suggest. The prophecy of Zechariah demonstrates a concern on Luke's part to incorporate material into his Gospel that signals a new era in God's dealings with his people. While N. T. Wright has proposed an interesting interpretation of 'forgiveness of sins' where it means 'return from exile', at least two passages in Luke's Gospel call this view into question. What is in fact offered, particularly in the closing words of Luke's Gospel, is release from personal guilt for people of every ethnic group who find in Jesus the fullest expression of covenant faithfulness on the part of the covenant God.

© Alistair I. Wilson, 2005

7. IN DEFENCE OF 'HEADSHIP THEOLOGY'

A. T. B. McGowan

Introduction

The remit I received for this chapter was to present a defence of federal (or covenant) theology. It is my intention to do so but with one qualification. Federal theology is not a monolithic scheme of thinking that, having appeared in the Reformation and post-Reformation periods, has since remained unchanged. Indeed, it has taken different forms over the centuries and there have been many internal disagreements. In this chapter, then, I do not feel any obligation to defend *every* historical occurrence of federal theology but rather to argue that there is a form of federal theology that, in my view, arises naturally out of a study of Scripture and that is able to draw together, in a coherent and systematic way, the main themes of Scripture.

In this chapter I hope to demonstrate that federal theology has been and can be expressed in different ways, depending upon the use made of the law–grace dichotomy. I will demonstrate this by focusing on two significant Scottish theologians, who each taught a federal theology that can be characterized as a theology of grace;

namely, Thomas Boston and John Murray. In doing so, I will highlight the fact that federal theology in the eighteenth century largely
divided into two camps: one that emphasized *grace* and one that
emphasized *law*. I will then demonstrate that a further debate over
the place given to law and grace caused a rift within twentieth-
century theology, centred on Westminster Theological Seminary. It
will be my contention that John Murray's reconstruction of the
notion of a covenant of works into what he called the 'Adamic
Administration' went part of the way to dealing with an incipient
problem within federal theology but that a further step has to be
taken, namely, speaking about a 'Messianic Administration', thus
turning aside from overemphasis on the covenants and refocusing
attention upon Adam and Christ as the two 'heads' of administration. This then leaves us free to see the covenant of grace as an
overarching theme, rather than as a counterpoint to a covenant of
works. Thus, I intend to chart a way forward for federal theology
that I shall rename 'headship theology'.[1]

Historical overview

Federal theology can be defined as that system of theology in
which the relationship between God and humanity is described in
covenantal terms, particularly the covenants of works and grace,
with some scholars adding a covenant of redemption. Alternatively,
it may be defined as that system of theology that centres on the parallel between Adam and Christ as representative heads of humanity.
   Federal theology teaches that God entered into a relationship
with Adam in Genesis 2:16, 17, whereby Adam was prohibited
from eating of the tree of the knowledge of good and evil. It is
taken that, if Adam had succeeded in obeying God during this
period of probation and had not eaten from the forbidden tree, he

---

1. I offer this argument tentatively and would value responses. It is my intention to work on a book on covenant theology, with a friend who is a
   biblical scholar, in the near future. Any help in identifying weaknesses in
   the argument would be much appreciated.

would have been granted eternal life. This would have involved the permanent conferral of existing blessings. It is further taught by federal theology that when God entered into that relationship with Adam he did not do so with Adam as a private individual but as representative of the human race, such that when Adam disobeyed God the judgment fell not only upon him as an individual but upon all humanity yet unborn (except Christ who was born of a virgin) whom Adam represented. Similarly, if Adam had obeyed God, then the permanent conferral of blessing would also have come to the entire human race. Federal theologians normally call this relationship between God and humanity the 'covenant of works'.

This notion of Adam as representative head is taken from Romans 5:12–21 and 1 Corinthians 15:21, 22 and 15:44b–49. The parallel in these verses is then carried forward such that Christ is conceived as the representative head of a new covenant, normally called the 'covenant of grace'. It is argued that Christ came as the second (or last) Adam and succeeded where Adam failed, and obeyed where Adam disobeyed, thus bringing salvation to all those whom he represented; namely, God's elect.

The whole federal scheme is normally set in the context of post-Reformation Calvinistic theology. Thus it is argued that God from all eternity elected a people for himself. When humanity fell through Adam's sin, God did not abandon the human race but, out of his love and mercy, sent his Son to be the last Adam. Christ died to pay the penalty for the sins of God's elect people, bearing the wrath of God in their place, having qualified himself for this position by his incarnation and by his obedience. The Holy Spirit then applies the work of Christ to the elect by effectual calling, regeneration, justification, sanctification and the other aspects of salvation, which are summed up in the doctrines that make up the *ordo salutis* (order of salvation).

This covenant theology seeks to be an an all-embracing system of thought, based on Scripture, and encompassing the whole scope of biblical teaching. For example, the sacraments are viewed as signs and seals of the covenant of grace.

The scholarly debate concerning the historical development of federal theology has largely taken place since 1979. In the course of this debate, several volumes have sought, among other things, to chart the history of federal theology.[2] Although these volumes represent different theological perspectives, both for and against federal theology, there is now growing agreement on the main line of development.

Federal theology arose within the Calvinistic strand of the Reformation, although there is disagreement among scholars as to Calvin's own position. Some have argued that there is a radical discontinuity between Calvin and the later federal theology,[3] whereas others argue that Calvin was the originator of federal theology.[4] Many who would hesitate to take this latter position would nonetheless argue that federal theology is a natural and legitimate development from Calvin's own thought.[5] It is certainly clear that

---

2. R. T. Kendall, *Calvin and English Calvinism to 1649* (Oxford: Oxford University Press, 1979). This was later republished with an additional preface and two appendices, although the body of the text and, indeed, the pagination, remained unchanged (Carlisle: Paternoster, 1997); D. A. Weir, *The Origins of the Federal Theology in Sixteenth-Century Reformation Thought* (Oxford: Clarendon, 1990); Charles S. McCoy and J. Wayne Baker, *Fountainhead of Federalism: Heinrich Bullinger and the Covenantal Tradition* (Louisville: Westminster/John Knox, 1991); David N. J. Poole, *Stages of Religious Faith in the Classical Reformation Tradition: The Covenant Approach to the Ordo Salutis* (Lampeter: Edwin Mellen, 1995).

3. Basil Hall, 'Calvin against the Calvinists', in G. E. Duffield (ed.), *John Calvin* (Grand Rapids: Eerdmans, 1966), pp. 18–37; Holmes Rolston III, 'Responsible Man in Reformed Theology: Calvin versus the Westminster Confession', *SJT* 23 (1970), pp. 129–156; *John Calvin versus the Westminster Confession* (Richmond: John Knox Press, 1972); M. C. Bell, 'Calvin and the Extent of the Atonement', *EvQ* 55 (1983), pp. 115–123; *Calvin and Scottish Theology: The Doctrine of Assurance* (Edinburgh: Handsel, 1985).

4. Peter A. Lillback, *The Binding of God: Calvin's Role in the Development of Covenant Theology* (Grand Rapids: Baker, 2001). Weir does admit one possible reference by Calvin to a prelapsarian covenant: *Federal Theology*, p. 10.

5. Paul Helm, *Calvin and the Calvinists* (Edinburgh: Banner of Truth, 1982); 'Calvin and the Covenant: Unity and Discontinuity', *EvQ* 55 (1983), pp. 65–81; Richard A. Muller, *Christ and the Decree* (Durham, NC: Labyrinth, 1986); 'Calvin and the "Calvinists": Assessing Continuities and

the covenant was very important in Calvin's theology.[6] The debate that took place between these three interpretations, together with those that do not fit neatly into any of these three categories,[7] has been called the 'Calvin versus Calvinism' debate.

Federal theology, as a two-covenant system, began with Zacharias Ursinus, Caspar Olevianus and their colleagues in Heidelberg, between 1560 and 1590.[8] There is no unanimous agreement as to the precise origins of the expression *foedus operum* (covenant of works), although Weir's argument that a prelapsarian covenant was first introduced into Reformed theology in 1562 by Ursinus and that Dudley Fenner, in 1565, first called it the *foedus operum*, is very persuasive.[9] This is supported by David Poole:

> The centre of covenant thought in the years immediately following 1562 was Heidelberg, the key figures being Ursinus and Olevianus. After that city's return to Lutheranism in 1576, continental covenant theology came to pivot on Herborn. The seeds of the notion of a first covenant preceding that of grace, had already been sown on the Continent, but it was Dudley Fenner who first introduced the *foedus operum* in his *Sacra Theologia* (Geneva 1585).[10]

Federal theology quickly took root and grew after this point. Its spread and development were helped by the fact that it received confessional status, in a very preliminary form, in the *Irish Articles* of 1615 and then more fully in the *Westminster Confession of Faith* of 1646.

Discontinuities between the Reformation and Orthodoxy', *CTJ* 30 (1995), pp. 345–375; *CTJ* 31 (1996), pp. 125–160; also a number of the essays in Carl R. Trueman and R. S. Clark (eds.), *Protestant Scholasticism: Essays in Reassessment* (Carlisle: Paternoster, 1999).

6. See *Institutes* 2.10 and 2.11.

7. A. N. S. Lane, 'The Quest for the Historical Calvin', *EvQ* 55 (1983), pp. 95–113.

8. Weir, *Federal Theology*, p. 115.

9. Ibid., pp. 99–114, 133–152.

10. *Stages of Religious Faith*, p. 162.

Since in this chapter I am focusing particularly on two Scottish theologians, it is useful to note that Scotland ultimately became a major centre for the development and promotion of federal theology, not least because the theological system became closely allied to political developments, which were also couched in covenantal language.[11] Federal theology had been introduced to Scotland by Robert Rollock at the end of the sixteenth century,[12] and by the seventeenth century it was the standard form of Reformed theology in Scotland, mainly because the Church of Scotland adopted the *Westminster Confession of Faith* in 1647 as its 'Principal Subordinate Standard'. There was never the same near universal commitment to federal theology in England, although men like William Perkins, William Ames and other Puritan scholars did have significant influence. On the continent the federal theology was strongest in Holland.

Law and grace: eighteenth-century debate

As the federal theology developed through the seventeenth century, tensions began to develop between those whose emphasis was on law and those whose emphasis was on grace. In Scotland this came to a head in the Marrow Controversy at the beginning of the eighteenth century.[13] The two positions that collided in this dispute may be represented by considering two of the leading protagonists, Principal James Hadow of St Andrews University and the Revd Thomas Boston, Church of Scotland minister in Ettrick. Hadow took the view that the gospel should be offered only to those who

---

11. For example, the political events surrounding the signing of the National Covenant (1638) and the Solemn League and Covenant (1643).

12. *Tractatus De Vocatione Efficaci* (1597). For English translation, see W. M. Gunn (ed.), *Select Works of Robert Rollock* (Wodrow Society, 1849), pp. 1–288.

13. For details of the controversy, see Donald Beaton, 'The "Marrow of Modern Divinity" and the Marrow Controversy', *Records of the Scottish Church History Society (c. 1925)*, vol. 1, pt 3, pp. 112–134; David Lachman, *The Marrow Controversy* (Edinburgh: Rutherford House, 1988).

were already showing 'signs of election' and that a universal offer of
the gospel was impossible because it would require a universal
atonement as its basis. He further insisted that repentance was a
condition of salvation. Boston resisted this by insisting that the
gospel must be preached 'to every creature without exception' and
that repentance flowed from regeneration and justification as a
result, rather than going before them as a *cause*. Both men held to
the *Westminster Confession of Faith* as their Principal Subordinate
Standard and both held firmly to a Calvinistic soteriology, stem-
ming from the Synod of Dordrecht (1618–19).

Clearly there were two schools within federal theology, both
claiming allegiance to the *Confession* and both claiming to be true to
the Calvinistic tradition. One of the key issues in this dispute concerns the relationship between law and grace. Hadow and his
associates accused the Marrowmen[14] of being antinomian, but it
can be demonstrated that, whereas Hadow was clearly neonomian,
Boston and his associates were not antinomian but rather anti-
neonomian.[15] These two schools persisted (and persist) within
federal theology.

The difference between these schools of thought within federal
theology, however, has often not been recognized, particularly
regarding their views on law and grace. For example, J. B. Torrance,
that single-minded enemy of federal theology, offered many criticisms of the system, not least that it involved giving priority to law
over grace.[16] Many of these criticisms are legitimate in respect of

---

14. As Thomas Boston and his associates were called during the Marrow
    Controversy.

15. See A. T. B. McGowan, *The Federal Theology of Thomas Boston* (Carlisle:
    Paternoster, 1997), pp. 156–159.

16. For a selection of his criticisms, see J. B. Torrance, 'The Incarnation and
    Limited Atonement', *EvQ* 55 (1983), pp. 83–94; 'The Covenant Concept
    in Scottish Theology and Politics and its Legacy', *SJT* 34 (1981), pp.
    225–243; 'Strengths and Weaknesses of the Westminster Theology', in A.
    I. Heron (ed.), *The Westminster Confession in the Church Today* (Edinburgh: St.
    Andrew Press, 1982), pp. 40–54; 'The Contribution of McLeod Campbell
    to Scottish Theology' *SJT* 26 (1973), pp. 295–311.

the Hadow school but are definitely *not* legitimate in respect of federal theology per se. Torrance argues that federal theology is based 'on contract law rather than on the grace and love of God',[17] but his blunderbuss approach to federal theology in all its forms conveniently ignores much of the evidence. For example, Thomas Boston's federal theology is clearly a theology of grace, in which he teaches that even the establishment of the covenant of works was the action of a gracious God in granting to his creatures undeserved favour. Torrance finds himself in the curious (and misguided) position of warmly agreeing with Boston's theology but having to argue that he is trapped in a federal system in which his marvellous insights do not appear in their best light![18]

This chapter argues in favour of the tradition represented by Thomas Boston, in which federal theology is to be viewed as a theology of grace, as over against those who emphasize law and conditionality.

Law and grace: twentieth-century debate

The variegated nature of federal theology was not solely an eighteenth-century phenomenon, however. In the twentieth century there was another dispute within federal theology, which again centred on issues of law and grace.

In the middle of the twentieth century no-one espoused the gracious federal theology of Thomas Boston more clearly than the late Professor John Murray of Westminster Theological Seminary. He was opposed, however, by his pupil (and later, his colleague),

---

17. See the short pamphlet by J. B. Torrance, *A Critique of Federal Theology in the Light of the Gospel: Was John Calvin a 'Federal' Theologian?* (Victoria: Burning Bush Society of Victoria, 1997), p. i.
18. In private conversation with the author during doctoral supervision. The same view was taken by Donald J. Bruggink, 'The Theology of Thomas Boston 1676–1732' (PhD thesis, University of Edinburgh, 1956); cf. also Bell, *Calvin and Scottish Theology*, p. 161; and T. F. Torrance, *Scottish Theology* (Edinburgh: T. & T. Clark, 1996), pp. 204–220.

Meredith Kline, who wanted to emphasize the starkness of the contrast between law and grace.[19] This debate has rumbled on below the surface since Murray died but has come to a head more recently with one of Kline's disciples, Mark Karlberg, claiming that Westminster Theological Seminary, in following Murray, Norman Shepherd and Richard Gaffin, has abandoned the legacy of Calvinistic theology and has become Barthian![20]

It is my intention to summarize and assess the views of these two schools within Westminster. I do this not simply to provide an assessment of a fascinating debate but rather to demonstrate that the issues between these two schools of thought within federal theology (those who emphasize law and those who emphasize grace) are at their clearest and sharpest in this encounter.

The key issue separating Murray and Kline is the issue of law and grace. Kline insists that a covenant of works was established by God with Adam and that this covenant was a legal covenant. Had Adam obeyed God perfectly during his probationary period, then he would have merited eternal life. This would not have involved grace at any point, merely obedience to the law, which was written on his heart. Prior to the fall, human beings were related to God by law, only afterwards was a relationship of grace necessary. On this view, we may only speak of grace after the fall and never before. Kline goes further and, following the English Puritan John Owen, views the law given at Sinai as a republication of the covenant of works, such that there is a radical discontinuity between the Abrahamic covenant and the Sinaitic covenant. Kline insists that the radical dichotomy between a covenant of works and a covenant of grace, undergirded by the radical dichotomy

---

19. For a useful summary of the debate (if somewhat biased towards Kline's position), see Jeong Koo Jeon, *Covenant Theology: John Murray's and Meredith Kline's Response to the Historical Development of Federal Theology in Reformed Thought* (Lanham, MD: University Press of America, 1999).

20. Mark W. Karlberg, *The Changing of the Guard: Westminster Theological Seminary in Philadelphia* (Unicoi, TN: Trinity Foundation, 2001). For a published collection of his writings on this same general theme, see Mark W. Karlberg, *Covenant Theology in Reformed Perspective* (Eugene, OR: Wipf & Stock, 2000).

between law and grace, is vital, not least in maintaining the doctrine of justification by faith.

One of the key points in Kline's position is that the biblical covenants between God and humanity are bilateral, conditional law-covenants. He writes:

> Historical priority belongs incontestably to law covenant since pre-redemptive covenant administration was of course strictly law administration without the element of guaranteed, inevitable blessings. By the same token promise covenant is disqualified from the outset as a systematic definition of covenant because it is obviously not comprehensive enough to embrace the pre-redemptive covenantal revelation. It remains, however, to show that law constitutes the ground structure of redemptive covenant administration and thus that a definition of covenant as generically law covenant would be applicable over the whole range of history as is necessary in a systematic theology of the covenant.[21]

This was what he proceeded to do in the remainder of the book.

John Murray, on the other hand, argues that it is inappropriate to use the term 'covenant of works' in respect of the relationship established by God in Genesis 2. He writes:

> There are two observations. (1) The term is not felicitous, for the reason that the elements of grace entering into the administration are not properly provided for by the term 'works'. (2) It is not designated a covenant in Scripture. Hosea 6:7 may be interpreted otherwise and does not provide the basis for such a reconstruction of the Adamic economy. Besides, Scripture always uses the term covenant, when applied to God's administration to men, in reference to a provision that is redemptive or closely related to redemptive design. Covenant in Scripture denotes the oath-bound confirmation of promise and involves a security which the Adamic economy did not bestow.[22]

---

21. Meredith G. Kline, *By Oath Consigned* (Grand Rapids: Eermans, 1968), pp. 29–30.

22. 'The Adamic Administration', in John Murray, *Collected Writings of John Murray* (Edinburgh: Banner of Truth, 1977), vol. 2, p. 49.

Rather, Murray refers to this relationship as the 'Adamic Administration'. This retains the relationship of solidarity between Adam and the human race but without positing a covenant as the necessary underpinning of this relationship. Murray also insists that the very establishment of this Adamic Administration was a gracious act of a sovereign God. God was under no obligation to do more for his creatures than he had already done. To offer the possibility of eternal life was an act of grace. Therefore, it is possible to speak of grace prior to the fall. In addition, following Galatians 3, Murray sees continuity between the covenant established with Abraham and the law given on Sinai, 450 years later. Sinai was not a republication of the covenant of works but rather a spelling out of the obligations of the covenant of grace. Murray writes:

> The view that in the Mosaic covenant there was a repetition of the so-called covenant of works, is a grave misconception and involves an erroneous construction of the Mosaic covenant, as well as fails to assess the uniqueness of the Adamic Administration. The Mosaic covenant was distinctly redemptive in character and was continuous with and extensive of the Abrahamic covenants. The Adamic had no redemptive provision, nor did its promissory element have any relevance within a context that made redemption necessary.[23]

Murray continues to affirm the parallel between Adam and Christ, between the Adamic Administration and the covenant of grace. In contrast to Kline, however, he emphasizes that all covenants between God and human beings are unilateral and are concerned with the administration of grace. He writes:

> From the beginning of God's disclosures to men in terms of covenant we find a unity of conception which is to the effect that a divine covenant is a sovereign administration of grace and of promise. It is not compact or contract or agreement that provides the constitutive or governing idea but that of dispensation in the sense of disposition. This central and basic concept is applied, however, to a variety of situations

---

23. Ibid., p. 50.

and the precise character of the grace bestowed and of the promise given differs in the differing covenant administrations. The differentiation does not reside in any deviation from this basic conception but simply consists in the differing degrees of richness and fullness of the grace bestowed and of the promise given.[24]

Headship theology

It seems to me that Murray greatly advanced the cause of Reformed theology by indicating that a relationship of solidarity between God and Adam could be established without the requirement of calling it a covenant. Further, he rightly noted that grace has priority over law in God's relationship with Adam. His assertion of continuity between the Abrahamic and Sinaitic covenants is also important; namely, that the Sinaitic covenant does not annul or cancel the earlier covenant but is rather a spelling out of the obligations of the covenant of grace.

There remain, however, two possible developments that arise naturally from the refinements to federal theology which Murray has already proposed. First, given the vital parallel between Adam and Christ in Romans 5 and 1 Corinthians 15, we might usefully go on to speak about a 'Messianic Administration' as the natural con-comitant of Murray's 'Adamic Administration'. Second, given Murray's rejection of the idea that law comes before grace, we might usefully revisit the notion that Adam had the law written on his heart.

It is my contention that by dealing with these two issues, there emerges the possibility of developing Reformed theology in the direction of what we might call 'headship theology', instead of federal, or covenant theology. I also believe that a strong argument can be made for the position that prior to the fall it is impossible to speak of *law*, in stark contrast to Kline's view that prior to the fall it is impossible to speak of *grace*. Some have taken the view that this

---

24. John Murray, *The Covenant of Grace: A Biblico-Theological Study* (London: Tyndale Press, 1954), pp. 30–31.

abandonment of the radical dichotomy between law and grace has implications for the doctrine of justification.[25] Let us then address these two issues: the Adam–Christ parallel in respect of two 'administrations of grace', and the issue of law prior to the fall.

The Adamic and Messianic Administrations

One of the problems in maintaining the federal theology concerns the covenants. As spelled out in the *Westminster Confession of Faith*, for example, there are two covenants, the covenant of works and the covenant of grace, sometimes referred to by theologians as the 'old covenant' and the 'new covenant'. Unfortunately, when Scripture speaks of the 'old covenant' it is not referring to a covenant of works as established in Genesis 2 but to the covenant established on Sinai. In order to take account of this problem, federal theologians were forced to the position that the covenant at Sinai was really the republication of the covenant of works and hence references to the 'old covenant' could be read as referring to the covenant of works. This, however, is deeply unsatisfactory from an exegetical perspective.

When we step back and ask what it is about the covenant of works and covenant of grace that was so central to Reformed theology as it developed in the late sixteenth century, we have to conclude that it is the parallel between Adam and Christ as recorded in Romans 5 and 1 Corinthians 15. The vital element of federal theology is that all human beings are either 'in Adam' or 'in Christ' and that death or salvation come by means of our relationship with one or other of these 'representative heads'. That is to say, the headship of Adam involves the imputation of sin and the headship of Christ involves the imputation of righteousness. It is, however, perfectly possible to maintain this relation of headship without positing covenants as the basis for the relationship.

---

25. I explored some of these implications in a paper to the Edinburgh Dogmatics Conference in August 2003. Jeon says, 'we cannot discuss the imputed righteousness of Christ in justification without the theological framework provided by the antithesis between Law and Gospel' (*Covenant Theology*, p. 21).

Murray partially accomplished this by speaking of the Adamic Administration instead of the covenant of works, thus freeing that relationship between God and humanity from the strictures of being called 'a covenant'. Why, then, can we not go further and speak of a 'Messianic Administration' where the emphasis is on union with Christ rather than upon the covenant of grace? By this means we can place the emphasis of Romans 5 and 1 Corinthians 15 where it belongs; namely, on headship solidarity. Either we are 'in Adam' as a result of that solidarity created by the establishment of the Adamic Administration in Genesis 2, or we are 'in Christ' as the result of a spiritual union with Christ.

Law prior to the fall?

The other key issue in charting a way forward for headship theology lies in the question of whether or not, prior to the fall, Adam was under law. There is a cluster of issues surrounding this problem. For example, if Adam had obeyed God perfectly during his probationary period, would his obedience have been meritorious and eternal life the just deserts of obedience rather than a gracious gift of God?[26] Or again, if Adam was under law, are all human beings related to God by law and only the elect related to God by grace?

If it is possible to demonstrate from Scripture that Adam did not have the law written on his heart (law conceived of here as a pre-publication of the law of Sinai), then a major hurdle to the development of a gracious headship theology will have been removed. One way forward would be to examine the work of a significant Scottish theologian, George Smeaton, who argued that Adam, prior to the fall, was indwelt by the Holy Spirit.[27]

---

26. See David B. McWilliams, 'The Covenant Theology of the *Westminster Confession of Faith* and Recent Criticism', *WTJ* 53 (1991), pp. 109–124.

27. See George Smeaton, *The Doctrine of the Holy Spirit* (Edinburgh: Banner of Truth, 1974), p. 178. For a useful analysis of this issue, see Robert Shillaker, 'The Federal Pneumatology of George Smeaton (1814–89)' (PhD thesis: Open University/UHI Millennium Institute, 2002).

Two preliminary points ought to be made here:

1. Man's problem is sin, not finitude. Pre-fall Adam did not require a Mediator.[28]
2. The relationship into which God entered with Adam offered the permanent conferral of blessings already enjoyed.[29]

One key to understanding the place of law prior to the fall is to ask what is meant by the biblical teaching that, post-fall, human beings became like God, knowing good and evil? Part of the serpent's temptation of Eve was to suggest that by eating of the forbidden tree she would become like God, knowing good and evil (Genesis 3:5). After the fall, in Genesis 3:22, we are told, 'The man has now become like one of us, knowing good and evil.' In one sense, then, what the serpent said has come true. But what does it mean? What is this knowledge of good and evil? How can our first parents be more like God after the fall than they were before?

There are several things that it cannot mean. It cannot mean that our first parents were morally or spiritually more like God after the fall, since they were now sinners. It cannot mean that they were more like God through an experimental knowledge of sin, because God does not know sin in that way. It cannot be that they had more real, God-given knowledge than they had before, because the knowledge of good and evil led to judgment and banishment.

One way of understanding Genesis 3:22 is to think about the sinful human desire for autonomy. With this focus, it could mean that our first parents became like God in the sense of making decisions about good and evil, in other words, deciding for themselves what was good and evil. This is the sin of fallen human beings, for only God can establish what is good and evil. When human beings try to do this they are trying to take the place of God. When governments do this they have abandoned God's Word. This analysis could provide us with a possible answer to the problem of law in relation to the post-fall situation.

---

28. For a contrary view, see McWilliams, 'Covenant Theology', p. 110.
29. See Murray, *Collected Writings*, vol. 2, pp. 47–50.

Dietrich Bonhoeffer may be regarded by some as an unlikely character to come to the assistance of federal theology, but I would like to argue that, in his *Ethics*,[30] he does just that. Bonhoeffer turns to the subject of the knowledge of good and evil at the very beginning of the book, when he offers a radical critique of all ethical systems. On a personal note I would say that, when I came to study this book, it transformed my thinking by helping me to see something I had not understood properly before. The first paragraph of the book caught my attention:

> The knowledge of good and evil seems to be the aim of all ethical reflection. The first task of Christian ethics is to invalidate this knowledge. In launching this attack on the underlying assumptions of all other ethics, Christian ethics stands so completely alone that it becomes questionable whether there is any purpose in speaking of Christian ethics at all. But if one does so notwithstanding, that can only mean that Christian ethics claims to discuss the origin of the whole problem of ethics, and thus professes to be a critique of all ethics simply as ethics.[31]

At first I could not see the point Bonhoeffer was making. In what sense is there a connection between the 'knowledge of good and evil' and Christian ethics? And how could this connection lead to the conclusion that Christian ethics 'professes to be a critique of all ethics simply as ethics'? As I read on, however, I began to see the significance of this line of argument. Bonhoeffer writes:

> Man at his origin knows only one thing: God. It is only in the unity of his knowledge of God that he knows of other men, of things, and of himself. He knows all things only in God, and God in all things. The knowledge of good and evil shows that he is no longer at one with this origin.[32]

In my exposition of federal theology I had always maintained that Adam's decision to take the forbidden fruit was an act

---

30. D. Bonhoeffer, *Ethics* (ed. E. Bethge; London: SCM, 1978).

31. Ibid., p. 3.

32. Ibid.

of self-declared autonomy, in which he (and all of us 'in him' since he was our federal head) became 'self-centred' instead of 'God-centred', but I had not seen before the significance of the 'knowledge of good and evil'. Then I recalled a systematic theology class in which I was explaining Adam's sin. I had said that Adam was (until Christ came as the last Adam) the only perfect man, and that he stood in complete equilibrium, able to choose good or evil without a sinful nature to produce a bias upon his will. One student asked how Adam knew what was good and evil. I gave the traditional answer about the law being written upon his heart. In other words, he knew 'by nature' what was good and what was evil. As I read Bonhoeffer, however, I realized that a proper exposition of Genesis 3 requires us to say that the knowledge of good and evil was not the possession of Adam before the fall 'by nature', but was the possession of Adam only after the fall. Indeed, it was his position as a direct result of that fall. Yet surely Adam did know what he ought to do and how he ought to live? Bonhoeffer explains that man has exchanged the knowledge of God, for the knowledge of good and evil. He writes:

> In the knowledge of good and evil man does not understand himself in the reality of the destiny appointed in his origin, but rather in his own possibilities, his possibility of being good or evil. He knows himself now as something apart from God, outside God, and this means that he now knows only himself and no longer knows God at all; for he can know God only if he knows only God. The knowledge of good and evil is therefore separation from God. Only against God can man know good and evil.[33]

This does not mean that Adam received any 'facts' that were not in his possession before; rather, it means, as Bonhoeffer points out, that his understanding of those facts changed dramatically:

> Man now knows good and evil. This does not mean that he has acquired new knowledge in addition to what he knew before, but the knowledge

---

33. Ibid., pp. 3–4.

of good and evil signifies the complete reversal of man's knowledge, which hitherto had been solely knowledge of God as his origin. In knowing good and evil he knows what the origin, God himself, can know and ought to know.[34]

From Van Til I had learned about the noetic effects of sin. Fallen man is unable to understand anything fully and properly because, without a God-centred worldview, nothing makes sense. Man may think that he possesses 'facts' and that one day he will be able to piece them all together and make sense of everything, but in fact there are no such things as 'brute facts', only 'God-interpreted facts'. That is to say, only when we think in a God-centred way do we understand how the various facets of our language fit together. We must think 'out of a centre in God'.[35]

Here in Bonhoeffer, however, we have an insight that enables us to expand upon this general theme. Fallen man, in his desire for autonomy, deliberately suppresses the knowledge of God, which is the possession of every human being (Romans 1). In this self-centred autonomous, knowledge-suppressing condition, man believes himself able to weigh up alternatives and make moral choices. In fact, this is impossible. Man can never be the arbiter of truth, and hence the moral and ethical decisions he makes are simply a sinful human substitute for the will of God. This means that even the 'best' decisions man makes and even his 'best' actions are as 'filthy rags' before God – not because they are inadequate or sinful per se but because they are the result of fallen man using his 'knowledge of good and evil' as a criterion for decision-making rather that the will of God. As Bonhoeffer says, 'Man knows good and evil, but because he is not the origin, because he acquires this knowledge only at the price of estrangement from the origin, the good and evil that he knows are not the good and evil of God but good and evil against God.'[36] The conclusion

---

34. Ibid., p. 4.

35. See the argument as developed in Cornelius Van Til, *The Defense of the Faith* (Philadelphia: Presbyterian & Reformed, 1976), especially ch. 3.

36. Bonhoeffer, *Ethics*, p. 5.

follows naturally: 'Man's life is now disunion with God, with men, with things, and with himself.'[37]

Fallen human beings, however, do not accept this assessment of their condition. Instead, they brazenly assert self-centredness and pretended autonomy as a positive lifestyle: 'Knowing of good and evil in disunion with the origin, man begins to reflect upon himself. His life is now his understanding of himself, whereas at the origin it was his knowledge of God. Self-knowledge is now the measure and the goal of life.'[38]

Bonhoeffer illustrates his argument by giving the example of the Pharisees in the New Testament who were constantly trying to trap Jesus with their questions:

> The Pharisee is that extremely admirable man who subordinates his entire life to his knowledge of good and evil and is as severe a judge of himself as of his neighbour to the honour of God, whom he humbly thanks for this knowledge. For the Pharisee, every moment of life becomes a situation of conflict in which he has to choose between good and evil. For the sake of avoiding any lapse his entire thought is strenuously devoted night and day to the anticipation of the whole immense range of possible conflicts, to the reaching of a decision in these conflicts, and to the determination of his own choice.[39]

Bonhoeffer then describes the conflict between Jesus and the Pharisees, pointing out that time and again the Pharisees tried to force him to make choices or complained about the decisions he did make. Jesus meantime often seemed to be unaware of what was being asked, so different were his answers from the 'either–or' alternatives offered to him in their questions. It is at this point that Bonhoeffer speaks of true freedom:

> The freedom of Jesus is not the arbitrary choice of one amongst innumerable possibilities, it consists on the contrary precisely in the

---

37. Ibid.
38. Ibid., p. 10.
39. Ibid., p. 12.

complete simplicity of His action, which is never confronted by a plurality of possibilities, conflicts or alternatives, but always only by one thing. This one thing Jesus calls the will of God. He says that to do this will is His meat. The will of God is His life. He lives and acts not by the knowledge of good and evil but the by the will of God. There is only one will of God. In it the origin is recovered; in it there is established the freedom and the simplicity of all action.[40]

If we now go back to reconsider the situation of Adam in the Garden before the fall, we are enabled to see matters more clearly. Adam before the fall had true freedom. He did not, however, possess 'by nature' the law, the knowledge of good and evil. What Adam possessed 'by nature' was a knowledge of God and of the will of God. Consequently, the choice he made in relation to the forbidden fruit was not a choice between a good act and an evil act but the choice between obedience to the will of God or disobedience to that will. The root of the sin was a belief that human beings were capable of standing apart from God as autonomous beings able to decide what was good and what was evil.

From this perspective we can see why Bonhoeffer could say that Christian ethics 'professes to be a critique of all ethics simply as ethics'. To engage in a study of ethics from the 'knowledge of good and evil' perspective rather than from the 'will of God' perspective is simply to make the mistake of the well-intentioned Pharisee and to find ourselves in opposition to Jesus.

If we accept this analysis, then we must say that Adam was not under law and that law comes after the fall. This interpretation solves several problems:

1. It enables us to argue that Adam, like Christ, was wholly without sin and knew only the will of God. He was not under law but under grace.
2. The priority of grace over law in God's dealings with humanity is established.

---

40. Ibid., p. 15.

3. The argument that Adam, like Christ, was indwelt by the Holy Spirit makes much more sense in a context of grace than a context of law.

4. Sinai becomes not the republication of a legal covenant of works but a spelling out of the obligations of the covenant of grace, wherein the integrity of Paul's argument in Galatians 3 is maintained.

The covenant of grace

Given that there is an undoubted peculiarity in talking about 'federal' theology without focusing on covenants,[41] where lies the significance of the covenant of grace? The answer is that, by developing a headship theology where the contrast is between Adam and Christ (contrasted in Romans 5 and 1 Corinthians 15), rather than between the covenants of works and grace (nowhere contrasted in Scripture), we are then free to see the covenant of grace as Calvin did; namely, as the overarching structure of biblical revelation embracing the whole redemptive process. This retains the vital importance of the covenant of grace, while releasing it from being a mere counterpoint to a perceived covenant of works.

We must also be careful, however, to note that these administrations were, in certain important respects, quite different. Although Adam and Christ both stood before God as representative heads whose obedience or disobedience was determinative for those whom they represented, the Messianic Administration involved much more. That is to say, Christ not only had to offer full and perfect obedience to God; he also had to pay the penalty for the sins of those who will be in heaven. In other words, there was passive obedience as well as active obedience and the former was no part of Adam's situation.

----

41. Since the very word 'federal' comes from the Latin *foedus*, meaning 'covenant'.

Conclusion

In defending federal theology, then, I am being very specific. I am not defending the federal theology represented by Principal James Hadow's neonomianism, nor the federal theology represented by Kline's law–grace dichotomy. The federal theology I am defending is the federal theology of Thomas Boston, which is a theology of grace, as adapted and clarified by John Murray and as further refined into headship theology.

8. COVENANTS, SPECIAL RELATIONSHIPS AND A PERFECTLY LOVING GOD

Harry Bunting

Introduction

A conference whose theme is 'The Covenant in the Bible and Theology' might reasonably be expected to concern itself with issues that presuppose the integrity of the covenant concept and, in that spirit, to address historical, textual and theological aspects of their subject matter. However, at least at some point, the discussion should recognize that biblical covenant relations give rise to questions that not only do not presuppose but directly call into question the integrity of the biblical covenants, and the discussion might be expected to inquire as to how such critical questions can best be answered. It is with one aspect of this task that I shall be chiefly concerned in the present chapter.

The chapter examines, most generally, whether perfect moral goodness is consistent with particular and partial affections; especially, whether or not a perfectly loving being can enter into preferential relationships with certain individuals or collectives at the expense of others. Two criticisms of covenant relations, one external to and one internal to the Hebraic-Christian tradition, will be examined. The examination will explore the extent to which recent philosophical discussions of concepts such as alienation, the personal, love and friendship can help to reconcile God's perfectly loving character with his very particular and partial covenant relationships with his chosen people, the Israelites, as portrayed in Scripture. I shall suggest that if these basic concepts are adequately understood, then the moral structure of covenant relations will become more clear, familiar objections to Old Testament ethics can be seen in a new light and supposed tensions between the ethics of the Old and New Testaments may perhaps be eased.

Covenant relationships

Our point of departure is the concept of a 'covenant' and with distinctions between some of the different kinds of covenant to be found in the Scriptures and in the history of theology. At the heart of the biblical concept of a covenant is the idea that there exists an agreement between God and certain individuals, such as Moses, or the whole of a chosen people, such as Israel. Although the Sinai covenant is at the spiritual heart of the Old Testament, nonetheless it is preceded by two other covenants, that with Noah (Genesis 9:8–17) and that with Abraham (Genesis 15 and 17); and, of course, the covenants of the Old Testament anticipate the new covenant, sealed by the blood of Christ, which is described as a 'better covenant' since it assures better promises (Hebrews 7:22; 8:6). The different covenants have various things in common: chiefly, as we have seen, they involve an agreement between God and various persons and collectives.

However, the different covenants do not have identical scope. The covenant with Noah, in which God pledged himself to continue life on earth, involved a unilateral commitment by God to all living things; and the new covenant relates to a kingdom whose membership is open to all, irrespective of race, gender or social status. By contrast the covenants with which I shall be concerned in this chapter are covenants that are in some sense limited as opposed to universal, in that they do not apply to the whole of the human race; and they are particular rather than general because they involve agreements between God and a specially chosen person or collective as opposed to a limited but otherwise undifferentiated group. Finally, they are bilateral rather than unilateral in that both parties to such agreements assume responsibilities and form the expectation of certain associated benefits.

The covenants with Abraham and at Sinai are perfect examples. The former guarantees to Abraham numerous offspring, beginning with the birth of Isaac (Genesis 17:19) and for their posterity promises the land of Canaan (Genesis 15:18). The condition for this is faith, and the covenant is preceded by a general commandment to walk before God and be blameless. The covenant on Sinai is similar in character. It involves God promising to give to the Israelites the land of Canaan, to confer various blessings on them, and to drive out the nations that would otherwise occupy the land. In return, Exodus 20:22–23:19 describes in great detail the social code of ordinances, the warnings and the exhortations associated with the covenant, together making up a document that is described in Exodus 24:7 as 'The Book of the Covenant'. Israel becomes God's partner, a people summoned to live in singleminded obedience to the claims of God, and great associated benefits are promised to Israel and to her leaders. Henceforth Israel's relationship to God is a special covenant relationship.

This chapter deals with covenants that are limited, particular and bilateral. Because these characteristics provoke much debate with regard to the appropriateness of covenants, they deserve our consideration.

Sceptical challenges, external and internal

The limited and particular nature of the covenant promises, the exclusive nature of the associated blessings and the dark and terrible punishments promised and carried out on those who were not included in the covenant relationship have invited the criticism and scorn of generations of critics. A concern with these aspects of Old Testament ethics was at the root of the second-century Marcion heresy, and they underlie two distinct lines of criticism of Old Testament covenants, one internal and the other external to the Judaeo-Christian tradition. The problem internal to the Christian faith concerns the consistency of these undoubtedly partial covenants with the perfectly loving nature of the God revealed in the New Testament; the problem external to the Christian faith questions the consistency of covenant partiality with the principles of fairness that are presupposed by any rational and objective morality.

One of the earliest recorded expressions of concern over the partiality of the Old Testament covenants is to be found in the work of Marcion,[1] and many later statements of these concerns are to some extent simply elaborations of themes that were developed by him.

Already by the first century AD the concept of a dual Godhead had developed within the broad Christian tradition, partly due to Gnostic influences. On the grounds that the just and righteous God of the Old Testament is other than and inferior to the God revealed in Christ, whose chief characteristic is loving-kindness, Marcion taught not only the existence of two 'Gods' but also the existence of two 'Christs'.

Marcion's main defence of his position is to be found in his book *The Antithesis*, where he systematically placed the statements of the Old Testament against the utterances of the New Testament, especially the sayings of Jesus and of Paul. The contrasts were final: they allowed for no higher synthesis. The two 'Gods' were distinct. However, Marcion also recognized two 'Christs', because he held that the Messianic prophecies were true and accurate prophecies, not to Jesus but to another Messiah.

Marcion's dualism was very influential, so much so that Tertullian found it necessary to devote five books to an attack on the position, and Irenaeus planned to publish a book refuting Marcionism but never carried out the project. On the positive side it should be noted that opposition to Marcionism was an important factor in the establishing of the distinctive Christian canon of Scripture, as it forced recognition of the existence of scriptures, true and false.

---

1. On the Marcionite heresy, see E. C. Blackman, *Marcion and his Influence* (London: Faber, 1948); H. Rashdall (ed.), *Principles and Precepts of Marcionism* (Oxford: Basil Blackwell, 1927); and Tertullian, *Adversus Marcionem* (ed. E. Evans; Oxford: Clarendon, 1972).

It is less important to trace in detail Marcion's arguments, the religion he built on the foundations provided by those arguments or the orthodox responses to them than it is to stress the character of Marcion's basic position. Marcion had identified a putative kernel of religious and moral truth in the New Testament and he believed that it was fundamentally inconsistent with the ethic of the Old Testament. This is a contrast many have felt even though they have refused to state it in bold terms or to draw Marcionite conclusions from it.

For example, Luther made an analogous distinction between *deus absconditus*, the God of law, justice and wrath, on the one hand, and *deus absolutus*, the God of love, grace, forgiveness and redemption, on the other hand. Luther never doubted that *deus absconditus* was one and the same God as was revealed in Jesus Christ. Yet his distinction showed an awareness of the tensions that gave rise to Marcionism, tensions recognized again and again in subsequent pietist and evangelical thought.

In the remainder of this chapter I shall draw a contrast between two forms that the basic line of sceptical argument can take and to explore possible apologetic responses to them. Hence I shall confront (1) an *internal* line of criticism, which argues that limited, bilateral and particular covenant relations of the Old Testament are at variance with the God of love revealed in the New Testament, and (2) an *external* line of criticism, which argues that covenant relations of the Old Testament are at variance with principles of rational, objective morality. I think that both of these worries are genuine worries that deserve to be sympathetically stated and answered if possible by the resources of moral theory and Christian apologetics. It is to this task that I now turn, commencing with the second line of argument, the externalist challenge.

The externalist challenge

What is the externalist and impartialist objection to covenant relations? To understand, we must take a short journey into modern ethical theory and note its impartialist tendencies.

Common to utilitarianism and rationalism was the contention that morality requires that the interests and well-being of all humans should be treated as being of equal moral worth. For utilitarians the happiness of any one person is of the same importance as the equal happiness of any other person; for Kant, the fact that all humans are endowed with reason entails that each person is equally worthy of respect. Flowing from these basic philosophical presuppositions there is a common understanding that a morally perfect being will be characterized by the virtue of impartiality and it is from this standpoint that the partiality of Old Testament covenant relations seemed so objectionable to so many Enlightenment thinkers. This point is fundamental to the externalist argument and so I shall expound it in a little more detail by reference to the utilitarian understanding of it.

According to utilitarianism the moral value of actions is a function of their utility; it is uniquely determined by the maximization of the well-being of all those affected by them. Now a point much stressed by utilitarianism is that the well-being of one person is as important as the equal well-being of any other person. Thus Mill famously declared, 'As between his own happiness and that of others, utilitarianism requires him to be as strictly impartial as a disinterested and benevolent spectator.'[2]

There is, therefore, an impartialism at the heart of Enlightenment moral theory and this impartialism forms the basis of the externalist criticism of covenant relations that are essentially partial in character. Kant expressed the point well when he wrote:

So far from Judaism forming an epoch belonging to the universal Church, or being itself this universal Church, it rather excluded the whole human race from its fellowship, as a peculiar people chosen by Jehovah for Himself, which bore ill-will to all other nations and was regarded with ill-will by them in return.[3]

---

2. J. S. Mill, 'Utilitarianism', in J. M. Robson (ed.), *Collected Works* (Toronto: Toronto University Press, 1969), vol. 10, p. 235.

3. Cited in E. W. Hengstenberg, *Dissertations on the Genuineness of the Pentateuch* (tr. J. E. Ryland; Edinburgh: T. & T. Clark, 1847), vol. 2, p. 453.

I have mentioned Kant, perhaps unfairly, as an example of critics of covenant relations; unfairly because his Christian pietism is far removed from some of the more prominent external critics of covenant relationships. Yet his moral theory provides a good example of the externalist standpoint: the demands of morality are dictates of reason and the categorical imperative enjoins an impartiality inconsistent with the partiality of covenant relations.

However, it was the English deists of the seventeenth and eighteenth centuries, rather than Kant, who brought these charges to prominence; it was they who taught the modern world to ridicule the partisanship of the Old Testament covenants.[4] When Lord Herbert of Cherbury published his *De Veritate* in 1624 he laid down the basic principles of deism: there is one supreme God worthy to be worshipped, and virtue and piety are central elements of the religious life. These were theses few orthodox Christians would want to challenge. Herbert and other influential members of the group such as John Toland, Anthony Collins and Matthew Tindal went on, however, to set up a dichotomy between reason and revelation and to attack as superstition, or at best to treat as ordinary human history, the contents of Scripture.[5] They were convinced that moral principles that can be known by reason alone can be used to evaluate all religious traditions. In particular they were hostile to what they referred to as 'the bibliology' of the Puritans, especially orthodox beliefs in prophecy and in supernatural miracles. And, of course, their 'mean esteem' of the Bible extended to a moral critique of the Old Testament. Prophets were invariably subjected to detailed moral examination and invariably found wanting in virtue.

The general consensus among the deists was that the Old Testament covenants represented primitive, vainglorious aspirations of

---

4. On the English deists, see P. Byrne, *Natural Religion and the Nature of Religion* (Edinburgh: Edinburgh University Press, 1988).

5. See J. Champion, *Republican Learning: John Toland and the Crisis of Christian Culture 1696–1722* (Manchester: Manchester University Press, 2003); and R. E. Sullivan, *John Toland and the Deist Controversy* (Cambridge, MA: Harvard University Press, 1982).

an insignificant race to personal and national greatness; the books of Genesis and Exodus represented projections of an early, albeit important, stage in the religious evolution of human religious consciousness. The deist rejection of any literal vocation for the nation of Israel followed partly from their general distrust of Scripture, its ambiguities and supposed historical errors dismissed in the name of gentlemanly reason.

However, deists found especially odious what they considered to be the conceit implicit in the whole account of Israel's divine calling and the viciousness that awaited any neighbouring tribes or nations who dared to challenge Israel's conception of its divine destiny. When Old Testament covenant relations were weighed in the balances of reason and morality they were found to be wanting. This is an important criticism and I shall shortly develop a detailed response to it; before doing so, however, it is worth dealing with a familiar response to the criticism that, while containing important insights, is not an adequate response if taken in isolation.

A very simple theological argument is usually used to counter the criticisms. This states that of course there was a particularism in the covenants of the Old Testament, but it was a particularism that carried with it the promise of a universal salvation available for all humanity. The election of Israel was just God's way of preparing one nation to be a means for the blessing of all nations. Besides, it was an election to service, not to privilege alone, a service that included ultimate benefit for all of the human race. And so it came about that when it had served its purpose this early exclusiveness was cast aside, the scaffolding was taken down and the door of salvation opened for all nations.

Now there is considerable force in this reply and it forms part of any comprehensive answer to rationalist objections to partialism. However, I do not think that it adequately answers the criticisms on its own. First, it acquiesces too easily to an exclusively impartialist conception of morality that is in itself seriously deficient. Secondly, it fails to answer the questions that most motivate the rationalist critic. Let us grant that God's redemptive plan is universal in scope and that it opens the door of salvation to the whole of the human race. The question still remains: Of the many options available, why did God have to realize his ends by such partial means? Why did his short-term blessings have to fall so exclusively on the nation of Israel? These issues are at the heart of the particularist objection and it is not clear to me that the long-term availability of salvation for the human race satisfactorily answers them. So long as we hold to impartialist moral foundations we shall continue to be troubled by the particularist nature of Old Testament covenant relations.

The objection has an analogy in recent work in moral theory and this analogy points to the direction in which a satisfactory reply to the externalist objection is to be found. The distinction between partial and impartial standpoints and the contention that the moral standpoint is necessarily impartialist are at the heart of the externalist challenge. However, these basic doctrines are in fact very controversial and moral philosophers in the second half of the twentieth century have had much to say about them. To antici-pate, some recent criticisms of the impartialist conception of morality are highly relevant in responding to the externalist chal-lenge. I shall argue that the moral standpoint should incorporate both partial and impartial elements and that, thus conceived, the moral standpoint can readily overcome Enlightenment criticisms of covenant relationships. It is to this argument that I shall now turn.

Central to the externalist critique and so the point of departure for a defence of covenant relations is the basic contention that rational morality is necessarily impartial in character. Plausible though this vision of morality may be, it has been challenged by contemporary moral philosophers and we may draw on their insights to question that impartialist vision. The aspect of the moral life that is most at odds with impartialist morality is what is some-times referred to as the 'personal' nature of common morality. By invoking this, the 'personal' philosophers are drawing our attention to the fact that autonomous moral agents typically construct their lives around projects. These projects co-ordinate and give unity to the lives of agents over long periods of time, they engage the desires and emotions of agents, and they also confer meaning on their lives.

Some of these projects, though temporally extended, may be quite narrow in scope. For example, suppose that a talented but impecunious young person wishes to undertake a lengthy period of study in medical school and that to make this possible a friend undertakes to support the student financially for the period in question; and suppose that the student only undertook the project on the assumption that the friend would indeed support her through the years of training. This would be an example of a narrow but temporally extended project.

A person's project might, however, be much more ambitious in scope: it might involve successfully leading a large business organization that provides employment for thousands of workers and makes an important contribution to the economy of a country. At the extremity the project might involve becoming the Secretary General of the United Nations and contributing to peace and reconciliation on a truly global scale. All of these are examples of projects, narrowly or widely conceived and they all give rise to moral responsibilities and commitments great or small.

Personal projects, widely or narrowly conceived, feature prominently in the lives of human beings. They are relevant to our present purposes because moral theories that place a stress on impartiality have great difficulty in accommodating personal projects. This is because the pursuit of personal projects often entails obligations that conflict with impartial morality, as we may see by taking a utilitarian construal of impartial morality. The supportive friend is confronted with demands that promise to generate more happiness than continued support of the medical student; the company manager and aspiring politician are confronted with opportunities that offer larger and more immediate utility gains. Twists in circumstances open up tensions between personal projects and the demands of impartial morality.

Different philosophers have diagnosed this tension in different ways. Some have argued that impartial morality compromises individual integrity, some have argued that it causes moral alienation, some have argued that it creates a form of moral schizophrenia. At root the objection is the same: impartial morality is at variance with the personal point of view. Bernard Williams is one such philosopher. He writes of the tension as follows:

> How can a man as a utilitarian agent come to regard as one
> satisfaction amongst others, and a dispensable one, a project or

attitude around which he has built his life just because someone else's projects have so structured the causal scene that that is how the utilitarian sums come out? The point is that he is identified with his actions as flowing from his projects and attitudes which in some cases he takes seriously at the deepest level, as what his life is about. It is absurd to demand of such a man, when the sums come in from the utility network which the projects of others have in part determined, that he should just step aside from his own project and decision and acknowledge the decision which utilitarian calculation requires. It is also to alienate him in a real sense from his action and the source of his action in his own convictions. It is to make him into a channel between the input of everyone's projects, including his own, and an output of optimistic decision; but this is to neglect the extent to which his actions and his decisions have to be seen as the actions and decisions which flow from the projects and attitudes with which he is most closely identified. It is thus, in the most literal sense, an attack on his integrity.[6]

Elsewhere Williams extends the critique to Kantian impartiality. He writes:

A man who has such a ground project will be required by utilitarianism to give up what it requires in a given case just if it conflicts with what he is required to do as an impersonal utility-maximiser when all of the causally relevant considerations are in. That is an absurd requirement. But the Kantian, who can do rather better than that, still cannot do well enough. For impartial morality, if the conflict really does arise, must be required to win; and that cannot necessarily be a reasonable demand on the agent. There can come a point at which it is quite unreasonable for a man to give up, in the name of the impartial good ordering of the world of moral agents, something which is a condition of his having interest in being around in the world at all.[7]

---

6. B. Williams, 'A Critique of Utilitarianism', in J. J. C. Smart and B. Williams, *Utilitarianism: For and Against* (Cambridge: Cambridge University Press, 1973), §5, pp. 116–117.

7. Ibid., p. 116.

Theories such as Mill's utilitarianism or Kant's rationalism are impersonal theories of morality because they interpret moral value as being a function of considerations that are indifferent to the projects of moral agents. However, if agents become divorced from their deepest projects, then they fail as moral agents irrespective of whether their actions accord with impersonally judged standards of rightness.

Williams also suggests that a person who is committed to an impersonal ethic is morally deficient because in some sense he or she is alienated. This concept of alienation is worth exploring in more detail. Marxists define alienation as occurring when the conditions and products of labour have become independent of the labourers in the sense of being determined by market forces that have a life of their own. The concept can be generalized, however. If a person is alienated from his situation (S) he would normally be expected to have a sense of loyalty towards S but in fact he does not have this loyalty. An agent can normally be expected to have formed loyalties, to friends and community, for example and he is alienated if he does not view his friends or community as his own and does not give to them the overriding consideration and care that the attachments merit. So in Williams's sense, people committed to impersonal morality are alienated in the sense that they fail to live up to what is required by their personal affections and attachments.

The analogy that Michael Stocker uses is schizophrenia.[8] People suffer from schizophrenia if their thoughts, feelings and attachments are radically disconnected. But this is exactly what the defender of impersonal morality experiences: as human beings situated in a certain social matrix, they are committed to certain relationships and projects, but as utilitarians or Kantians they are committed to inconsistent relationships and projects.

In response to criticisms of impersonal morality the American philosopher Samuel Scheffler has developed what he calls a 'hybrid conception' of ethics.[9] This theory is of philosophical interest in

---

8. M. Stocker, 'The Schizophrenia of Modern Ethical Theory', *JP* 73 (1976), pp. 453–456.

9. S. Scheffler, *The Rejection of Consequentialism* (Oxford: Clarendon, 1982).

its own right, since it qualifies impartialism so as to render permissible aspects of the moral life that, counter-intuitively, are ruled out by simple impartialist theories. However, it is of special interest in the present context because it provides a framework within which the integrity of covenant relationships can be defended against impartialist criticisms.

Scheffler's point of departure is critique of utilitarianism from the standpoint of personal integrity: he accepts that Williams has shown that impartialist accounts fail to do justice to the integrity of the moral agent and that any simple form of impartialism is unacceptable for this reason. He therefore endorses Williams's contention that impersonal moral theories place intolerable burdens on and ask for unacceptable sacrifices from individuals. As a corrective to what he sees as impartialist excesses, Scheffler proposes an account that incorporates 'an agent-centred prerogative'. This qualifies impartialism by making it permissible for agents to devote energies and resources to their personal projects in a way that is out of proportion to the weight that would be acceptable in a strictly impartialist moral standpoint. On this account agents are no longer required always to pursue the projects and commitments prescribed by an impartialist calculus of duty. Scheffler's theory is genuinely 'agent-centred' in that it allows people's projects to override impartialist requirements. Thus the patron is permitted to support the medical student, the father is permitted to give preferential treatment to his own children and the aspiring diplomat is permitted to pursue his career at the expense of the hungry and the needy.

Returning to our central theme, it seems to me that not only is Scheffler's 'hybrid theory' rationally preferable to an unqualified impersonal morality, but I believe that the partiality of Old Testament covenants can be explained and justified by reference to such a theory. However, the defence is slightly more complicated and its elaboration enables us both to revisit what I called the standard response to the charge of partiality and to answer an obvious objection to hybrid theories in the process.

An obvious objection to hybrid theories of morality is that they are too permissive; and there is substance to the objection. Surely, not just any conceivable agent-centred prerogative can play the role that Scheffler accords it in constructing a moral theory. For example, a person might devote an extensive, and wholly disproportionate part of her life to a personal whim, such as becoming the local table-tennis champion or to collecting eighteenth-century clocks or to breeding a special type of Welsh corgi dog, and in so doing neglect other potentially much more valuable opportunities for service, which she is uniquely well placed to render.

Scheffler, however, does not wish to defend such eccentric obsessions. Not just any personal commitment can be justified by reference to agent-centred prerogatives. The hybrid theory should have a 'seriousness condition' built into it to the effect that only projects that serve important personal ends and are central to the integrity and personal fulfilment of a person can play the role of agent-centred prerogatives. And any successful appeal to such prerogatives should surely also satisfy an 'other-regarding clause' to the effect that the fulfilment of the prerogatives contributes significantly to the well-being of other people. The examples of the patron, the father and the aspirant diplomat certainly satisfy both the 'seriousness' and the 'other-regarding' constraints that I have described. Bernard Williams's example of the painter Gauguin, who abandoned his family to perfect his work as an artist, is also a good example of the context in which agent-centred theories can operate.

If the foregoing argument is correct, therefore, the externalist criticism of covenant relationships is based on a contrast between impartial morality, on the one hand, and partial Old Testament morality on the other hand and on the contention that the former is a rationally preferable morality. However, we have also seen that a morality which systematizes all of our deeply held moral convictions, especially our convictions about integrity and personal relationships, will not be totally impartial in every respect. A system that combines impartiality with limited partiality, constrained by a seriousness condition, is in certain respects a more rational morality. We have also seen that Old Testament covenant relationships fit comfortably within such a hybrid moral system. Therefore the externalist objection to covenant relationships fails.

An internal challenge

I return to what I earlier described as the internal challenge to the integrity of covenant relationships, the challenge posed by the apparent inconsistency of the very exclusive loving relations that characterized Old Testament covenants between God and his people on the one hand, and the very inclusive loving nature of the God who is revealed in the New Testament. The problem is how one can be reconciled with the other. To appreciate the gap between the two we need only look in brief at the apparently contrasting conceptions of God's love that are to be found in the Old and New Testaments; especially at the particularity of the one and the universality of the other.

Let us note briefly the particularity of God's love in the Old Testament covenants, especially the intimate personal language in which it is expressed. We read that Abraham is the friend of God (Isaiah 41:8; 2 Chronicles 20:7) and Yahweh is his guest (Genesis 18); Israel is described as the people of Yahweh and he is their God (Exodus 6:7; Leviticus 26:12; Deuteronomy 26:17); Israel is attached to God in the closest of possible relations, as his personal possession, as a people set aside to be a kingdom of priests of which Yahweh is king and in which all Israelites, by fulfilling the statutes of the covenant, together assume the offices of a priesthood; elsewhere the description of the relationship is even more intimate – one of father to son (Exodus 4:22; Deuteronomy 14:1) or of husband to wife (Hosea 1 – 3; Isaiah 50:1) or in terms of the intimacy of lovers throughout the Song of Solomon.

By contrast with the love expressed in the Old Testament covenants consider the way in which the love of God is elaborated in the New Testament. The God of the New Testament is a God who loves without qualification and without distinction and a God whose love in no way depends on the qualities or responses of the objects of his love. Central to the Christian message is its universal appeal. The Christian message, to 'Jews or Gentiles – bond or free' was a message that presupposed only the common humanity and the common moral experience of its hearers: that the human race has undergone a moral catastrophe, the most serious consequence of which is our alienation from God, the ground of all goodness; that God has provided redemption, freely available to all who accept it in faith and repentance; that the fellowship to which acceptance of salvation provides access is indifferent to race, culture, social or historical situation: that obedience to the will of God is the badge of Christian discipleship: and that obedience to God is expressed in a heart given over to unqualified love of others. Christ's teaching on the mountain ends with an injunction to be perfect, summing up a lengthy exposition of what is involved in loving not only one's neighbour but also one's enemies (Matthew 5:43–48). This principle is described by James (James 2:8) as the fulfilment of the 'royal law'; love is described (repeated in Romans 13:10); John exhorts his readers to love not 'in word or talk but in deed and in truth' (1 John 3:18, ESV); and he adds, 'And this is his commandment, that we believe in the name of his Son Jesus Christ and love one another, just as he has commanded us' (1 John 3:23, ESV). Christian perfection, therefore, finds its all-embracing unity in obedience to the Law of God, manifesting itself (Matthew 22:37–40) in unqualified love – with all the heart, soul and mind – for others.

To conclude, let us notice the contrast in two brief passages. Old Testament particularity: 'For you are a people holy to the LORD your God; the LORD your God has chosen you out of all the peoples on the face of the earth to be his people, his treasured possession' (Deuteronomy 7:6; repeated in 14:2). New Testament universalism: 'If you really fulfil the royal law according to the Scripture, "You shall love your neighbour as yourself" you are doing well. But if you show partiality you are committing sin and are convicted by the law as transgressors' (James 2:8–9, ESV).

When discussing external criticisms we saw that philosophical clarity can help to overcome moral objections to covenant relations, and in connection with internal criticisms I want to attempt a resolution along the same lines. That is, I shall make various philosophical distinctions and argue that in the light of them internal objections to covenant relations no longer seem so serious. Happily the process involves becoming clearer about some of the fundamental concepts in theological ethics and this is a worthwhile project even if my arguments in defence of covenant relations are not entirely conclusive. The philosophical distinctions in question concern the nature of love, the various forms it can take and the way in which different forms of love are related to each other.[10] Three forms of love important to distinguish are instrumental, non-instrumental (or end) and pure love.

Instrumental love

Ties of identity and belonging often develop between members of a group who share common goals. Sometimes these ties develop spontaneously; sometimes they are cultivated artificially so as to enhance the interests of the group. Often in such cases the ties give rise to genuine affection between members of the group, and the fact that the friendships are instrumental need not lead us to disparage their value. Their usefulness may, of course, be the spark that gives rise to other and better kinds of affection and, of course, most friendships, however exalted, are useful on at least some occasions in at least some ways. However, instrumental friendships are not the best kinds of friendships, so let us turn to two better kinds.

Non-instrumental (end) love

Aristotle says that 'those who are most truly friends love each other by virtue of their nature, i.e. for being the person that they are'.[11] This captures nicely the fact that parties to non-instrumental love value each other for the distinctive features they each possess, for the qualities that make them the people they are. In such relationships the friends value each other and wish each other well as ends in themselves. They take pleasure in being together because of the people they are. Hence these affections have a significantly

---

10. At this point I am indebted to the work of N. K. Badhar. See especially
    the articles N. K. Badhar, 'Friends as Ends in themselves', *PPR* 48 (1987),
    pp. 1–23; and N. B. Kapur, 'Why it Is Wrong Always to be Guided by the
    Best: Consequentialism and Friendship', *Ethics* 101 (1991), pp. 483–504.
11. Aristotle, *Nicomachean Ethics* 1156a.18–19.

different focus than instrumental friendships because an instrumental friend is replaceable, whereas an end friend is irreplaceable. However, a purer form of friendship is commonly identified with the love of God, and this is what, to borrow an expression from Robert Adams, might be called 'pure love'.

Pure love

In the context of a criticism of Plato's concept of love, Gregory Vlastos contrasts pure love with non-instrumental love as follows: 'The cardinal flaw in Plato's theory is that it does not allow for love of the whole person, but only love of that abstract version of persons that consists of the complex of their best qualities.'[12] This captures very well the central aspect of the contrast. Pure love has as its object the loved one and not any complex of qualities that the loved one may possess. Other writers have hinted at the nature of such love.

According to Kierkegaard 'love to one's neighbour makes a man blind in the deepest and noblest and holiest sense, so that he blindly loves every man'.[13] Such love is the love that God has for all human beings. It is unconditional, it is without thought of gain, it is indifferent to value in its object. For this reason Kierkegaard describes such love as 'lost love' because it is 'the direct opposite of rational calculation'.[14] Luther describes such love as 'an overflowing love which says "I love thee, not because thou art good for I draw my love not from thy goodness as from an alien spring; but from mine own well-spring".'[15]

Kierkegaard and Luther both argue that a life organized around the principle of pure love is the best of all possible lives and that it is completely different from a life organized around other kinds

---

12. G. Vlastos, 'The Individual as an Object of Love', in *Platonic Studies* (Princeton: Princeton University Press, 1973), p. 31.

13. S. Kierkegaard, *Works of Love* (tr. H. Hong and E. Hong; New York: Harper & Row, 1962), p. 80.

14. Quoted in A. Nygren, *Agape and Eros* (tr. P. S. Watson; New York: Macmillan, 1939), pt 2, vol. 2, p. 514.

15. Ibid., p. 512 n. 1.

of affection, though lives characterized by pure love may contain elements of the other affections in them.

We have seen that love may manifest itself in at least three forms – instrumental love, end love and pure love – and it is now time to draw together the various threads of the discussion, to re-examine the moral foundations of covenant relationships in the light of our new understanding of the complexities of loving relationships and to attempt to diffuse standard internal criticisms in the light of our account.

God's love for Israel, as recorded in the Old Testament, is a compound of instrumental love, end love and pure love and it is only if we recognize this diversity that we can see that God's equal love for the whole of the human race is consistent with various forms of partiality in his relations with different persons and collectivities. Let us reflect, then, on the character of God's relations with some of the various parties who cross the biblical stage.

First, the children of Israel and their leaders were chosen to be God's partners in the unfolding plan of redemption for the human race. God's relationship with them was an instance of instrumental love that marked off the relationship from the relationship God had with other nations. God therefore treated the Israelites in ways that were different from the ways in which he treated other nations; he also treated certain individual Israelites differently from the ways in which he treated others. This is made clear from God's assurance to Abraham that through him all of the nations of the earth would be blessed. God's love for his chosen people involved instrumental love, therefore, in the context of which God would bless some and punish some of his chosen people. Such partiality, however, is intelligible in terms of the overall objectives of God's plans and it is consistent with the seriousness condition that must characterize any departure by a perfect being from straightforwardly impartial courses of action.

Secondly, God's love for Israel involved non-instrumental, end love because the relationship between God and Israel was a personal relationship characterized by the same feelings of attraction, frustration, disappointment, anger, relief, pleasure and joy that are characteristic of all intense loving relationships.

Thirdly, God's love for Israel involved pure love; because God freely gives this love to all human beings including the people of Israel.

There is therefore no inconsistency between God's love revealed in the New Testament on the one hand and the very partial love of God expressed in the covenants with Abraham and at Sinai, unless it is assumed that pure love is inconsistent with instrumental love. I would like to conclude by offering one argument why, at least in connection with a perfectly loving being, there is no such inconsistency.

An understandable human reason for thinking that instrumental love and pure love are inconsistent is that in corrupted and sinful creatures like ourselves instrumental love is almost always directed towards entirely selfish ends. And, certainly, pure love is inconsistent with instrumental love of that form. However, there is no reason why a morally perfect being should not enter into instrumental relationships in pursuit of pure ends, and when this takes place it gives rise to special affections internal to those distinctive relationships and projects. In the case of God's partial love for Israel the instrumental affections are affections directly linked to overall goals that are motivated by pure love. And so when we understand the compatibility of some forms of pure love with instrumental love, we can see how the standard internal objections to covenant relationships can be overcome.

The single most pervasive error underlying all rationalist objections to covenant relationships is the idea that a perfectly loving God will necessarily bring about the equal happiness or (even more absurdly) the equal pleasure of all human beings. There is no reason whatever to believe that this is true, but the idea underpins much rationalist argument against covenant relationships.

Conclusion

In summary, I have distinguished between external and internal moral criticism of the integrity of covenant relationships. I have argued that external criticisms can be met by recognizing that God's love for the people of Israel expressed in covenant relations is an instance of an agent-centred prerogative constrained by appropriate seriousness conditions, and so is an instance of a hybrid theory that is morally preferable to straightforward impartial conceptions of ethics. I have argued that internal criticisms can be met by disambiguating the concept of partiality and by recognizing the compatibility of instrumental, end love and pure love in the character of a morally perfect being.

More generally, our discussion has implications for the nature of biblical exposition. Many academic disciplines combine to enrich our understanding of the meaning of Scripture. However, it is not sufficiently recognized that philosophy, especially moral philosophy, is one of those disciplines. As this essay will have made clear, I believe that an understanding of the development of God's redemptive plans cannot be fully grasped or influential criticisms of it rebutted without a sound knowledge of the foundations of moral theory. And this is something that is insufficiently recognized by theologians in the Reformed tradition.[16]

---

16. I am grateful to members of the Philosophy section of The Tyndale Fellowship whose comments forced me to clarify numerous aspects of this chapter. I wish to express my gratitude also to Mr Effiong Udoeyop for his consideration and kindness during my writing of this chapter.

9. GOD'S COVENANT – GOD'S LAND?

Colin Chapman

Introduction

This chapter is a contribution at a particular point in time to a heated debate in which biblical interpretation, theology, contemporary international politics and interfaith relations are inextricably intertwined. Most observers agree that among Christians in the US who call themselves 'evangelical', the majority (estimated by some to be as many as 70 million) support a particular policy towards the Israeli–Palestinian conflict largely because of the way they interpret the Bible and understand eschatology. The fact that the West Bank and Jerusalem are part of the land promised to Abraham and his descendants is more significant for them than the fact that Israel's continued occupation of the West Bank since 1967 is illegal, according to international law as defined by the UN Charter.

Few issues discussed at this conference can have more immediate implications for the well-being of so many people – not only in the Middle East but throughout the world. I suggest that what is at stake is nothing less than our understanding of God, our witness to the gospel and the credibility of the Christian church, especially in the Middle East and in relation to the Jewish people and the House of Islam.

I wrote *Whose Promised Land?*(*WPL*) in Beirut in the early 1980s, and after its first publication in 1983 revisions were published in 1985, 1989, 1992 and 2002. The book attempts to do three things: (1) give a historical account of the events leading up to the establishment of the state of Israel in 1948 and developments since then, attempting to explain the nature of the conflict in its own terms; (2) trace the theme of the land from Genesis to Revelation, questioning the popular view that the covenant with Abraham gives the Jewish people a divine right to the land for all time and that the recent return of Jews to the land and the establishment of the Jewish state should be seen by Christians as the fulfilment of OT prophecies; and (3) explore alternative ways of using Scripture to interpret the significance of what has been unfolding in the land in recent years and to develop a genuinely Christian perspective on the conflict.

In what follows I am attempting to explain the assumptions underlying *WPL* and respond to criticisms of the book from a number of different sources. David Torrance, for example, speaks of the book as 'an important, thought-provoking book, which continues to exercise an unhappy political, biblical and theological influence'.[1] And Melanie Phillips describes the book as 'a poisonous travesty which uses theology to de-legitimise Israel', adding that 'this book will influence not just anti-Israel but anti-Jewish feeling'.[2] Of the seven major issues I want to address, the first two have to do with biblical interpretation; the third and fourth are related to theological issues; five and six concern Christian responses to the Jewish people and the world of Islam; the seventh has to do with the question of political involvement.

---

1. David Torrance, Review of *Whose Promised Land?*, in *Shalom* magazine, November 2002. See a further review at <http: || www.apologetics.fsnet. co.uk/chapman-torrance.htm>.

2. Melanie Phillips, online seminar at the Centre for Jewish–Christian Relations, Cambridge, 14 May 2002.

Covenant and land: What is the place of the land in biblical covenants, and how is the land to be understood in the context of the 'new covenant'?

If Walter Brueggemann is right in saying that the land is 'a central, if not the central theme of biblical faith',[3] Christians need to recognize its importance and appreciate how it is understood in both testaments. I have suggested in *WPL* that the four strands of the Abrahamic covenant (concerning the land, the nation, the covenant relationship and the blessing), which are outlined in Genesis 12, 15 and 17, need to be taken together as a kind of 'package deal' in such a way that the understanding of each strand is related to the others and the fulfilment of the promise concerning the land cannot be separated from the fulfilment of the other promises.

The Mosaic covenant at Sinai is portrayed not as a new covenant but as one that exists alongside the Abrahamic covenant. What is new is the explication of the law and the detailed stipulations which describe the blessings and the curses that will follow upon the keeping or the breaking of the covenant. Teaching about the land in Deuteronomy states explicitly that breaking the covenant will lead to expulsion from the land, but that repentance in exile will be followed by a return to the land (Deuteronomy 29:1–30). Thus while the Abrahamic covenant 'is identified in scripture as irrevocable and based on pure promise', the Mosaic covenant comes with 'strictly conditional promises and sanctions relating to the land and Israel's national election'.[4] The Davidic covenant can be seen as 'a further extension of the Sinai covenant',[5] and what is new is the promise that David will always have a descendant sitting on his throne and the fact that that promise is unconditional (2 Samuel 7:1–16, especially 11b–16). The Davidic covenant cannot therefore be described simply as a 'sign of the covenant' in the way that

---

3. Walter Brueggemann, *The Land: Place as Gift, Promise and Challenge in Biblical Faith* (London: SPCK, 1978), p. 3.

4. Michael S. Horton, *Covenant and Eschatology: The Divine Drama* (Louisville: John Knox, 2002), p. 237.

5. F. C. Fensham, 'Covenant', in *NBD*.

David Torrance does, making a distinction between the Abrahamic covenant and the 'signs of the covenant', which include 'the temple and its worship, the priesthood and the sacrifices, the creation of the kingship of David'.[6] In the light of God's covenant love for his people, the prophets speak a double message of judgment and hope. And when Jeremiah speaks of 'a new covenant' (Jeremiah 31:31–34), some conclude that the covenant made at Sinai had been 'so totally broken that it could be replaced only by a new covenant',[7] while others like Michael Horton see it as 'a renewed Abrahamic (rather than Mosaic) covenant'.[8] The Abrahamic, Mosaic and Davidic covenants therefore hang together, and constitute a major theme running through the whole OT.

The Gospels describe the life and ministry of Jesus in terms of a fulfilment of the covenant promises in the OT. In Luke, for example, the annunciation to Mary speaks of Jesus occupying 'the throne of his father David'; *he himself* (not his descendants) 'will reign over the house of Jacob for ever . . .' (Luke 1:30–33). The songs of Mary and Zechariah describe the birth of Jesus as fulfilment of the covenant made with Abraham (Luke 1:54–55; 72–73). In response to John the Baptist's doubts, Jesus relates his miracle of healing to Isaiah's poetic description of the return of exiles from Babylon (Luke 7:18–23; Isaiah 35:1–10). Jesus at the Last Supper looks forward to a new exodus that is about to be completed, and speaks of 'the new covenant in my blood' (Luke 22:20). And Jesus explains to the two disciples on the road to Emmaus that he has carried out the redemption of Israel described in Second Isaiah and the other prophets – although not in the way they had expected (24:25–32). Thus the Gospels consistently interpret the coming of Jesus in the light of the previous covenants. I have argued in *WPL* that the comparative silence about the land in the Gospels suggests that in the understanding of the NT writers, Jewish hopes centred on the land and the restoration of Israel had now been fulfilled and transformed through the coming of the

---

6. Torrance, Review of *Whose Promised Land?*

7. Fensham, *NBD*.

8. Horton, *Covenant and Eschatology*, p. 134.

kingdom.[9] Because of the unity of the two testaments, therefore, while in the OT there is a series of covenants and what comes in Jesus is 'a new covenant', they are all linked together in 'one covenant of grace'.[10]

There are two main ways in which this approach has been challenged. The first argues that this interpretation of the land promise in the NT is based on an argument from silence. 'When the NT is silent on matters repeatedly affirmed in the OT,' says David Torrance, 'be it the Land or the Ten Commandments, the NT is simply accepting and affirming or confirming what was earlier said in the OT, not denying it.'[11] My answer, following writers like W. D. Davies,[12] is that since Matthew 5:5 ('Blessed are the meek, / for they will inherit the earth/land') is the only unmistakeable reference to the land in the teaching of Jesus, and since the overarching concept that holds together the whole of the teaching of Jesus is the coming of the kingdom, it seems reasonable to conclude that the land must from now on be understood in the context of the kingdom that has come in and through Jesus.

It can also be pointed out that the argument is not actually based on silence, because alongside the almost total absence of affirmation about the significance of the land in the NT, land terminology is used by several different writers, but in every case with new meanings. Paul, for example, speaks of the promise that Abraham would inherit 'the world' rather than 'the land' (Romans 4:13). Both Paul and Peter use the word *klēronomia* (used frequently in the Greek version of the OT to refer to the land) to speak about the inheritance of all Christian believers (Acts 20:32; 1 Peter 1:4). The book of Acts, which describes the gradual spread of the gospel from Jerusalem (Acts 1:5–8), can be seen as the NT counterpart to the book of Joshua, which describes the gradual conquest of the land,

---

9. Chapman, *Whose Promised Land?* (rev. ed.; Oxford: Lion/Grand Rapids: Baker, 2002), pp. 150–172.

10. Horton, *Covenant and Eschatology*, p. 230.

11. Torrance, Review of *Whose Promised Land?*

12. W. D. Davies, *The Gospel and the Land: Early Christianity and Jewish Territorial Doctrine* (Berkeley: University of California Press, 1974).

beginning from Jericho. The writer to the Hebrews speaks of the land as 'the rest' and reinterprets the promise of the land in terms of the experience of every Christian believer; and in the list of all the privileges that belong to believers in Jesus the focus has moved from Mount Sinai and Jerusalem to 'the heavenly Jerusalem' and to 'Jesus the mediator of a new covenant' (Hebrews 12:18–24). If words and ideas associated so closely with the land are used by NT writers – but transformed – in this way, the argument cannot be said to be based on silence.

The second objection is that a theme in the OT that is as physical and material as the land cannot be spiritualized. David W. Torrance, for example, writes:

> The New Testament re-affirms the Old although it carries it to a higher dimension. The Gospel witnessed to in the New as well as in the Old Testament has a physical and material dimension in space and time and does have a literal fulfilment in Christ. If we separate the spiritual dimension of the Gospel which supposedly belongs to the New Testament from the material dimensions of the Gospel which belongs (with the spiritual) to the Old Testament, then ultimately we must accept a dualism between soul and body and between a person's spiritual and material needs. This I believe is unbiblical.[13]

If this argument is pressed in relation to the land, however, why is it not pressed in relation to any of the other major themes of the OT? In what sense could Christians say that the temple, the priesthood, the sacrificial system have 'a physical and material dimension in space and time' and 'a literal fulfilment in Christ'? Pressing the necessity for a 'literal fulfilment' of everything that is material and physical in the OT would make it difficult, if not impossible, to see Jesus as the new temple or to see his death as the one sacrifice that does away with the need for all sacrifice. If the physical element in an OT theme has to be reaffirmed even when it is carried 'to a higher dimension', how could it ever be acceptable to see *a person* (Jesus) as the fulfilment of *a thing* (the land, the temple, the sacrificial

---

13. Torrance, Review of *Whose Promised Land?*

system or the monarchy)? The logic of this objection virtually rules out reinterpretation of OT themes in the light of the incarnation and atonement. They have to retain for ever the 'material dimensions' that they have in the OT.

I conclude therefore that the land promise cannot be isolated from all the other strands of the covenant that speak about the nation, the covenant relationship and blessing for all the peoples of the world and put in a separate category of its own that demands a literal fulfilment after Christ. If we accept that, in the words of Michael S. Horton, 'It is Jesus Christ as the mediator of the covenant that occupies center stage and unites the drama of redemption in its Old and New Testament acts,'[14] covenant promises concerning the land have to be taken alongside everything else in the OT and interpreted in the light of the coming of the kingdom in Jesus. As we shall see, there is little or nothing in the NT to suggest that the disciples after the ascension continued to believe that Jewish sovereignty over the land had any significance for the kingdom of God, which had begun to come through Jesus.

Biblical exegesis: Are there not at least two ways of reading the key biblical texts?

In the debate about the significance of the land there is a fundamental divide between two approaches, which I will simply label as 'dispensational'/'millennial' and 'covenant'. The 'dispensational'/'millennial' view insists that OT promises and prophecies about the land that have not already been fulfilled must be fulfilled literally in the future. The 'covenant' approach sees all the promises and prophecies fulfilled in the coming of Christ and therefore tends to see no special theological significance in the establishment of the Jewish state. The tensions between these two approaches can be illustrated by noting the different interpretations of three key texts.

---

14. Horton, *Covenant and Eschatology*, p. 230.

The parable of the fig-tree (Mark 13:28–31; Matthew 24:32–35; Luke 21:29–31)

Dispensationalists and restorationists interpret this parable as a prediction of the revival of the Jewish nation in the land. Jesus has already cursed the fig-tree on his way to Jerusalem (Matthew 21:18–19), acting out the physical destruction of the temple and, some would say, the nation. Since the fig-tree represents Israel, the sprouting of the leaves must represent the revival of the nation in the end times.

This interpretation, however, can be challenged at two points. Firstly, the identification of the fig-tree with Israel is far from clear. The vine is clearly a symbol for Israel (e.g. Psalm 80:8–16; Isaiah 5:1–7), but while 'sitting under his own vine and fig-tree' is a metaphor for security and prosperity and the withering of the fig-tree is a metaphor for disaster and judgment, nowhere in the OT is Israel clearly represented by the fig-tree. None of the Bible dictionaries I have consulted suggests that the fig-tree is a symbol for Israel.

Secondly, the verses immediately after the parable indicate that it is pointing to events that are going to happen *in the near future*. 'The point of the parable is clear,' says I. H. Marshall. 'Certain events convey the unmistakable message to any observer that a climax is about to happen.'[15] Similarly, John Nolland writes:

> Despite the series of attempts to apply *hē genea tautē*, 'this generation', to something other than the generation of Jesus' contemporaries, all the alternatives (the Jewish people; humanity; the generation of the end-time signs) are finally artificial and represent imposition based upon some supposition brought to the text . . . Many try to make 'this generation' to mean something different to the generation of Jesus' contemporaries but all the alternatives offered are finally unnatural and are proposed as ways out of a problem rather than as natural readings of the text. I cannot avoid the conclusion that the Lukan Jesus

---

15. I. H. Marshall, *The Gospel of Luke: A Commentary on the Greek Text* (NIGTC; Exeter: Paternoster, 1978), p. 779.

anticipated that all that he prophesied would run its course in a single generation.[16]

It seems therefore that the parable of the fig-tree can hardly bear the weight put on it by dispensationalists and restorationists.

The future of Jerusalem (Luke 21:24)

In Luke's version of the eschatological discourse Jesus says, 'Jerusalem will be trampled on by the Gentiles until the times of the Gentiles are fulfilled' (NIV); 'until their day has run its course' (NEB); 'until their time is up' (TEV). The discussion concerning this verse revolves around the question of what, if anything, is implied about the future status of Jerusalem *after* the judgment has taken place. The dispensationalist/restorationist interpretation of this verse is that Jerusalem will cease to be under Gentiles and come once again under the control of the Jews. The fact that this happened in June 1967 indicates the profound theological significance of this event and points to the imminence of the second coming.

Alfred Plummer long ago pointed out the ambiguity of this verse and the variety of different interpretations that have been proposed.[17] Of the six options he outlined, recent scholarship seems to favour the interpretation that the Gentiles (Romans) will themselves one day come under divine judgment. Thus John Nolland suggests that the 'times of the nations (Gentiles)' refers to

> the period for a judgement on the gentile nations that corresponds to the judgement on Jerusalem ... The underlying pattern here of judgement upon Jerusalem/Judah/Israel followed by judgement upon the instrument of their judgement may be found in Isaiah 10:12–14, 33; 47; Jeremiah 50–51; Daniel 9:26–27 and compare Ezekiel 38; Habakkuk 1:11–2:3.[18]

---

16. John Nolland, *Luke 18:35–24:53* (WBC; Dallas: Word Books, 1993), pp. 1007–1010.

17. Alfred Plummer, *The Gospel according to St Luke* (Edinburgh: T. & T. Clark, 1922), p. 483.

18. Nolland, *Luke 18:35–24:53*, pp. 1002–1003.

Other recent commentators raise the possibility that it may refer not to judgment on the Gentiles but rather to the mission to the Gentiles. Thus Joel B. Green writes,

> with v 25 Jesus' eschatological discourse turns not to consider the place of Israel in God's plan but to the end time, marked by the coming of the Son of Man . . . In this case, 'the times of the Gentiles' would mark a temporary season that would give way to the consummation of God's purpose in the eschatological fulfillment. At the outset of Acts, the question of the place of Israel in God's eschatological aim remains unanswered (Acts 1:6–8); there, as here, the focus is shifted from speculation about Israel to mission among the Gentiles. 'Times of the Gentiles' then, has a dual reference in this co-text. It manifestly relates to the role of the Gentiles as God's agents in the prophesied destruction and subsequent occupation of Jerusalem. More than this, however, it portends the proclamation of the good news among the Gentiles.[19]

I have not yet found any commentary suggesting that the clear implication in Jesus' prediction is that Jerusalem will one day be returned to Jewish sovereignty. And even if it can be argued that there is a vague hint in these words that Jerusalem will one day revert to Jewish rule, the text gives no indication of the significance of such a development. The emphasis in Jesus' words is on the significance of the coming destruction of Jerusalem (which will take place in the lifetime of many of his hearers) rather than on the status of Jerusalem in the more distant future. He is silent about the future of the land; but the fall of Jerusalem is to be an act of divine judgment, compared in a shocking way to the judgment on Babylon described by Isaiah. Whereas the OT prophets predicted judgment, exile *and* a return to the land, Jesus predicts destruction and exile, but says nothing about a return to the land. Instead of predicting the restoration of Israel, he speaks about the coming of the kingdom of God through the coming of the Son of Man.

---

19. Joel B. Green, *The Gospel of Luke* (NICNT; Grand Rapids: Eerdmans, 1997), p. 739.

The kingdom of God and the sovereignty of Israel (Acts 1:6–8)
The dispensationalist/restorationist interpretation popular in evangelical circles was summed up many years ago by G. Campbell Morgan in these words:

> Christ rebuked, not their conception that the kingdom is to be restored to Israel – for that He never rebuked – but their desire to know when it would take place . . . A popular interpretation of this is that Christ said to them: There is to be no restoration of the kingdom to Israel. Christ did not say so. What he said was: It is not for you to know the times or seasons. You have other work to do.[20]

Some recent commentators accept that the restoration of sovereignty is not rejected, but emphasize that the focus of attention moves from the question of Jewish sovereignty to the mission of the church and the redefinition of the identity of Israel. C. K. Barrett, for example, writes, 'It is not denied . . . that there will be a time when the kingdom is restored to Israel, though the book as a whole makes clear that Israel, the people of God, is receiving a new definition.'[21]

In *WPL* I have suggested that this incident and the meeting of the risen Jesus with the two disciples on the road to Emmaus (Luke 24:13–35), taken together, represent a significant turning point for the disciples. Until this point they have been thinking like first-century Jews, believing that the coming of the kingdom of God has a great deal to do with the Jewish people and their hopes for a restored Jewish state in the land. Thus when they ask him, 'Lord, are you at this time going to restore the kingdom to Israel?' (Acts 1:6, NIV) or 'is this the time at which you are to restore sovereignty to Israel?' (REB), they are 'wedded still to the popular notion of the kingdom of God as something political and that its coming would see the ingathering of the tribes . . ., the

---

20. G. Campbell Morgan, *The Acts of the Apostles* (Glasgow: Pickering & Inglis, 1946), p. 19.
21. C. K. Barrett, *The Acts of the Apostles* (ICC; Edinburgh: T. & T. Clark, 1994), p. 77.

restoration of Israel's independence and the triumph of Israel over its enemies'.[22]

In the light of Jesus' strong rebuke to the disciples on the road to Emmaus ('How foolish you are, and how slow of heart to believe all that the prophets have spoken!' Luke 24:25), I believe that Jesus' reply to the disciples in Acts 1:7–8 is intended not only to correct their idea about *the timing* of the fulfilment of these events, but to challenge *the very idea itself*. I therefore follow Calvin's interpretation of their question when he says, 'There are as many mistakes in this question as there are words.'[23] Jesus' reply therefore expresses a mixture of disappointment and exasperation: 'Have you still not understood that the kingdom of God is not a physical entity that is tied only to the Jewish people or to the land, but is a spiritual reality that will include people of all races and reach to the ends of the earth?' This interpretation takes verses 7 and 8 closely together, with verse 7 pointing to the negative and verse 8 the positive: 'not this . . . but this'. Thus, according to Barrett:

> The connection with the preceding verse is important, and there is no
> doubt that a measure of contrast is intended. 'Not the kingdom for
> Israel (Acts 1:6), but the power of the Holy Spirit for the church
> (Maddox).' Verse 8 therefore 'supplies the corrective to the particularism
> of the Apostles' question in verse 6'.[24]

A further argument to support this interpretation is that nothing else in the book of Acts supports the idea that the return of Jewish sovereignty would have any significance for the kingdom of God. Stephen's speech in Acts 7 plays down the significance of the land by pointing out that many of the significant events in Israel's history (like the call of Abraham and the exodus) took place outside the land. Clare Amos suggests that because of the references to the 'glory of God' in the speech, when Stephen is described as seeing

---

22. Chapman, *Whose Promised Land?*, pp. 169–172.

23. John Calvin, *Commentary on the Acts of the Apostles* (tr. W. J. D. McDonald;
    Grand Rapids: Eerdmans, 1989), p. 29.

24. Barrett, *Acts of the Apostles*, p. 78.

the glory of God as he dies, Luke is implying that 'now "glory" has finally disappeared from the temple. Jerusalem . . . is no longer privileged by special presence'.[25] At the Jerusalem Council James quotes Amos 9:8–15 to argue that the restoration of Israel was not something still in the future, but something that *had already taken place*. The inclusion of Gentiles in the church is described as something whose happening is a *result* of the restoration of Israel (Acts 15:17). The rebuilding of David's fallen tent (15:16) leads on to Gentiles seeking the Lord (15:17); and the first stage of Israel's restoration is linked to the second by the word *hopōs*, 'that', 'so that', 'in order that': 'I will restore it, / *that* the remnant of men may seek the Lord, / and all the Gentiles . . .' (my emphasis).

I conclude therefore that the dispensational/millennial interpretation cannot be sustained by detailed exegesis of these key texts. One further issue that needs to be addressed in this context is the question of whether it is possible to interpret prophecy in more ways than one. Even if we grant that OT promises and prophecies have been fulfilled in Christ, isn't it possible in some cases to see *both* a spiritual interpretation *and* a literal or physical interpretation of prophecies relating to Christ and his coming? R. T. Kendall, formerly of Westminster Chapel, London, for example, accepts most of the argument in *WPL*, but wants to leave the door open for a possible literal fulfilment. 'Is there nothing whatever in the Bible', he asks, 'that makes Israel's becoming a nation in 1948 a fulfilment of some prophetic expectation?'[26]

My approach in *WPL* has been to distinguish three different kinds of fulfilment (in the original context of the prophet; in the first coming of Christ; and the end times) and to suggest that only when we have exhausted these kinds of fulfilment should we go on to ask whether biblical prophecy is being fulfilled in contemporary history. Since Zechariah's prophetic words 'They will look on me, the one they have pierced' (Zechariah 12:10) are related in

25. Clare Amos, 'Serving at the Table of Jesus, Servant of Others', in David Thomas and Clare Amos (eds.), *A Faithful Presence: Essays for Kenneth Cragg* (London: Melisende, 2003), p. 119.

26. R. T. Kendall email, 30 March 2003.

John to the crucifixion (John 19:37) and in Revelation to his second coming (Revelation 1:7), I am open *in principle* to prophecies being interpreted in more ways than one. But I have yet to find a convincing example of prophecy related by NT writers to the first coming of Christ that can also be related clearly to contemporary events. Some of the attempts in recent years (like seeing the union of Egypt and Syria in 1959 as a literal fulfilment of Isaiah 19:23–25) have been very unconvincing.[27]

The most powerful argument to my mind, however, is the Christological one. If Ezekiel's vision of a restored temple in Jerusalem is seen by Christians as a way of pointing forward to the incarnation, could it *also and at the same time* be interpreted as an architect's blueprint of a temple that will at some time in the future be built in Jerusalem? If the sacrificial system is fulfilled in Christ, is it not a denial of the finished work of Christ on the cross to suggest that the sacrificial system will one day have to be reinstated in a restored temple in Jerusalem? If the apostle John interpreted Ezekiel's vision of water bubbling up from under the temple in Jerusalem and flowing down to the Dead Sea in the light of Jesus and saw the vision fulfilled in the gift of the Holy Spirit (John 7:37–39), could this same vision ever be related by Christians to contemporary irrigation schemes on the West Bank? If Jesus the Messiah has broken down 'the dividing wall of hostility' between Jews and Gentiles in order to create 'one new humanity' (Ephesians 2:15 NRSV), is it not a step backwards rather than forwards to expect special divine blessings being given to Jews through their return to the land? The discipline of detailed exegesis lends little support to the dispensationalist/restorationist interpretation of the key texts.

Dispensationalism and restorationism: Is covenant theology compatible with dispensationalism and restorationism?

Dispensationalism provides many Christians with a theological basis for supporting Zionism because it teaches with dogmatic

---

27. Chapman, *Whose Promised Land?*, Appendices 1–2, pp. 311–328.

certainty that the return of Jews to the land and the establishment of the Jewish state will lead at any time to the rapture of the church and the time of tribulation, which will include (according to many) the rebuilding of the temple in Jerusalem and be followed by the battle of Armageddon, the return of Christ and the inauguration of Christ's millennial rule. Timothy Weber goes so far as to say that 'the key to this entire prophetic plan is the re-founding of Israel as a nation state in Palestine. Without Israel the whole plan falls apart'.[28] This set of dispensational beliefs is described by Stephen Sizer as

> one of the most influential theological systems within the universal church today. Largely unrecognized and subliminal, it has increasingly shaped the presuppositions of fundamentalist, evangelical, Pentecostal and charismatic thinking concerning Israel and Palestine over the past 150 years . . . dispensationalism is now 'a theological system that in all probability is the majority report among current American evangelicals' (Gerstner).[29]

Restorationism shares many of the assumptions of dispensationalism about the interpretation of the OT, but does not usually accept all the details of the various dispensational schemes. The starting point for restorationists is summed up by Tim Price in a review of *Whose Promised Land?* as follows:

> Since its foundation in 1809 CMJ [The Church's Mission to the Jews] has been led by people who, on reading the Scriptures, have concluded that God has not finished with the Jewish people and indeed the return of the Jewish people to their ancient homeland is a necessary prerequisite for the Return of Christ . . . Many of CMJ's leaders themselves have held different theological positions concerning the nature of the coming kingdom of God. However, underlining all of

---

28. Timothy Weber, 'How Evangelicals Became Israel's Best Friends', *Christianity Today*, 5 October 1998, p. 41.

29. Stephen Sizer, 'Dispensational Approaches to the Land', in P. Johnston and P. Walker (eds.), *The Land of Promise: Biblical, Theological and Contemporary Perspectives* (Leicester: Apollos, 2000), p. 142.

them has been the fundamental conviction that Christ will physically
return for his own people the Jews, once more re-gathered in their
land, before establishing his physical reign on earth prior to the New
Heaven and New Earth.[30]

Although there are differences between dispensationalism and
restorationism, those who identify with these two positions are
all agreed over four basic convictions: (1) on the basis of the
Abrahamic covenant Jews have a divine right to the land for all
time; (2) the return of Jews to the land since the 1880s is to be
seen as a fulfilment of prophecy; (3) the establishment of the state
of Israel has special theological significance because of what it
means for the Jews and indicates that the second coming will soon
take place; (4) Christians should not only support the idea of a
Jewish state, but (at least in general terms) support what it stands
for and defend it against attack. When every allowance is made for
differences between the various forms of dispensationalism and
between dispensationalism and restorationism, these four convictions form a solid core of beliefs they all share.

These four convictions are based on two major assumptions
that need to be examined.

1. *The insistence on literal interpretation.* Cyrus I. Scofield wrote,
'Not one instance exists of a "spiritual" or figurative fulfilment of
prophecy . . . Jerusalem is always Jerusalem, Israel is always Israel,
Zion is always Zion . . . Prophecies may never be spiritualized, but
are always literal.'[31] Robert K. Whalen describes this insistence on
literalism as part of the response of evangelical Christians to the
growth of liberalism in the nineteenth century: 'Premillennialists
realized that their treasured eschatology was lost if they failed
to insist on an inerrant (or "literal") interpretation of the Bible.'
He describes the outlook of the early nineteenth-century premillennialists as

---

30. Tim Price, Review of *Whose Promised Land?*, *Shalom* magazine,
     September–October 2002, p. 22.
31. Cyrus I. Scofield, quoted in Sizer, 'Dispensational Approaches', p. 145.

essentially legalistic, in that they treated the Bible as a contract between God and humanity, best understood as a series of sequential governing clauses – the dispensations. This mind-set, in turn, reveals the chasm that steadily opened during the first half of that century between certain Evangelicals and more liberal Protestant thought.[32]

I suspect it is becoming harder and harder to find serious biblical scholars within the evangelical community – both in the UK and the US – who are prepared to argue for such a wholesale rejection of 'figurative fulfilment'. From our perspective today the basic weakness of this assumption is that, as we have already seen, the NT writers do not seem to be bound to this kind of literal interpretation of the land theme and other major themes in the OT.

2. *The distinction between Israel and the church.* Dispensationalists insist that the distinction between the Jewish people (Israel) and the church remains even after the first coming of Christ. Therefore although individual Jews can become Christians during the present period of grace, the promises of an earthly kingdom that were given to Israel as a nation (including all the promises of material blessing for the Jewish people in the land) have to be fulfilled literally in the millennial kingdom after the second coming. This assumption leads to the position that, in the words of Whalen,

> Although Christianity may seem to supersede Judaism, it is, in reality, just a temporary detour . . . a 'parenthesis' in sacred history, necessitated by the Jews' faithlessness to the covenant . . . 'Israel' is the eventual fulfilment of God's covenant with the Jews. The 'church' is what God has done in the meantime.

He suggests that in this scheme Christianity is reduced to 'a sort of historical warm-up act before the main attraction'.[33]

There are probably very few scholars in the UK who are willing

---

32. Robert K. Whalen, *Encyclopedia of Fundamentalism* (ed. Brenda E. Brasher; London: Routledge, 2001), p. 135.

33. Ibid., p. 138.

to argue from the NT for this understanding of the relationship between the biblical Israel and the church. C. H. Dodd writing in the 1930s about the hope of national resurrection expressed in verses like Hosea 6:2, argued that 'The resurrection of Christ *is* the resurrection of which the prophets spoke.'[34] In the late 1970s R. T. France wrote that Jesus 'saw himself as in some way the heir to Israel's hopes'.[35] These same ideas have been powerfully developed more recently by N. T. Wright: 'Jesus was claiming in some sense to represent Israel in himself . . . he regarded himself as the one who summed up Israel's vocation and destiny in himself.'[36]

> Through the Messiah and the preaching which heralds him, Israel is transformed from being an ethnic people into a worldwide family . . . The Christians regarded themselves as a new family, directly descended from the family of Israel, but now transformed . . . they claimed to be the continuation of Israel in a new situation.[37]

If the two basic assumptions of dispensationalism and restorationism are fatally flawed, the whole system appears to be undermined. In this situation the covenant theology of the Reformed churches, developed especially by Calvin in the sixteenth century and refined by others in the seventeenth century, offers a convincing alternative. This system insists that the covenant of grace, in the words of M. Eugene Osterhaven, 'lies at the heart of Scripture' and 'runs throughout the two Testaments as a golden chain holding them together, with Christ the connecting link'. The covenant first made with Abraham eventually came, through the work of Christ, to include Gentiles who are now grafted into Israel. There is therefore continuity between the two covenants, with Jesus establishing a new form of the covenant. 'This teaching of

---

34. C. H. Dodd, *According to the Scriptures*, quoted in R. T. France, 'OT Prophecy and the Future of Israel', *TynBul* 26 (1975), p. 68.

35. Ibid.

36. N. T. Wright, *Jesus and the Victory of God* (London: SPCK, 1996), p. 537.

37. N. T. Wright, *The New Testament and the People of God* (London: SPCK, 1992), pp. 447, 457.

the unity of the covenant of grace is fundamental to the Reformed understanding of the church. The Christian church is the new covenant form of the people of God, the Israel of this age.'[38]

For many years I believed that dispensationalist and restorationist beliefs should come into the same category as beliefs about baptism, church government and spiritual gifts, where Christians must learn to live with a variety of views, accepting one another and remaining in fellowship even when they disagree strongly. In recent years, however, I have found it harder to keep them in this category. If the whole theological system is profoundly misguided because of its insistence on literal interpretation and its failure to appreciate how OT promises and hopes have been reinterpreted in the light of the coming of Christ, can it really be put on the same level as beliefs about infant or adult baptism, where there are good reasons for accepting different interpretations of Scriptures? And if these beliefs, when worked out in practice in the real world of the Middle East today, seem to support a fundamental injustice and weaken the church in its mission both among the Jewish people and the Muslim world, how can it be put into the same category as beliefs about bishops and presbyters, speaking in tongues and prophecy?

In 1944 the General Assembly of the Presbyterian Church of the US condemned dispensationalism as 'out of accord' with the church's confession.[39] In 1987 John Stott went much further in a private interview with Don Wagner: 'I have recently come to the conclusion that political Zionism and Christian Zionism are biblically anathema to Christian faith.'[40] The Middle East Council of Churches condemns Christian Zionism in the strongest possible terms.[41] I suspect that what holds back many from using the word

38. M. Eugene Osterhaven, *Encyclopedia of the Reformed Faith* (eds. D. K. McKim and D. F. Wright; Edinburgh: St. Andrews Press, 1992), p. 87.

39. Ibid., p. 105.

40. John Stott, quoted by Donald E. Wagner in *Anxious for Armageddon: A Call to Partnership for Middle Eastern and Western Christians* (Scottdale, PA: Herald, 1995), p. 80.

41. See, for example, 'What Is Western Fundamentalist Christian Zionism?', Middle East Council of Churches, Limassol, 1988; and many issues of

'heresy' is the awareness that dispensationalism is still the view held by the majority of evangelicals in the US and that anathematizing others can easily bring fellowship and fruitful dialogue to an end. In the British context restorationists dissociate themselves from many of the wilder excesses of American dispensationalism. But if several of the starting points and the consequences are the same for both, is there not a case for raising the same issue in relation to the more moderate forms of restorationism?

Replacement theology and supersessionism: How do we describe the relationship between Judaism and Christianity, between the Jewish people and the church? What are the alternatives to replacement theology?

A new intensity was injected into this debate by Melanie Phillips in an article published in the *Spectator* of 16 February 2002, in which she mounted a spirited attack on replacement theology, defining it as the belief that 'the Jews have been replaced by the Christians in God's favour and so all God's promises to the Jews, including the land of Israel, have been inherited by Christianity'.[42] The arguments for the unacceptability of 'replacement theology' are well summarized in the document *Sharing One Hope? The Church of England and Christian–Jewish Relations: A Contribution to a Continuing Debate*:

> The theory that the Christian Church has simply superseded or replaced the Jewish people, who no longer have any special place in God's calling, is widely seen to be untenable for a number of reasons. Theologically, it seems to call into question the faithfulness of God, 'who does not abandon those he calls'. Scripturally, it fails to do justice to the subtlety of the New Testament witness regarding Israel, in particular to Paul's sustained reflections on his 'kindred according to the flesh'. Historically,

---

News Report, Middle East Council of Churches <http: || www. mecchurches.org>.

42. Melanie Phillips, 'Christians Who Hate Jews', *Spectator*, 16 February 2002.

it inevitably led to the Christian accusations of Jews' 'God-forsakenness' which were at the root of the 'teaching of contempt'. Pastorally, a misunderstanding of the meaning of 'Old Testament' as 'out of date', 'outworn' or 'superseded' continues to feed negative attitudes to Judaism, and can cause grave offence to Jewish people, as well as diminishing Christian appreciation of the entire scope of the biblical witness.[43]

In a chapter in *WPL* entitled 'The Condemnation of Anti-Semitism' I argued that Paul's image of the wild branches being grafted into the cultivated olive in Romans 11:17–24 was intended to correct possible attitudes of arrogance on the part of Christians towards Jews.[44] I suggested that Paul's understanding of the relationship between 'Israel' and 'the church' could never be described as being 'supersessionism' or 'replacement theology', and quoted N. T. Wright: 'Paul is writing, with all the eleven chapters of theology behind him to say that "Gentile Christians" have not "replaced" Jews as the true people of God.' Wright believes that properly understood, Paul's argument could have provided the church with 'the best antidote it could have had for identifying and combating some of the worst evils of the Third Reich'.[45]

Unfortunately it seems that however much I try to distance myself from replacement theology, I am still told that I teach it and that I therefore continue 'the long tradition of arrogance towards the Jewish people . . . which has fuelled contempt, hatred and anti-semitism borne out of a false Church triumphalism'.[46] At a seminar in Cambridge in June 2002 Melanie Phillips described *WPL* as 'replacement theology masquerading as a dispassionate analysis of the tragedy of Israel and the Palestinians'. She argued that it is 'not

43. *Sharing One Hope? The Church of England and Christian–Jewish Relations: A Contribution to a Continuing Debate* (London: Church Publishing, 2001), p. 20.

44. Chapman, *Whose Promised Land?*, pp. 245–250.

45. N. T. Wright, *The Climax of the Covenant: Christ and the Law in Pauline Theology* (Edinburgh: T. & T. Clark, 1991), pp. 282–283.

46. Price, Review of *Whose Promised Land?*, p. 22.

just a form of anti-Zionism, but directly attacks Jewish religion, history and identity'.[47] A footnote in the recent Church of Scotland report 'Theology of Land and Covenant' sums up my position in the same way: 'Suggestions that the promise of the land to Israel are now invalid tend conversely towards some form of replacement theology; e.g. Colin Chapman . . .'[48] Sadly, therefore, It seems that anyone who cannot accept a two-covenant or a dispensationalist/restorationist theology is automatically labelled as holding replacement theology. Since it is so widely regarded as being 'a bad thing', it seems to have become a convenient way to 'give the dog a bad name'.

If we ask what the alternatives are to replacement theology or supersessionism, the Anglican report outlines three different views about the relationship between the Jewish people and the church that are held by Christians: *one covenant, two parallel covenants, two totally different religions.* The only real option of these three for evangelical Christians is probably the one-covenant view. Many statements of this position, however, fail to address the difficult issue of the consequences of the parting of the ways between Judaism and Christianity. If Christians see themselves as inheritors of the promises made to the descendants of Abraham, how do they think of Jewish people who have not seen Jesus as their Messiah? Does the unwillingness of Jewish people to recognize his Messiahship ultimately matter? Does it make any difference to their status within the one covenant and their enjoyment of the privileges of the covenant?

In turning to the NT, the first problem we need to address is the subject of judgment and punishment. Melanie Phillips sums up her perception of the traditional Christian view as the belief 'the Jews must be punished by the loss of their homeland for their refusal to believe in Christ'.[49] Jane Clements of the Council of Christians and Jews (CCJ) tells me that her main criticism of *WPL* revolves around the theme of judgment and my understanding

---

47. Phillips, 'Christians Who Hate Jews'.

48. *Theology of Land and Covenant*, Church of Scotland Report, May 2003.

49. Phillips, 'Christians Who Hate Jews'.

that in the eschatological discourses (especially in Luke) 'Jesus sees the coming destruction of Jerusalem as a judgement from God . . . simply because the people had failed to recognize the time of God's coming in the person of the Messiah'. She comments, 'This punishment theme is the one calculated to poison relations with the Jewish people – understandably. . .'[50]

My response is to ask whether the language of judgment in the teaching of Jesus is different in principle from that of the law and the prophets. It may be much easier to accept it in the context of the destruction of Jerusalem and the Babylonian exile because it was so far back in history and lasted for only seventy years, and because idolatry and disobedience to the law in the sixth century BC were much more obviously deserving of judgment than the inability of orthodox Jews in the first century AD to see a Jewish teacher as the incarnate Messiah.

But in the understanding of the Gospel writers we are not just talking about the rejection of a prophet, but the inability of people to recognize a much more significant divine visitation. In Luke's account of Jesus' saying concerning Jerusalem, the hardest words 'because you did not recognise the time of God's coming to you' (19:44) come immediately after his weeping over the city. While it is natural to want to soften the harshness of Jesus' words and to get away from the language of punishment, it is difficult to see how the idea of judgment can be taken out of the eschatological discourses completely.

A second problem in dealing with biblical texts has to do with the tension between verses of this kind that speak in terms of judgment and those that emphasize that the covenant promises still stand for the Jewish people. In 1 Thessalonians 2:14–16, for example, the theme of judgment predominates with Paul's statement 'The wrath of God has come upon them at last (or fully).' The letter to the Hebrews urges Jewish believers in Jesus who are tempted to return to their traditional Judaism to see Jesus as the one who inaugurates a 'new covenant' that is so much better than the 'old': 'The former regulation is set aside . . . and a better hope is

50. Email, 3 June 2003.

introduced ... Jesus has become the guarantee of a better covenant'
(7:18–19, 22). 'The ministry Jesus has received is as superior to
theirs as the covenant of which he is mediator is superior to the old
one, and it is founded on better promises... By calling this covenant
"new", he has made the first one obsolete; and what is obsolete and
ageing will soon disappear' (8:6, 13). 'You have not come to a mountain ... But you have come ... to Jesus the mediator of a new
covenant' (12:18–24). The language of Hebrews inevitably seems to
call in question the validity and relevance of what has been replaced
or superseded.

In Romans 9 – 11, however, Paul seems to be able to hold *both*
themes together in tension. He recognizes on the one hand the
serious consequences of the rejection of the Messiah when he says,
'Israel has experienced a hardening in part ...' (11:25); he speaks of
'their transgression ... their loss ...' (11:12); and 'they were broken
off because of unbelief ... God did not spare the natural branches'
(11:20–21). At the same time he refuses to believe that the covenant
with his people has been abrogated: 'I ask then: Did God reject his
people? By no means ... God did not reject his people, whom he
foreknew' (11:1–2). 'Theirs is the adoption as sons; theirs the divine
glory, the covenants, the receiving of the law, the temple worship
and the promises' (9:4); 'as far as election is concerned, they are
loved on account of the patriarchs, for God's gifts and his call are
irrevocable' (11:28–29).

If Paul was able to hold these different emphases in balance,
Christians today seem to find it hard to hold them together. Some
are unwilling to accept the full implications of the statements that
'they are loved on account of the patriarchs' (11:28) and 'God's
gifts and his call are irrevocable' (11:29), while others seem unwilling to accept what is implied by the vivid metaphor of being
'broken off because of unbelief' (11:20). David Torrance, for
example, speaks of 'a covenant within a covenant', meaning that
unbelieving Jews still have a call to service: 'Israel is God's servant,
and continues to be God's servant, through whom God challenges
the world.' Thus, while Jews and Gentiles who believe in Jesus are
gathered into the Abrahamic covenant and 'become the common-
wealth of Israel', he says that at the same time 'there is also the
covenant with all Israel, the unbelieving Israel, who are still made to

subserve the purposes of God and whom God still uses even in unbelief to testify to the world'.[51] Language like this suggests that one side of the paradox is ignored in favour of the other, since unbelief seems to make no difference whatsoever to the status of Jewish people within the covenant.

Is it possible, therefore, to describe the relationship between Judaism and Christianity in terms that (1) avoid the unacceptable aspects of replacement theology, (2) are faithful to all the different emphases of Scripture, but at the same time (3) recognize Judaism as a living faith with a vitality and integrity of its own, and (4) avoid giving unnecessary offence to Jewish people? Are we saying that the only way to maintain a relationship of mutual respect between Christians and Jews is for Christians to avoid any negative judgments on Judaism? Is the price of good Jewish–Christian relations not only the rejection of replacement theology but also the bracketing or watering down of Christian beliefs about Jesus as Messiah? I take comfort from the contribution of Jonathan Gorsky at the same Cambridge seminar, in which he not only put his finger on the nub of the issue but also pointed to possible ways forward:

> The theological difficulty is rooted in the universality of Christian beliefs – the coming of Christ is seen as being of ultimate and incomparable significance for all humanity – but this need not forestall a proper appreciation and respect of non-Christian traditions, and an on-going endeavour to understand their place in the Divine economy. With respect to Judaism the celebrated Vatican II document Nostra Aetate gave a novel emphasis to the passage in Romans, especially 11:28–29 . . . and remains the foundation of Catholic–Jewish relations. The passages in Romans have also been important for Anglican and Protestant reflection, especially in the impressive new document of the Leuenberg Fellowship of post-Reformation churches, which emphasizes the unresolved tensions of Christian and Jewish beliefs in a manner that is deeply respectful of Judaism . . . We are already a long way from the 'replacement' model, and there is every reason to expect further progress

---

51. Torrance, Review of *Whose Promised Land?*

as theological research interacts with Jewish–Christian dialogue, mutual understanding and personal friendship.[52]

Other Jewish concerns: How can Christians avoid anti-Semitism? Is recent criticism of Israel rooted in hatred of Jews and Judaism?

What we have been witnessing in Britain since 2002 is a heightened level of anxiety and fear in the Jewish community. Melanie Phillips's *Spectator* article in February 2002 began with an account of a meeting of a group of Jews and Christians who met to discuss 'the churches' increasing hostility to Israel'. At this meeting the Christians said that 'The hostility to Israel within the church is rooted in a dislike of the Jews . . . the real reason for the growing antipathy . . . was the ancient hatred of Jews rooted deep inside Christian theology and now on widespread display once again.' She went on to claim that it is replacement theology which lies at the heart of this prejudice, because it seeks to delegitimize the state of Israel by saying that it is 'fundamentally illegitimate and shouldn't be there at all'.[53] She ended the article with the words 'For the Jews, caught between the Islamists' blood libels on one side and Christian replacement theology on the other, Britain is suddenly a colder place.' Jane Clements of the CCJ, commenting on Phillips's article, writes:

> This article worried a great many in the Jewish community – some even had their bags packed, expecting a Christian backlash in Britain any moment. It sounds astonishing, but I am not exaggerating. We had to put on a special seminar about it with leaders of the Jewish community.[54]

---

52. Jonathan Gorsky, Cambridge Seminar, Centre for Jewish–Christian Relations, 14 May 2002.

53. Phillips, 'Christians Who Hate Jews'.

54. Email, 3 June 2003.

Dr Jonathan Sacks, the Chief Rabbi, analyses the problem in these terms:

> Today there is a slide from opposition to Israeli policies to opposition to the very existence of Israel to attacks on Jews. Whenever we see a slide from a political problem to the demonisation of a whole group we are in the presence of a very dangerous trend indeed. All of history tells us this. The second is that it is bringing together a strange coalition of radical Islamists, the anti-American Left and the extreme Right, groups who would otherwise have virtually nothing in common. Whenever an attack on a group unifies otherwise disparate groups then again we are in the presence of a dangerous phenomenon that can be manipulated to political ends.[55]

Our first response to this situation must be to recognize the fear of Jewish people and to admit that they have good reason to be afraid when they hear the rhetoric of some Palestinians, some Muslims and some Christians. Language of this kind needs to be strongly challenged, wherever it comes from, and Christians have a special responsibility to be alert to anything that feeds the fears of Jews. Many also would want to commend Melanie Phillips when she says:

> It is perfectly proper to criticise Israel's behaviour. I myself am deeply critical of the occupation of the disputed territories, the settlements, and the 'Greater Israel' philosophy of the ruling Likud party. I believe it is wrong to rule another people, that the Israelis have undoubtedly behaved reprehensibly from time to time since all occupations are corrupt, and that the Palestinian longing for a state of their own which lives in peace with Israel should be granted.

These words sum up the heart of Palestinian anger, which has led to the recent escalation of the conflict. The problem arises, however, when she goes on to say that 'a line is being crossed into anti-Jewish

---

55. Quoted by Ruth Gledhill in 'Church Leaders Condemn Attacks on Jews', *The Times*, 1 December 2003.

hatred'. Who, we may ask, is in the position of umpire to decide when the line between legitimate criticism of Israel and anti-Semitism has been crossed?

One has only to mention the present government opposition in Israel, movements like 'Peace Now' and 'Rabbis Against the Demolition of Houses', writers like Amos Oz, David Grossman and Benny Morris, and rabbis like Marc Ellis, to make the point that many Jews, both within and outside Israel, have been extremely critical of Israel and its policies and asked fundamental questions about the Zionist vision. A chapter entitled 'A Crisis for Zionism' in *WPL* explores five main themes: (1) Zionists have generally been unable to come to terms with the Palestinians, (2) violence was implicit in the original vision of Zionism, (3) a Jewish state requires a majority that has political power, (4) a Jewish state inevitably contains an element of racial and/or religious discrimination, and (5) a Jewish state has not solved the problem of anti-Semitism.[56] There are no *political* arguments of this kind that I have used which have not been put forward by Jews. It must surely be possible both for Jews and non-Jews to criticize the policies and actions of the Israeli government and to offer a critique of Zionism without being accused of being anti-Semitic.

My answer to Melanie Phillips at this point, therefore, is that I accept without question the existence of the state of Israel, its right to exist and its legality in terms of international law. I am not delegitimizing the Jewish state nor arguing for the view that 'Israel is fundamentally illegitimate and shouldn't be there at all'. I accept its existence, but feel obliged to point out some of the problems and ambiguities in the very concept of a Jewish state. I also strongly challenge the *theological* justification for the state of Israel that is presented by Christian Zionists, which I regard as thoroughly spurious. If some Jews and many Christians use their scriptures as the justification for Jewish claims to ownership of the whole land and for political sovereignty, I have every right to challenge the way that Scripture and theology are being used for political purposes.

---

56. Chapman, *Whose Promised Land?*, pp. 261–268.

The Islamic dimension: How do we respond to the Islamic opposition to Zionism? Does the Islamic dimension totally change the nature of the conflict?

David Torrance was critical of earlier editions of *WPL* for not taking seriously enough the Islamic dimension in Palestinian and Arab responses to Zionism. Although the 2002 revision included a whole chapter on 'Zionism and Islam', he is still critical, saying that I seriously underestimate 'the part which the religion of Islam has played throughout this entire conflict'. He believes that 'However important the political crisis in the Middle East is, the conflict is primarily religious and it is the religious dimension which has made it so difficult and intractable.'[57]

If we are trying to understand the conflict that has developed since 1880, what we are dealing with is a clash of two nationalisms, with two people laying claim for different reasons to the same piece of land. The present crisis was triggered by an explosion of anger over Israel's illegal occupation of the West Bank and its refusal to comply with UN resolutions since 1967. The majority of the dispossessed happen to be Muslims and have inevitably responded to their tragedy in Islamic ways. Islam has provided the ideology and a major part of their motivation for fighting what they perceive to be an injustice. The root of the problem, however, is not Islam but dispossession. If the Palestinians had been largely Christian, their rhetoric would have been different and they might not have had the vociferous support of Christians all round the world. But they would have felt the same indignation felt by others who have been uprooted from the land in which their ancestors have lived for centuries.

It is also important that non-Muslims attempt to understand the Islamic worldview. Many of the statements by Israeli politicians, by people in the West and by Christians are often cynical, derogatory or dismissive of Islamic claims and show an appalling ignorance and lack of sensitivity. Islamic claims to the land and Jerusalem are based on a number of verses in the Qur'an, Muhammad's

---

57. Torrance, Review of *Whose Promised Land?*

connection with the land, teaching about Jerusalem in Islamic tra-dition including a number of eschatological themes, the place of Jerusalem in Islamic history, the Islamic response to Western Christian aggression in the Crusades, and the place of the land in popular religious tradition.[58] Non-Muslims are not expected to accept this whole package of Islamic beliefs. But they should at least know what they are talking about and show the same kind of respect for Islamic beliefs that they show for Jewish and Christian beliefs.

In a chapter entitled 'Israel as a Focus for the Anger of Muslims against the West',[59] I have argued that a serious attempt on the part of the West (and especially the US) to understand the anger of Palestinians, Arabs and Muslims and to deal with this conflict in a more even-handed way would go a long way – perhaps even a very long way – towards defusing the anger that many Muslims feel towards Israel and the West. This will not happen, however, if Western governments continue to defend themselves and respond by venting their own anger, disappointment and frustration on the Muslim world. Many Americans have felt that what happened on 11 September 2001 was so traumatic that they are justified in putting all their energies into 'the war against terrorism' – including the 'terrorism' of those who resist Israel's illegal occupation of the West Bank. An alternative response is for people in the West to stand back and ask themselves, 'Why are these people so angry?' If they can separate the religious and the political issues, and if on reflection they can admit – first to themselves and then perhaps gradually to others – that at least *some* of the anger may be justified, then it is possible for dialogue to begin.

If in this dialogue Muslims are listening to non-Muslims, they will have understood the different reasons why many in the West support the state of Israel. They will also no doubt have under-stood that many others in the West have considerable sympathy

---

58. Chapman, *Whose Promised Land?*, pp. 289–298.

59. Colin Chapman, 'Israel as a Focus for the Anger of Muslims against the West', in Theodore Gabriel (ed.), *Islam and the West after 9/11* (Oxford: Ashgate, forthcoming).

for the Palestinian cause, but are beginning to have genuine concerns about the Islamic ideology with which it has come to be associated. They are alarmed at the resurgence of Islamism in groups like Hamas, Islamic Jihad and Hizbullah and the resultant conflict and division within the Palestinian movement, and appalled at the suicide bombings and the terrorism directed against Israeli civilians that are sanctioned, if not actually encouraged, by particular kinds of Islamic teaching. They understand that these actions often spring from a profound despair, but fear that ultimately they are likely to be counter-productive, because they play into the hands of hard-line Israeli governments. When they hear the expectation of some, if not many, that any future Palestinian state would have to be an Islamic state, they begin to be concerned about the status of Christians and other non-Muslims in such a state.

For these reasons many sympathizers in the West fear that the more the Palestinian cause is argued and fought *in Islamic terms*, the more it is likely to lose support from the rest of the world. The stronger the emphasis on Islam, the less sympathy they can expect from non-Muslims. The Palestinian cause is strong enough to stand on its own as a cause based on internationally accepted understandings of human rights, and does not need the underpinning of Islamic ideas in order to be supported in the West. A more nuanced response of this kind, I submit, is a better way to understand the Islamic dimension of the conflict than the view that the basic problem is not political but religious, and that the root of the problem is Islam.

Theology and politics: What has theology to do with politics?

Three attitudes are common among Christians that seem to raise special problems in relation to this issue.

1. *Christians should not get involved in politics.* 'I have felt no inner peace in getting involved in politics as such,' writes R. T. Kendall. 'I never ONCE got into politics during my 25 years in London.' But he then

goes on to explain how his interest in the Israeli–Palestinian conflict and a meeting with Yassir Arafat have drawn him in a small way into the politics of this conflict. 'The irony is, I am being called on to do what I can in the Middle East. But again I shall stick to theology – as before.'[60]

Different people clearly have different ministries, and one could hardly expect every Christian to be politically involved. But should Christians not be concerned about justice, and are they not called to do something when they see injustice being done before their eyes? It is sad that the word *dikaiosynē* has generally been interpreted by Protestants in terms of personal, individual right-eousness before God. If in some contexts it were translated 'justice', and if we were to read the familiar Beatitude as 'Blessed are those who hunger and thirst to see right prevail' (Matthew 5:6, REB), might this encourage a few more Christians to take a political stance on issues of this kind?

2. *Theology first, politics later.* This is the view that theology has priority over politics. We need to get our interpretation of Scripture and our eschatology worked out *first*, and *only then* should we start thinking about politics. Unfortunately, this approach usually means starting with one particular theology, which is almost invariably dispensationalist or restorationist. All the history is therefore seen through this particular lens. David Torrance, for example, recognizes that Israel may have committed wrongs, but sees them as God's servants and instruments for carrying out his will:

> God uses the sinful state of Israel as representative of all the sinful states of the world, that through them he might demonstrate his power to the world and show that all nations are sinful and accountable to God . . . God is not responsible for the injustices that have taken place. Nonetheless I believe that God was behind the restoration of the Jews to the land and the creation of the state of Israel. I deplore the way that the Palestinians have been treated and

---

60. Email, 30 March 2003.

am concerned for their suffering, as I hope all Christians are. Their
injustices and suffering should not, however, hinder or prevent
us seeing the hand of God at work . . . Because God is in this
situation . . . we should not as Christians look on the situation purely
politically. God is using tiny, unbelieving, sinful Israel to challenge
spiritually the whole of Islam and to challenge the world as he seeks
to bring us to that day when every people and nation will bow the
knee and confess that Jesus is Lord.[61]

Despite the references here to injustice and suffering, there is
no naming of dispossession or illegal occupation, and no real
protest about any actions or policies of the state, simply because
the whole process is given a theological interpretation and therefore justified as part of the build-up to the second coming. The
Palestinian problem is seen largely as a question of Palestinian
refugees who have only themselves and the surrounding Arab
countries to blame. This theology seems to me to produce a very
distorted understanding of human affairs, in which God and his
Christ seem to be supporting a profound injustice.

In my own case, what first drew me into the controversy about
the Palestinian issue was the feeling that what I was reading in the
Christian books in the West did not square with what I could see
on the ground in the Middle East. I have never been a particularly
political animal in the British context. But a sense of indignation
over what has been happening in the whole region and bewilder-
ment about the views of Western Christians, combined with a
deep conviction that the credibility of the Gospel is at stake have
kept me involved over the years.

3. *There is no hope for a solution unless Jews and Palestinians accept Christ or
before Christ comes again.* 'The only hope for the Middle East', says
Tony Higton, 'is for Arabs, Palestinians and Jewish people to turn to
Christ.'[62] According to David Torrance, 'Only in Christ can there be

---

61. Torrance, Review of *Whose Promised Land?*

62. Tony Higton, quoted by Andy Peck in 'Whose Land?' *Christianity and
Renewal*, August 2002, p. 15.

real reconciliation.'[63] 'God will not let true peace prevail', writes R. T. Kendall, 'until the people of Israel get right with God . . . The way forward for peace in Israel generally and Jerusalem particularly . . . is theological not political or through a military solution . . . This is what must be preached. Nothing else will bring peace to Jerusalem.'[64]

Such comments hardly bring a message of hope to terrified Israeli Jews in Jerusalem waiting for the next suicide bombing or to Palestinians whose towns have been occupied by Israeli tanks and who have watched their olive trees being uprooted and their land confiscated for the building of Jewish settlements. Would these Christians say the same thing in relation to Northern Ireland, arguing that the problem will only be solved when Protestants and Catholics become 'real Christians'? Political problems require political solutions, and to say that the only solution is a spiritual one may in some cases be an excuse for not even bothering to work out what the problem is all about. While it may seem to some observers that the political problems are insoluble, others would say that political solutions to the immediate crisis are there staring at us in the face and could be implemented quite soon if only there were sufficient determination among all the interested parties.

One might also have thought that Christians who are interested in biblical prophets might have imbibed some of their fire and indignation about what was going on around them. While looking into the future they were also interpreting the past and commenting on the present, making moral judgments about society and local, national and international politics. Elijah predicted a drought, but also rebuked Ahab for murdering Naboth and stealing his vineyard, and declared the judgment that would fall on Ahab's head for doing so. I look in vain for this kind of moral sensitivity in the writings of those who think that their theology enables them to understand the real nature of this conflict.

---

63. Torrance, Review of *Whose Promised Land?*
64. Email, 9 April 2003.

Conclusion

I end with a series of images to remind myself that I am not talking about ideas, but about the suffering of many human beings, to declare my sympathies and to express my hopes about how the gospel might touch those involved in the conflict.

I am troubled at the picture of Jews in London with their bags packed, fearing anti-Semitic attacks, and understand the fear of Israeli Jews that they could easily face another Holocaust. But I have little sympathy for the settlers on the West Bank who claim that the Bible has given the land to them, and wish they could be persuaded that the only way of guaranteeing their future in the land is to make peace with the Palestinians. And I wish they could see that Isaiah's Suffering Servant might not only be a picture of the Jewish people, but could also point to Jesus of Nazareth.

I feel with the Palestinian refugees all round the Middle East who still have the keys of the houses they left behind in 1948 or 1967, and with Palestinians on the West Bank and Gaza who run short of water while they see the green lawns and the swimming pools in the illegal settlements next door. I can understand the anger of Muslims all over the world, and can see why young men and women are offering themselves for suicide missions out of a mixture of despair, rage and hope for martyrdom, even though I cannot accept the Islamic ideology that undergirds their protest. And I wish they could see in the example of Jesus other ways of responding to injustice.

I fear for America, the only superpower, that has set itself up as the policeman of the world, but is unable to be impartial in this particular conflict and is being perceived more and more by the rest of the world as the new Rome. I pray for American evangelical/fundamentalist Christians who are so convinced that their country is on the winning side because of its support for 'God's people' in the Middle East, but have little sense of justice and no idea of the message that they are communicating to the Muslim world. I wish their eyes could be opened to understand the conflict in less theological and more personal terms, and to see that there might be other ways of interpreting Christian Scripture in relation to this conflict.

If any of these prayers might be answered even in a small way, the world might be able to rejoice that the promises *about the land in the covenant* really have been fulfilled in a way that *brings blessing to all peoples of the earth*.